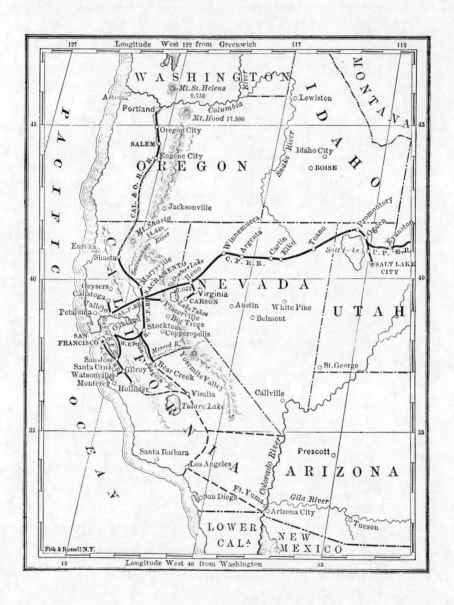

CALIFORNIA:

FOR

HEALTH, PLEASURE, AND RESIDENCE.

A BOOK FOR TRAVELLERS AND SETTLERS.

By CHARLES NORDHOFF,

AUTHOR OF "CAPE COD AND ALL ALONG SHORE," &c., &c.

A DOUBLE ELEPHANT BOOK

TEN SPEED PRESS
Berkeley, California

First published in 1873. For further information, write to:

1☉

TEN SPEED PRESS
P. O. Box 7123
Berkeley, California 94707

Cover design by Nancy Austin
Book production by Hal Hershey

Library of Congress Catalog Card Number: 91-050670
ISBN 0-89815-418-9

First Ten Speed Press printing, 1974
Printed in the United States of America

1 2 3 4 5 — 95 94 93 92 91

TO

GENERAL E. F. BEALE,

IN MEMORY OF

PLEASANT DAYS AT THE TEJON.

PREFACE.

THERE have been Americans who saw Rome before they saw Niagara; and for one who has visited the Yosemite, a hundred will tell you about the Alps, and a thousand about Paris. Now, I have no objection to Europe; but I would like to induce Americans, when they contemplate a journey for health, pleasure, or instruction, or all three, to think also of their own country, and particularly of California, which has so many delights in store for the tourist, and so many attractions for the farmer or settler looking for a mild and healthful climate and a productive country.

When a northern American visits a tropical country, be it Cuba, Mexico, Brazil, or Central America, he is delighted with the bright skies, the mild climate, the wonderful productiveness of the soil, and the novel customs of the inhabitants; but he is repelled by an enervating atmosphere, by the dread of malarious diseases, by the semi-barbarous habits of the people, and often by a lawless state of society. Moreover, he must leave his own country, and is without the comfort and security he enjoys at home. California is our own; and it is the first tropical land which our race has thoroughly mastered and made itself at home in. There, and there only, on this planet, the traveler and resident may enjoy the delights of the tropics, without their penalties; a mild climate, not enervating, but healthful and health-restoring; a wonderfully and variously productive soil, without tropical malaria; the grandest scenery, with perfect security and comfort in traveling arrangements; strange customs, but neither lawlessness nor semi-barbarism.

The first part of this book will interest mainly travelers and tourists, and in it I have aimed to give a plain and detailed statement of the routes across the continent, and of what the traveler should see by the way; of the notable sights of California, and how they may best be visited; and a table of expenses, and of the time needed for different excursions. There is also a chapter on health resorts for invalids, and there are some hints to sportsmen. Consumptives will find in Southern California a climate remarkably mild and healing.

The remainder of the book is devoted to accounts of the agriculture and fruit culture of Southern California, a region almost unknown, and just now opened to settlement by the completion of several lines of railroad; and which, by reason of its fine healthful climate, its rich soil, and its remarkably varied products, deserves the attention of farmers looking for pleasant homes and cheap and fertile lands, combined with a climate the best, probably, in the United States.

Parts of the book have appeared in *Harper's Magazine*, the *Tribune*, and the *Evening Post*, but the whole has been revised and much new matter added.

CONTENTS.

14 CONTENTS.

APPENDIX.

ILLUSTRATIONS.

VIEW FROM THE CLIFF HOUSE, SAN FRANCISCO.

CALIFORNIA:
FOR HEALTH, PLEASURE, AND RESIDENCE.

CHAPTER I.

THE WAY OUT.

THOUGH California has been celebrated in books, newspapers, and magazines for more than twenty years, it is really almost as little known to the tourist—a creature who ought to know it thoroughly, to his own delight—as it was to Swift when he wrote, in his description of the flying island of Laputa,

"The continent of which this kingdom is a part extends itself, as I have reason to believe, eastward to that unknown tract of America westward of California, and north to the Pacific Ocean, which is not above a hundred and fifty miles from Logado," and so on.

California is to most Eastern people still a land of big beets and pumpkins, of rough miners, of pistols, bowie-knives, abundant fruit, queer wines, high prices —full of discomforts, and abounding in dangers to the peaceful traveler. A New Yorker, inefficient except in his own business, looking to the government, municipal, State, or Federal, for almost every thing except his daily dollars; overridden by a semi-barbarous foreign population; troubled with incapable servants, private as well as public; subject to daily rudeness from car-drivers and others who ought to be civil; rolled helplessly and tediously down town to his business in a lumbering omnibus; exposed to inconveniences, to dirty streets, bad gas, beggars, loss of time through improper conveyances; to high taxes, theft, and all kinds of public wrong, year in and year out—this New Yorker fondly imagines himself to be living at the centre of civilization, and pities the unlucky friend who is "going to California." He invites him to dine before he sets out, "because you will not get a good dinner again till you return, you know;" he sends him, with his parting blessing, a heavy navy revolver; and shudders at the annoyances and dangers which his friend, out of a rash and venturesome disposition, is about to undergo.

Well, the New Yorker is mistaken. There are no dangers to travelers on the beaten track in California; there are no inconveniences which a child or a tenderly reared woman would not laugh at; they dine in San Francisco rather better, and with quite as much form and a more elegant and perfect service, than in New York; the San Francisco hotels are the best and cheapest in the world; the noble art of cooking is better understood in California than anywhere else where I have eaten; the bread is far better, the variety of food is greater; the persons with whom a tourist comes in contact, and upon whom his comfort and pleasures so greatly depend, are more uniformly civil, obliging, honest, and intelligent than they are anywhere in this country, or, so far as I know, in Europe; the pleasure-roads in the neighborhood of San Francisco are unequaled anywhere; the common country roads are kept in far better order than anywhere in the Eastern States; and when you have spent half a dozen weeks in the State, you will perhaps return with a notion that New York is the true frontier land, and that you have nowhere in the United States seen so complete a civilization—in all material points, at least—as you found in California. Moreover, the cost of living is to-day less in California by a third than in any Eastern State; it is, at this time, the cheapest country in the United States to live in.

If this seems incredible to what out there they call an Eastern person, let him reflect for a moment upon the fact that New York receives a constant supply of the rudest, least civilized European populations; that of the immigrants landed at Castle Garden, the neediest, the least thrifty and energetic, and the most vicious remain in New York, while the ablest and most valuable fly rapidly westward; and that, besides this, New York has necessarily a large population of native adventurers; while, on the other hand, California has a settled and permanent population of doubly picked men.

"When the gold was discovered," said a Californian to whom I had expressed my wonder at the admirable *quality* of the State's population, "wherever an Eastern family had three or four boys, the ablest, the most energetic one, came hither. Of that great multitude of picked men, again, the weakly broke down under the strain; they died of disease or bad whisky, or they returned home. The remainder you see here, and you ought not to wonder that they are above your Eastern average in intelligence, energy, and thrift. Moreover, you are to remember that, contrary to the commonly received belief, California has a more settled population than almost any State in the Union. It does not change; our people can not 'move West,' and very few of them return to the East. What we have we keep, and almost all, except the Chinese, have a permanent interest in the State. Finally," added this old miner, who is now a banker, and whom you could not tell from a New Yorker, either in his dress or the tones of his voice, or in the manner in which he transacts business, and who yet has not been "home," as he calls it, for seventeen years — "finally, you must remember that of our immigrants who came from China, not a single one, so far as is known, but knew how to read, write, and keep at least his own accounts on his own abacus when he passed the Golden Gate. We are not saints out here, but I believe we have much less of a frontier population than you in New York." And my experience persuades me that he was right.

Certainly in no part of the continent is pleasure-traveling so exquisite and unalloyed a pleasure as in California. Not only are the sights grand, wonderful, and surprising in the highest degree, but the climate is exhilarating and favorable to an active life; the weather is so certain that you need not lose a day, and may lay out your whole tour in the State without reference to rainy days, unless it is in the rainy season; the roads are surprisingly good, the country inns are clean, the beds good, the food abundant and almost always well cooked, and the charges moderate; and the journey by rail from New York to San Francisco, which costs no more than the steamer fare to London, and is shorter than a voyage across the Atlantic, is in itself delightful as well as instructive. Probably twenty Americans go to Europe for one who goes to California; for one who has seen the Yo Semite, a hundred will tell you of the Alps, and a thousand about Paris; yet no American who has not seen the Plains, the Great Salt Lake, the Sierra Nevada, and the wonders of California, can honestly say that he has seen his own country, or that he even has an intelligent idea of its greatness. It is of this journey from New York to San Francisco that I wish to give in this chapter such an accurate and detailed account as will, I hope, tempt many who contemplate a European tour to turn their faces westward rather, sure that this way lies the most real pleasure.

You may purchase tickets for California in any of the larger Eastern towns and cities; and you may go out by way of Chicago or St. Louis as you prefer. The journey really begins at one or the other of these places.

From Chicago three railroads, the Burlington and Missouri, the Chicago and North Western, and the Chicago and Rock Island, lead to Omaha. All three are well managed; the Burlington and Missouri road, one of the best built in the whole country, has a special attraction to tourists in its Pullman dining-cars, which run with every through train, and are a great convenience, as well as an attractive novelty.

From St. Louis you may either go direct to Omaha, or, if you desire to take Colorado on your way, you may go, either from St. Louis or Chicago, over the Kansas Pacific Railroad, the only one on which still, in the season, buffalo are seen, to Denver. At Denver you have your choice of diversions in Colorado, with Mr. Bowles's admirable book, "The Switzerland of America," to show you the way; and when you are done, you pass from Denver to Cheyenne, where you join the overland train.

You are to understand that all these lines make connection with the Pacific Railroads, and that all roads lead to San Francisco. Now that the bridge at Omaha is completed, you may, if you desire it enough, charter a Pullman car in New York, Chicago, or St. Louis, or, indeed, at any point you please, and go through to the Pacific without change of cars.

The traveling time from New York to San Francisco, if you go through without stopping, is seven days.

In practice, the tourist bound to California will do well to stop two days in Chicago and one day in Salt Lake City, in which case he would get to San Francisco in ten days, and with surprisingly little fatigue, and he will have seen several very remarkable sights on the way.

For instance, though Chicago itself was burned and is not yet entirely rebuilt, the ruins are worth seeing; and near at hand, accessible by frequent trains, he may find one of the most characteristic sights of our continent, the great Chicago stock-yards—a city whose inhabitants are cattle, sheep, and hogs, and where these creatures are so well cared for that many a poor human being supposed to have an immortal and amenable soul, living in a New York tenement house, is neither so cleanly lodged nor so well protected against harm or cruelty.

This city of the beasts has streets, sewers, drains; it has water laid on; it is lighted with gas; it has a bank, an exchange, a telegraph-office, a post-office, an admirably kept hotel; it has even a newspaper—else it would not be an American city. It has very comfortable accommodations for 118,350 residents—

namely, 21,000 head of cattle, 75,000 hogs, 22,000 sheep, with stalls for 350 horses. It contains 345 acres of land; and when all this is prepared for use, 210,000 head of cattle can be lodged, fed, and cared for there at once, and with the certainty that not one will suffer or go astray.

It has thirty-five miles of sewers; ten miles of streets and alleys, all paved with wood; three miles of water-troughs, all so arranged that the water may be stopped off at any point; 2300 gates, which are the front-doors, so to speak, of the place; 1500 open pens, heavily fenced in with double plank; 100 acres are covered with pens for cattle, and all these are floored with three-inch plank; 800 covered sheds for sheep and hogs; and seventeen miles of railroad track connect this city of the beasts with every road which runs into Chicago. It has two Artesian wells, one 1032, the other 1190 feet deep, which, being spouting wells, send the water into huge tanks forty-five feet high, whence it is distributed all over the place in pipes. Fourteen fire-plugs are ready to furnish water in case of fire; immense stacks of hay and large granaries of corn contain the food needed for the beasts; and, I believe, a train of palace cattle cars now bears the emigrant animals from this their city comfortably to the Eastern butchers.

Of course, as the "lower animals" do not help themselves, a considerable force of men is needed to attend upon those gathered here. The company receives and cares for all animals sent to it. It has thus taken in, penned, fed, watered, littered, and taken account of 41,000 hogs, 3000 cattle, and 2000 sheep in a single day, and that without accident, hitch, or delay. From 175 to 200 men are constantly employed in this labor; and to accommodate these and their families numerous cottages have been built, while a town-hall for public meetings and lectures, a church, a Sunday-school, and a well-kept day-school provide for their instruction and amusement. The hotel, which has bath-rooms, and is in other respects well fitted, is for the use of the drovers and owners of cattle, whom business brings hither. At the Exchange sales are effected, and the news of a sale may be sent to Maine or Texas by telegraph from the same room, while the money paid may be securely deposited in the bank, which is under the same roof. Thus you will see that this amazing town is completely furnished in every part; and it will not be the least part of your surprise and pleasure to find that the whole business, which near New York often involves painful brutalities, is here conducted as quietly as though a Quaker presided over it, and with as much care for the feelings of the dumb brutes as though good Mr. Bergh were looking on all the time.

It will cost about two millions when it is completed; is a pecuniary success, as it deserves to be; and when you hear that so long ago as 1869 Chicago received and sent off 403,102 head of cattle, 1,661,869 hogs, and 340,072 sheep, and that it will probably remain for years one of the greatest cattle markets in the world, you will see the need for such elaborate arrangements as I have described, and, if you are a humane person, will be pleased that these immense droves of animals are kindly cared for and comfortably lodged and fed on their way to a market. Most of the people employed in the yards are Americans.

Among such a multitude of beasts as are here received Mr. Buckle's law of averages would tell you that there will be a certain few monstrosities; and you will probably be shown one or two Texas steers which look much more like elephants or mammoths than horned oxen; perhaps a two-headed sheep, or a six-legged hog; and, indeed, when I saw the stables they contained a collection which would have turned the face of a Chatham Street exhibitor green with envy.

The Union Stock-yards lie but half an hour from the centre of Chicago, and there is no reason why ladies and children should not visit them if the weather is fine. I do not know of a more instructive or remarkable sight for tourists.

If you want to see how private enterprise and good taste can provide for the pleasant lodging of men and women, turn from this city of the beasts and go out to Riverside Park.

It always seemed to me that it would be the summit of human felicity to have a handsome house in the New York Central Park, and thus to seem to own and control, and to really enjoy as a piece of personal property, that fine pleasure-ground. When the Tammany Ring was in the height of its power this thought was also entertained by its chiefs, who for some time nursed and fondled a proposition that "a few eminent citizens" should be allowed, "under proper restrictions," to build themselves fine houses in the Park. It is not difficult to guess who would have been the eminent citizens to share among themselves this happy privilege; and New York may thank *Harper's Weekly*, the *Times*, and Thomas Nast that their ambitious scheme has come to naught. Their names would have begun with a T and an S and a C and an H.

Well, a company of capitalists in Chicago conceived the idea that it would be possible and profitable to buy a piece of ground near that city, lay it out as tastefully and improve it as thoroughly as the New York Central Park, and then sell it off in lots to people of taste and wealth. It needed some faith to begin such an undertaking; but if you go to Riverside you will see Central Park roads, drives, and paths; you will find gas and water supplied as though it were a city; you will find tasteful public buildings; a hotel, which was a place of refuge for multitudes of Chicago people after the great fire, and which is a favorite summer resort; and you will see a good many people living already with Central Park surroundings, and with all the comforts and social advantages of the city and the country combined.

Perhaps you will wonder whether co-operation is not a good thing for the wealthy as well as the struggling poor, and whether the many who prefer to live in the suburbs of great cities would not do wisely and save money if they would—having found a region they like—unite to improve it upon some general and tasteful plan.

And whatever you may think of Chicago in ruins, or of the future of that stirring place, when you have seen Riverside and the Union Stock-yards you will acknowledge that Chicago capitalists have known how, in the words of the old tavern signs, to provide " first-rate accommodations for man and beast."

At Chicago or St. Louis the journey to California really begins. In the East we make journeys by rail; west of Chicago men live on the cars. In the East a railroad journey is an interruption to our lives. We submit to it, because no one has yet been ingenious enough to contrive a flying-machine, and the telegraph wires do not carry passengers by lightning; but we submit to it reluctantly, we travel by night in order to escape the tedium of the journey, and no one thinks of amusing himself on the cars. When you leave Chicago you take up your residence on the train. The cars are no longer a ferry to carry you across a short distance: you are to live in them for days and nights; and no Eastern man knows the comfort or pleasure of traveling by rail until he crosses the Plains.

I suspect that part of our discomfort in making a railroad journey comes from its brevity. You are unsettled; the car, on a common journey, is but a longer ferry; and who ever thought of taking his ease on a ferry-boat? You can not fix your mind on the present; your constant thought is of when you will get there. Now the journey to San Francisco takes not a few hours, but a number of days; and when you are safely embarked on the train at Chicago, you leave care behind in the dépôt, and make yourself comfortable, as one does on a sea-voyage.

Moreover, until you have taken this journey, you will never know how great a difference it makes to your comfort whether your train goes at the rate of forty or at twenty-two miles per hour. This last is the pace of the iron horse between Omaha and San Francisco; and it is to the fierce and rapid rush of an Eastern lightning express what a gentle and easy amble is to a rough and jolting trot. It would not be surprising to find that the overland journey will, by-and-by, create a public opinion in favor of what New Yorkers would call slow trains. Certainly a lightning express rushing through from Chicago to San Francisco would not carry any one, except an express-man, a second time. At forty or forty-five miles per hour the country you pass through is a blur; one hardly sees between the telegraph poles; pleasure and ease are alike out of question; reading tires your eyes, writing is impossible, conversation impracticable except at the auctioneer pitch, and the motion is wearing and tiresome. But at twenty-two miles per hour travel by rail is a different affair; and having unpacked your books and unstrapped your wraps in your Pullman or Central Pacific palace-car, you may pursue all the sedentary avocations and amusements of a parlor at home; and as your housekeeping is done—and admirably done—for you by alert and experienced servants; as you may lie down at full length or sit up, sleep or wake, at your choice; as

INTERIOR OF A PULLMAN PALACE-CAR, PACIFIC RAILROAD.

your dinner is sure to be abundant, very tolerably cooked, and not hurried; as you are pretty certain to make acquaintances on the car; and as the country through which you pass is strange, and abounds in curious and interesting sights, and the air is fresh and exhilarating—you soon fall into the ways of the voyage; and if you are a tired business man, or a wearied housekeeper, your careless ease will be such a rest as certainly most busy and overworked Americans know how to enjoy.

I tell you all this in some detail, because it was new to me, and it is worth while to be spared the unpleasant forebodings of weariness and lack of occupation which troubled me when I was packing my trunk for 'Frisco.

You write very comfortably at a table in a little room called a drawing-room, entirely closed off, if you wish it, from the remainder of the car, which room contains two large and comfortable arm-chairs and a sofa; two broad, clean, plate-glass windows on each side, which may be doubled if the weather is cold; hooks in abundance for shawls, hats, etc., and mirrors at every corner. Books and photographs lie on the table; your wife sits at the window, sewing and looking out on long ranges of snow-clad mountains, or on boundless, ocean-like plains; children play on the floor, or watch at the windows for the comical prairie-dogs sitting near their holes, and turning laughable somersaults as the car sweeps by. You converse as you would in your parlor at home; the noise of the train is as much lost to your consciousness as the steamship's rush through the waters; the air is pure, for these cars are thoroughly ventilated; the heating apparatus used seems to me quite perfect, for it keeps the feet warm, and diffuses an agreeable and equal heat through all parts of the car. This is accomplished by means of hot-water pipes fastened near the floor.

As at sea, so here, the most important events of the day are your meals. The porter calls you at any hour you appoint in the morning; he gives you half an hour's notice of breakfast, dinner, or supper; and the conductor tells you not to hurry, but to eat at your ease, for he will not leave any one behind. Your beds are made up and your room or section swept and aired while you are at breakfast, or before, if you are early risers; you find both water and fresh towels abundant; ice is put into the tank which supplies drinking-water, at the most improbable places in the great wilderness; and an attentive servant is always within call, and comes to you at intervals during the day to ask if you need any thing to make you more contented.

About eight o'clock—for, as at sea, you keep good hours—the porter, in a clean gray uniform, like that of a Central Park policeman, comes in to make up the beds. The two easy-chairs are turned into a berth; the sofa undergoes a similar transformation; the table, having its legs pulled together, disappears in a corner, and two shelves being let down furnish two other berths. The freshest and whitest of linen and brightly colored blankets complete the outfit; and you undress and go to bed as you would at home, and, unless you have eaten too heartily of antelope or elk, will sleep as soundly.

Thus you ride onward, day after day, toward the setting sun, and unless you are an extremely unhappy traveler, your days will be filled with pleasure from the novel sights by the way. At Burlington you cross the Mississippi over a noble bridge, and will be surprised to see what a grand river the Father of Waters is nearly sixteen hundred miles above its mouth. At Omaha you cross the Missouri, there a variable, turbid, but in the early spring a narrow river, which yet requires a bridge more than a mile long when the stream is bank-full. This new bridge at Omaha was built by the engineer to whom New York is indebted for the iron bridge at Harlem, T. E. Sickles, and it is a remarkable work to be done so far from the appliances of civilization.

From Chicago to Omaha your train, if you have taken the Burlington and Missouri road, will carry a dining-car, which is a great curiosity in its way. I expected to find this somewhat greasy, a little untidy, and with a smell of the kitchen. It might, we travelers thought, be a convenience, but it could hardly be a luxury. But in fact it is as neat, as nicely fitted, as trim and cleanly, as though Delmonico had furnished it; and though the kitchen may be in the forward end of the car, so perfect is the ventilation that there is not even the faintest odor of cooking. You sit at little tables which comfortably accommodate four persons; you order your breakfast, dinner, or supper, from a bill of fare which contains a quite surprising number of dishes, and you eat, from snow-white linen and neat dishes, admirably cooked food, and pay a moderate price.

It is now the custom to charge a dollar per meal on these cars; and as the cooking is admirable, the service excellent, and the food various and abundant, this is not too much. You may have your choice in the wilderness—eating at the rate of twenty-two miles per hour—of buffalo, elk, antelope, beef-steak, mutton-chops, or grouse.

Beyond Omaha, unless you have taken seats in a hotel-car, you eat at stations placed at proper distances apart, where abundant provision is made, and the food is, for the most part, both well cooked and well served. These hotel stations are under the supervision and control of the managers of the roads, and at many of them, especially on the Central Pacific road—in California, that is to say—your meals are served with actual elegance. Sufficient time is allowed—from thirty to thirty-five minutes—to eat; the conductor tells you beforehand that a bell will be rung five minutes before the train starts, and we always found him obliging enough to look in and tell the ladies to take their time, as he would not leave them behind.

There is a pleasant spice of variety and adventure in getting out by the way-side at the eating stations. We saw strange faces, we had time to look about us, the occasional Indian delighted the children, we stretched our legs, and saw something of our fellow-passengers in the other cars. Moreover, if you have a numerous party desirous to eat together, the porter will telegraph ahead for you to have a sufficient number of seats reserved, and thus you take your places without flurry or haste, and do not have your digestion spoiled by preliminary and vexatious thoughts about pushing for a good place. In short, these trains are managed for the pleasure and accommodation of the passengers. The journey would, I suppose, be unendurable else.

The sleeping-car, but for which the journey to the Pacific by rail would be extremely uncomfortable, but by whose help it is made a pleasure-trip, owes its development and perfection to Mr. George M. Pullman, who is the inventor and patentee of most of the ingenious devices by which the traveler's comfort is secured in these cars. Of course he is an American. He began life poor; and was once a miner in Colorado. He is now President of the Pullman Car Company, which has five hundred sleeping, drawing-room, and hotel cars on different railroads, and is building more, at the rate of three finished cars.

GEORGE M. PULLMAN.

for every week of the present year. The company are also building a new kind of day cars, to be put on such short routes as that between New York and Washington; and will presently run a daily hotel-car from Chicago to Ogden, in which you may sit and sleep, and have your meals served at any time you may choose to order them. It is planning, and will fit up this year, near Chicago, extensive car-works of its own on grounds large enough to contain also the cottages of the thousand workmen who will be there employed, and it is said that these grounds are to be planned with special regard to the convenience of the men and their families. The company has already found it expedient to keep and furnish, near the dépôts in all the great cities, rooms where conductors and porters may, at the end of a journey, bathe, change their clothes, make out their reports, and read, write, or amuse themselves. Mr. Pullman thinks that as he requires much from his men, and as they are picked men, trained with care, it is an advantage to the company to furnish them such a home at the ends of the great routes of travel, where they may make themselves comfortable and at ease. Certainly it is a humane thought, and likely, besides, to give him the command of responsible servants.

The Pullman cars are constantly improving. The Russian Grand Duke traveled last winter in perhaps the most commodious and perfect manner in which any one ever traveled by rail. He had in one train a day car, in which he and his companions could sit at ease, read, write, or amuse themselves as in a parlor; a dining or hotel car, into which they walked to breakfast or dinner; and a sleeping-car. No doubt the impressions he got of this kind of pleasure-traveling will facilitate Mr. Pullman's entrance into Russia, where, as well as in England, Germany, and France, the Pullman Company will within two years have placed their cars, as arrangements are now making for that purpose.

The superiority of the American sleeping-cars is in their cleanliness, the perfection of their heating and ventilating contrivances, and the presence of every thing which can make a car convenient to live in. There is nothing like them in Europe, and all European travelers in this country have been surprised and delighted with them. The Pullman Company is successful, as it deserves to be. It now runs cars on nearly one hundred roads, the railroad companies generally owning one-half the stock of the cars they use, and thus having a mutual interest. The Pullman Company sells to the public what the railroad company in such cases does not furnish—the sleeping-car accommodations. You may now ride in Pullman cars over sixty thousand miles of railroad. The Pullman Company already employs over two thousand persons, and in its new car shops will employ one thousand more, and all this vast business has grown from the smallest beginnings.

One of the pleasantest ways to travel across the continent, though not, I think, the way in which you will see most of the people, is to make the journey with a party of friends numerous enough to fill, or nearly fill, a car. To show you at what cost—exclusive of the regular railroad fare—such a company may travel, I give here some extracts from a little book issued by the company for the information of travelers:

"The Pullman Palace-Car Company is ready to furnish excursion parties with sleeping, drawing-room, and hotel-cars for a trip to San Francisco or elsewhere on these terms:

"For a regular sleeping-car, containing twelve open sections of two double berths each, and two state-rooms of two double berths each (in all twenty-eight berths), with conductor and porter, seventy-five dollars per day.

"For a drawing-room car, containing two drawing-rooms, having each a sofa and two large easy-chairs by day, and making up at night into two double and two single berths, three state-rooms having each two double berths, and six open sections of two double berths each (in all twenty-six berths), with conductor and porter, seventy-five dollars per day.

"For a hotel-car, containing two drawing-rooms, as above described, one state-room having two double berths, and six open sections of two double berths each (in all twenty-two berths), and having also, in one end, a kitchen fully equipped with every thing necessary for cooking and serving meals, with conductor, cook, and two waiters, eighty-five dollars per day.

"The conductor, if desired, will make all arrangements for the excursionists with the railroads for procuring transportation of the car; and in the case of their taking a hotel-car, will also act as steward, purchasing for them the requisite provisions for the table.

"The car is chartered, with its attendants, at a certain rate per day from the time it is taken until we receive it back again.

"We have no facilities for securing special rates of railroad fare, and would suggest that, in case an excursion is organized, application be made to any ticket agent who is empowered to sell through tickets, and the best rates of railroad fare obtained from him to and from the terminal point of the proposed trip.

"We can forward a car from our head-quarters in Chicago to any point which the excursionists may designate as their starting-place."

The Pullman hotel-car is one of the most ingenious as well as one of the most convenient of all modern arrangements for travel. It can seat forty persons at the tables; it contains not only a kitchen—which is a marvel of compactness, having a sink, with hot and cold water faucets, and every "modern convenience"—but a wine closet, a china closet, a linen closet, and provision lockers so spacious as to contain supplies for thirty people all the way from Chicago to the Pacific if necessary; its commissary list contains, as I ascertained by actual count, 133 different articles of food; it carries 1000 napkins, 150 tablecloths, 300 hand-towels, and 30 or 40 roller-towels, besides sheets, pillow-cases, etc., etc. And unless you are of an investigating turn, you would never know that the car contained even a kitchen.

Whenever a sleeping-car arrives at the end of a journey, it is laid over for twenty-four hours. Thereupon the porter gathers up the soiled linen for the laundry, and a force of men and women enters the car and takes out of it bedding, carpets, and every movable thing; all are beaten with rods and hung up to air; and meantime the whole car is aired, and the wood-work dusted, rubbed, and scrubbed in the most thorough manner. This is the manner of their housekeeping.

On the whole, a company of three or four can travel the most enjoyably across the continent; and there is no reason why a man should not take his children, if they are ten years old or over, as well as his wife. Four fill a drawing-room comfortably, three or four can be comfortable in a section on a sleeping-car; and in California, if you have three or four in your party, you can travel as cheaply by private carriage as by stage to all the notable sights of the State which you do not reach by rail, and thus add much to the comfort and pleasure of such journeys.   On the cars you are sure to make pleasant acquaintance, and probably to your advantage, for you will find persons who have been over the route before, ready to point out curious objects to you.   And from the hour

PULLMAN DINING-CAR.

you leave Omaha you will find every thing new, curious, and wonderful; the Plains, with their buffalo, antelope, and prairie-dogs; the mountains, which, as you approach Cheyenne, lift up their glorious snow-clad summits; the deep cañons and gorges which lead from Wasatch into Ogden, and whose grim scenery will seem to you, perhaps, to form a fit entrance to Salt Lake; the indescribable loveliness and beauty of the mountain range which shelters the Mormon capital; the extended, apparently sterile, but, as long-headed men begin to think, really fertile alkali and sage-brush plain; the snow-sheds which protect the Central Pacific as you ascend the Sierra; and, on the morning of the last day of your journey, the grand and exciting rush down the Sierra from Summit to Colfax, winding around Cape Horn and half a hundred more precipitous cliffs, down which you look out of the open "observation-car" as you sweep from a height of 7000 feet to a level of 2500 in a ride of two hours and a half.

A grander or more exhilarating ride than that from Summit to Colfax, on the Central Pacific Railroad, you can not find in the world. The scenery is various, novel, and magnificent. You sit in an open car at the end of the train, and the roar of the wind, the rush and vehement impetus of the train, and the whirl around curves, past the edge of deep chasms, among forests of magnificent trees, fill you with excitement, wonder, and delight.

When we had seen the Wasatch Cañons we thought the glory of the journey must be over, but the lovely mountains about Salt Lake gave us new delight; and last, as though nature and man had conspired to prepare a series of surprises for the traveler to California, comes the grand stormy rush down the Sierra, followed, as you draw down to the lower levels, by the novel sights of men actually engaged in gold mining: long flumes, in which they conduct the water for their operations, run for miles near the track; and as you pass below Gold Hill you may see men setting the water against great hills, which they wash away to get out the gold from the gravel which bears it. The entrance into California is to the tourist as wonderful and charming as though it were the gate to a veritable fairy-land. All its sights are peculiar and striking: as you pass down from Summit the very color of the soil seems different and richer than that you are accustomed to at home; the farm-houses, with their broad piazzas, speak of a summer climate; the flowers, brilliant at the road-side, are new to Eastern eyes; and at every turn in the road fresh surprises await you.

On the plains and in the mountains the railroad will have seemed to you the great fact. Man seems but an accessory; he appears to exist only that the road may be worked; and I never appreciated until I crossed the Plains the grand character of the old Romans as road-builders, or the real importance of good roads. We, too, in this generation are road-builders. Neither the desert nor the sierra stops us; there is no such word as "impossible" to men like Huntington; they build railroads in the full faith that population and wealth will follow on their iron track.

And they seem to be the best explorers. The "Great American Desert," which we school-boys a quarter of a century ago saw on the map of North

America, has disappeared at the snort of the iron horse; coal and iron are found to abound on the plains as soon as the railroad kings have need of them; the very desert becomes fruitful, and at Humboldt Wells, on the Central Pacific Railroad, in the midst of the sage-brush and alkali country, you will see corn, wheat, potatoes, and fruits of different kinds growing luxuriantly. with the help of culture and irrigation; proving that this vast tract, long supposed to be worthless, needs only skillful treatment to become valuable.

One can not help but speculate upon what kind of men we Americans shall be when all these now desolate plains are filled; when cities shall be found where now only the lonely dépôt or the infrequent cabin stands; when the iron and coal of these regions shall have become, as they soon must, the foundation of great manufacturing populations; and when, perhaps, the whole continent will be covered by our Stars and Stripes. No other nation has ever spread over so large a territory or so diversified a surface as ours. From the low sea-washed shores of the Atlantic your California journey carries you over boundless plains which lie nearly as high as the summit of Mount Washington. Americans are digging silver ore in Colorado, three thousand feet higher than the highest point of the White Mountains. At Virginia City, in Nevada, one of the busiest centres of mining, the traveler finds it hard to draw in breath enough for rapid motion; and many persons, when they first arrive there, suffer from bleeding at the nose by reason of the rarity of the air. Again, in Maine half the farmer's year is spent in accumulating supplies for the other and frozen half; all over the Northern States the preparation for winter is an important part of our lives; but in San Francisco the winter is the pleasantest part of the year; in Los Angeles they do not think it needful to build fireplaces, and scarcely chimneys, in their houses. And one people, speaking the same language, reading the same books, holding a common religion, paying taxes to the same Government, and proud of one common flag, pervades these various altitudes and climates, intervisits, intercommunicates, intermarries, and is, with the potent help of the railroad, fused constantly more closely together as a nation. What manner of man, think you, will be the American of 1972, the product of so many different climes, of so various a range as to altitude?

I wrote that on the plains and on the mountains the railroad is the one great fact. Whatever you notice by the way that is the handiwork of man, appears to be there solely for your convenience or safety who are passing over the road. On the Union Pacific you see miles upon miles of snow-fences. On the Central Pacific, thirty or forty miles of solid snow-sheds, thoroughly built, and fully guarded by gangs of laborers, make the passage safe in the severest snow-storms. Great snow-ploughs, eleven feet high, stand at intervals on the plains and in the mountains, ready to drive, with three or four, or even seven or eight, locomotives behind them, the snow out of the cuts. The telegraph accompanies you on your whole long journey. Coal mines are opened to furnish fuel to your locomotive. At intervals of a hundred miles, night and day, you hear men beating the wheels of the train to see if they are sound. Eating-stations furnish you your meals; ice is supplied on the way; laborers stand aside in the desert and on the mountains as the train sweeps by, and close up behind it to repair the track or keep it in order. There is a Chinaman and a half on every mile of the Central Pacific Railroad; and this road is not only a marvel of engineering skill and daring, running through a most difficult country, and abounding in deep rock-cuts, tunnels, and snow-sheds, but you will find its road-bed everywhere firm and solid, as though it had been laid for years, the cuts clean and clear, and on every part of the work an air of finish and precision, which shows the confidence of its owners, and the thorough spirit in which it was conceived and completed, and is maintained.

COOKING-RANGE, PULLMAN PALACE-CAR, UNION PACIFIC RAILROAD.

You reach San Francisco by passing through the great Sacramento plain, one of the famous wheat fields of the State, to Vallejo, whence you sail down the magnificent bay of San Francisco to the city; and thus you have, to the last hour of your journey, some new scene opening to your eyes, and when you go to sleep in your hotel at last, may dream of the Cliff House ride as a pleasure still to come.

I close this chapter with a few detailed directions to tourists, such as I should myself have been glad of when I first made the journey.

1. At Ogden your train will connect with the regular train for Salt Lake City, which place you reach the same evening. The Townsend House is kept by a Mormon, the American by a Gentile. An omnibus conveys you to either. Go to Brigham Young's theatre in the evening, if you like, and see his rocking-chair in the aisle, and the large space set apart in the box tier for his children. Rise early the next morning and walk about for an hour, and you may see almost the whole place. After breakfast get a carriage, and tell the driver to take you to the Tabernacle and the Menagerie—the last contains a number of native animals well worth seeing—and to show you the principal objects of interest. You will have time for a leisurely dinner before the cars start, and

will yet have seen all that Salt Lake City affords to the traveler—for it is not easy for non-residents to see the inside of a Mormon house.

2. At Salt Lake City buy a little gold for California; they take greenbacks in Utah.

3. In San Francisco you can exchange your greenbacks for gold notes, which are more convenient than coin, and just as serviceable.

4. Eat only two meals per day on your journey, as you are not exercising nor working. After you enter California you will find both fruit and flowers for sale on the train—signs of civilization which do not attend you on an Eastern train.

5. From Ogden, when you start westward, telegraph to the Grand Hotel, the Occidental, the Lick House, or wherever you mean to stay in San Francisco, for rooms. The cost is a trifle, and it is a convenience to have your apartments ready for you when you arrive.

6. In planning your journey you will desire to know how much time is required, and what the expense of your trip will be. Here are three schedules or time-tables for tours of various lengths, and a general estimate of expenses.

FOR A FIVE WEEKS' TOUR.

	DAYS.
From Chicago to San Francisco	5
At Salt Lake	1
San Francisco and the surroundings	5
The San José Valley, to the Almaden Mine	3
The Geysers	2
The Yosemite and Big Trees. (This gives you one day in the Calaveras grove and five in the valley.)	12
Return to Chicago	5
Total	33

FOR A SIX WEEKS' TOUR.

From Chicago to San Francisco	5
At Salt Lake	1
San Francisco and surroundings	8
The San José Valley and Almaden Mine	3
Santa Cruz, Watsonville, Pescadero, etc.	4
The Geysers	3
The Yosemite and Big Trees	12
Lakes Tahoe and Donner	2
Virginia City	1
Total	39

FOR A NINE WEEKS' TOUR.

Take the last, and add—

To Los Angeles and San Diego and back	14
To Mount Shasta and return	6
Total	59

If you can spare more time, you should add a week to your Yosemite journey, which would give you opportunity to make the tour of the valley's outer rim, which can be done by ladies now without discomfort.

In going to the Yosemite, go in by way of Merced, which, though a little longer ride, gives you Inspiration Point as your first view of the famous valley; and pass out the other way, as that leads, by way of Chinese Camp and Sonora, through one of the most famous of the "placer diggings," to the Calaveras Grove of Big Trees. Next I put the cost of the journey:

Fare by railroad from Chicago to San Francisco	$118
Return	118
To Salt Lake and return	5
To San José and return	10
To the Geysers and return	26
To the Big Trees, Yosemite, and return	38
Railroad and stage fares for five weeks' tour	$315
To this add, for sleeping-cars, about $3 per day—ten days	30
	$345

Add, for hotel accommodations, $3 50 per day, which is the usual price; and for carriage hire in seeing the Almaden mine, $5; for horses and guides in the Yosemite, $5 per day; for meals on the railroad, $2 per day. In all, $125 will pay your hotel and carriage bills, horse and guide in the Yosemite Valley, railroad meals, etc.; and this, added to $345, makes $470. This is a liberal and not a close estimate; and if you allow $500 for a five weeks' tour to California and back, you will have enough to pay the slight premium on gold, and to buy some curiosities to take home with you. And you will have stopped at first-class hotels everywhere, and used a carriage wherever it was convenient.

To see Lake Tahoe, Donner Lake, and Virginia City will cost you twenty dollars more, including hotel bills. These you should see on your way home, getting off the Central Pacific train at Truckee, and resuming your place at Reno, when you have made the trip, without extra charge. Allow three days, and engage your sleeping-car accommodations at Sacramento, for a given day, on your way to Truckee.

To Los Angeles you go by steamer; fare $18 each way, which includes meals and state-rooms. The sail is a lovely one, with land in sight all the way. Try to secure a berth on the land side, as the coast affords continuously fine views. The steamer lands you at San Pedro. Thence by cars to Los Angeles the fare is $2 50. From Los Angeles you should drive to the Mission San Gabriel, where are the finest orange orchards. The drive will cost you from three to five dollars. At San Diego you see a fine bay and a growing city, which now waits for railroad connections.

To Santa Cruz, Watsonville, and Pescadero the round trip should cost you from twenty to twenty-five dollars, and ten dollars less if you start from San José, after having seen the New Almaden quicksilver mines, and thus save the return to San Francisco.

INTERIOR OF PULLMAN SLEEPING-CAR, PACIFIC RAILROAD.

You will find good hotels everywhere, though often, in the country, plainly furnished. The bread is good, food is always abundant, and generally well cooked, and the beds are clean, and almost always good. The stage-drivers, landlords, and others with whom a traveler has to do are civil and obliging, and I have never heard of attempts at extortion.

The tourist should take with him Croffut's excellent "Trans-Continental Guide," which is sold on the cars, and which gives distances, elevations, etc., of all the stations, and many other interesting particulars. Also Hutchings's "Wonders of California," published by Widdleton in New York; and Professor Whitney's admirable "Yosemite Guide-Book."

OBSERVATION-CAR.

CHAPTER II.

SIGHTS BY THE WAY.—SALT LAKE CITY.

ON the way from Ogden to Salt Lake a singular piece of good fortune be-
fell us. Mr. Hooper, the Utah delegate in Congress, came down with us.
When the train got in, we found that Brigham Young, many of his elders and
chief officers, and their wives and daughters, had come up from Salt Lake City
to welcome Mr. Hooper, and accompany him home. They, with their band
and singers, filled two cars, and by the intervention of Mr. Hooper, another car,
containing the party of which I was a member, was taken on as part of this
train. We had hardly started, in this special train, when Mr. Hooper asked us
all into Mr. Young's car, and we were presently introduced to what somebody
called "all the nobility" of Salt Lake.

I believe the ladies of our party never thought to find themselves in such
strange quarters. After some general greetings we were seated in the two
cars for our ride of thirty-nine miles to Salt Lake City; and, being properly
introduced, fell as naturally into conversation as though we had been in New
York. Brigham Young—President Young he is formally called when you are
presented, but Brother Brigham his people often call him—took a seat beside

one of the ladies of our party, with two others in front of him, and conversed affably all the way down.   Mrs. Young fell to my lot—a handsome and clever person, well made up in every way.   Mrs. Young — I mean another Mrs. Young, also handsome and clever—was seated beside another gentleman.   I believe six or seven of Mr. Young's wives were distributed through the cars, and quite a number of his children.

Brigham Young is a tall, stout, full-faced, robust man, who looks more like a hearty, beef-eating English squire than any thing else—until you come to look into his pale blue, keen eyes.   Then he looked to me like a man extremely on his guard, and a man capable of showing his teeth.   He wore black, with a silk hat, and carried loosely about his neck — the day being a little cool — a somewhat conspicuous rose-colored scarf.   This color was worn also by one of his wives.

Mr. Young talked very freely with the ladies near whom he sat, explaining to them the methods of irrigating the land, the extent of his preaching tours, and the value of Salt Lake in the future.   Mrs. Young—Mrs. Amelia Young, I suppose she might be called—explained to me in like manner many objects of interest along the road.   Once only she touched upon polygamy—and then in the most casual manner.   Seeing some Indians, I asked if the saints had made any thing of these people.   She replied that the girls, if taken early and trained, make excellent and faithful servants.   "Mr. Young," said she, "has had one in his house for many years, and she is a very good woman, and would not return to her people."   I proceeded to ask some further particulars about this Indian woman, to which Mrs. Young replied, with not the least embarrassment, "I can't tell you; she is not my servant; she lives with another of Mr. Young's wives"—Sister Eliza, I think she said—"who is not here to-day."

To one of our ladies a daughter of Mr. Young related that her father had fifty-five children; that he was a very good and indulgent father; that he could not very well meet them all together at every meal, and therefore took breakfast with one half of them on one day, and with the other half at another time.

One Mrs. Young related to some of the ladies that Mr. Young takes no dinner, but only two meals per day.   He breakfasts at the Beehive House, and takes tea at the Lion House.   These are his two principal houses.   She added that all his wives do not live in these houses, some having houses of their own; and Mr Young goes occasionally to take a meal with one or the other of these.

A Miss Young added that her father is fond of dancing, and an excellent dancer (he is only seventy years of age, you know); and that balls are given in the theatre and elsewhere, occasionally, where he dances with great liveliness. I heard this, too, from others.   He seemed to me heavy and slow-motioned for a dancer, but he is an extremely well-preserved man, with the florid complexion of a person who lives much out-of-doors.

We had just passed through Echo and Weber Cañons, and the Devil's Gate—mile after mile of the grandest, strangest, and rudest scenery—like a long opium dream; and now, on our way to Salt Lake City, all this was changed, and we were enchanted by a gentler aspect of nature—distant mountain peaks, their snowy tops seen across the broad expanse of the lake: the beautiful Rock Island in the lake, and every view lovely and inviting where before it was grand but lonely.

At three or four hamlets along the road the train was stopped, and the country children, ranged in line—boys and girls, with banners like a Sunday-school procession in the border parts of our country, took off their hats and cheered their delegate, Mr. Hooper, who responded in a very few grateful words—words which had a curious and, to me, not unpleasant Old Testament tone—a brother returning to his kindred from afar off, blessing God that he finds all safe, and commending all to the God who has built up their Zion.

In the evening our whole party was invited to the theatre, where I saw the celebrated rocking-chair — placed in one of the aisles — in which Young sits; and his own private box, which was occupied by nine or ten young girls and some young men, who, we were told, were Brigham's children. Two of his married daughters took prominent parts in the play. The house was thin; and, during the performance, three officers quietly removed an escaped prisoner, who had sought concealment in the theatre.

The next day, of course, we saw the lions of Salt Lake City. The place is laid out with very broad streets, and lies on a hill-side. What strikes you as a pleasant arrangement is, that down every gutter a torrent of water rushes. This is for irrigation, and is turned off into the gardens by the way, doing its work, by the watchful care of "Water Masters," in turn for every one, poor and rich alike.

The dwellings are generally small, mostly of adobe, or unburned brick, and placed in gardens, in which fruit-trees of various kinds were budding and blossoming. I ate here apples better by far than any I have tasted for years in the East; and Salt Lake is famous for its fine peaches, pears, and apples. In one garden I saw strawberry plants in magnificent condition, and the fruit-trees everywhere looked very healthful, though they have for five years past suffered from grasshoppers.

In the upper part of the city—somewhat overlooking it, and spreading along almost its whole breadth—lie first the Tabernacle, then the vast granite foundations of the Temple, then the Tithing House and (jealousy inclosed in a high wall of stone) Brigham Young's houses, and farther on his stables, his woolen-mills, and the houses of some of his wives.

This inclosure, within which you get peeps only, through one or two narrow and half-closed doors, and which you can not overlook from any convenient place above, has the air of an Eastern harem. All is still and apparently lifeless within. The two largest houses are marked, one by a bee-hive and the other by a lion; and with an odd frankness, if it was not mere heedlessness, Brigham has put over the gate which leads to his inclosure and to his factories a bee-hive, the emblem of industry, in the claws of an enormous and rapacious-looking eagle.

Salt Lake need not hold any mere pleasure traveler more than a day. You can drive all over it in two hours; and when you have seen the Tabernacle— an admirably-arranged and very ugly building—which contains an organ, built in Salt Lake by an English workman, a Mormon named Ridges, which organ is second in size only to the Boston organ, and far sweeter in tone than the one of Plymouth Church; the Menagerie, within Brigham Young's inclosure, which contains several bears, some lynxes and wild-cats — natives of these mountains—and a small but interesting collection of minerals and Indian remains, and of the manufactures of the Mormons; the Temple Block; and enjoyed the magnificent view which is seen from the back of the city of the valley and the snow-capped peaks which lie on the other side—a view which you carry with you all over the place—you have done Salt Lake City, and have time, if you have risen early, to bathe at the sulphur spring. The lake lies too far away to be visited in one day. If you stop, as our party did, at the Mormon hotel—the Townsend House it is called—you will find an abundance of good food, admirably cooked, and plainly but well served; and you may perhaps, if you keep your eyes open, see an active-looking, vigorous young woman eating her breakfast alone at the end of the room, who is one of the three wives of the proprietor. Scandal relates that this one manages the cooking and service—one of the others being too old, and another too pretty, to work. Thus at the Townsend you may chance to get a peep at Mormondom.

For my part, I rose—thanks to the boisterous care of a friend—at five o'clock, walked over nearly the whole place between that hour and eight, and drove over it all again later in the day, and I give you here, with some diffidence, the impression it made upon me.

In the first place, considering what an immense quantity of good land there is in these United States, I should say that Brigham Young made what they call in the West "a mighty poor land speculation" for his people. "If we should stop irrigation for ninety days, not a tree, shrub, or vine would remain alive in our country," said a Mormon to me as I walked through his garden. "Not a tree grew in our plains when we came here, and we had, and have, to haul our wood and timber fourteen to twenty miles out of the mountains," said another. The soil, though good, is full of stones, and I saw a terraced garden of about three acres, built up against the hill-side, which must have cost ten or twelve thousand dollars to prepare.

That is to say, Young marched his people a thousand miles through a desert, to settle them in a valley where almost every acre must have cost them in

GREEN BLUFFS, 1500 FEET ABOVE THE AMERICAN RIVER,
SEVENTY-ONE MILES FROM SACRAMENTO.

labor and money to get it ready for agricultural use, I should say, not less than one hundred dollars. An Illinois, or Iowa, or Missouri, or Minnesota farmer, who paid a dollar and a quarter an acre for his land in those days, got a better farm, ready made to his hand, than these people got from Brigham, their leader, only after the experience of untold hardships (which we will not now count in), and of at least one hundred dollars' worth of labor per acre when they reached their destination.

The whole settlement of Salt Lake City tells of this. There is an air of strain and hardship about every thing. After twenty-five years of hard work, unceasing industry, their houses are small and mean; their gardens are badly kept; the whole place has the cheap, shabby, and temporary look of a new settlement. The Tabernacle is a huge, vast building; it will accommodate thirteen thousand people with seats, but the plaster is rough; the pews—models of comfort in their shape—are unpainted; the magnificent organ, which it took five years and a half to build, has a case very well shaped, but of shabby stained pine; and in the whole city, the high wall around Brigham Young's houses is the only permanent and respectable structure I saw—the only evidence of luxury, for it is a substantial wall.

Moreover, unless I am deceived, the younger generation—the children of Utah—show in their forms the bad fruit of this hard life. They seemed to me, as I studied them in the car coming down, and on the streets the next day, under-sized, loosely built, flabby. Certainly the young girls were pale, and had unwholesome, waxy complexions. The young men were small and thin, and

looked weak. Now this is not—so Gentiles here say—the result of polygamy.
It seemed to me more the result of poor living in the early days; of a too hard
struggle with life while these youth were babes.

I should say, then, that Brigham Young, prophet and leader of his people,
made a huge blunder when he brought them so far for so little. Moses led his
people through the wilderness, but he landed them in Canaan, flowing with
milk and honey. Brigham was a very poor sort of Moses.

But, said a Mormon to whom I gave these impressions, "President Young's
object was to isolate the people from the world, and this he accomplished."

To that I should say, polygamy was the only reason for the seclusion of the
Mormons. If it had not been for polygamy every State was open to the Mormons, and their industry and thrift would have been welcomed in Missouri,
Iowa, or Minnesota. It is to polygamy, then, that the long journey and the
lasting hardships, the too severe toil, the under-sized children, have to be
charged.

Well, not one-tenth of the men in Utah are, or can afford to be, polygamists.
Polygamy is in· the nature of things, like slavery, an aristocratic institution.
Brigham Young can afford sixteen wives; a prosperous hotel-keeper can afford
three; a merchant may, if he does well, support several women; but the laborer, the farmer, the poor man struggling to make himself a home, can not afford
to make half a dozen homes for half a dozen wives.

I should say, then, that it is for the luxury of the favored few, for Young,
for his elders and counselors and the prosperous Mormon leaders, in order that
they might gratify their bestial propensities, that this cruel migration was set
on foot; and this is the only plea which Brigham Young can offer, to shield
himself from the charge of a disgraceful blunder.

And now, if he lives to be eighty, he will see his whole system crumble.
The Utah Railroad and the Utah silver mines are killing polygamy, and when
that is broken up, Mormonism, no longer peculiar, will take an inconspicuous
place among the religions of our continent. A friend said to me, "I see a
great change in Salt Lake since I was there three years ago. The place is
free; people no longer speak in whispers. Three years ago it was unsafe to
speak aloud in Salt Lake City about Mormonism, and you were warned to be
cautious. Now the Gentile may, and does, say what he likes.

But Brigham has great influence over his people. Here is an impressive
example of it, as also of the way in which he uses it: some years ago an out-
lying settlement of Mormons was formed, near what they believed to be the
Montana border, but safely within Utah. With the patient industry of these
people, they made themselves comfortable homes, planted, as is their way, vines
and fruit-trees and gardens, and, having conquered the wilderness, began to be
prosperous. Last year their vines were to bear their first full crop, and they
looked forward with joy to the event. But a new survey of the state line

showed this settlement to lie within Montana.   The news was carried to Brigham Young; and shortly afterward the whole of these Mormon settlers abandoned their pleasant homes, leaving behind houses, tilled lands, fruit-trees, vines, all that their patient labor had created, and at Young's orders returned to Utah.   That is Mormonism.

One thing Young's supporters claim for him, which will probably have to be allowed.   They say that he brought hither, without cost to the Government, a multitude of the most ignorant and thriftless people of different European countries; that he has known how to work up this unpromising raw material into a population notable for its industry, its peaceful and orderly habits, and for some—not all—of the best qualities of free citizens; that he has done this by a system of co-operation which has enabled him to bring out from obscure and distant parts of Europe, and across half the continent of America, men, women, and children so poor that they could never have come at their own charges; that the system of migration which he perfected has protected the emigrant and his family against suffering and wrong on the way, and provided him at once, on his arrival at his destination, with a home and work; and introduced him into a society where he fell naturally into habits of industry, was taught how to labor, and was kept from temptations to vice.

To a certain extent this is true; the Mormon leaders, themselves mostly commonplace, and often vulgar, men, have certainly known how to work up very poor material into a tolerable form of citizen; and this part of their system is well worth the study of intelligent men, and deserves the attention of the railroad capitalists who are now, in different parts of the west, trying to settle Europeans on their lands.

C. P. HUNTINGTON.

CHAPTER III.

THE CENTRAL PACIFIC RAILROAD.

YOU enter California by one of the most notable and remarkable objects it contains—I mean the Central Pacific Railroad. All the world has heard of the great Mont Cenis Tunnel; and travelers tell us perpetually of sights and public works in Europe; but if the Americans were not the most modest people in the world, they would before this have made more famous than any European public work the magnificent and daring piece of engineering by whose help you roll speedily and luxuriously across the Sierra Nevada from Ogden to San Francisco. But we Americans have too much to do to spend our time in boasting. When we have accomplished some great thing, we turn to something still greater, if it is at hand; and it is a curious commentary upon this characteristic that the man whose daring, determination, resistless energy, and clear prevision did more than any thing else to build this great road—I mean C. P. Huntington—has already turned away to another enterprise, in parts almost equally difficult—the Chesapeake and Ohio Railroad.*

You take the cars of the Central Pacific Railroad at Ogden, at a level of 4200 feet above the sea, and the locomotive draws your train over many miles of an alkali desert, in parts of which water had to be drawn forty miles for the men who built the road; up the Sierra to a height of 7017 feet, where the snow lay sixty feet deep one winter while the road was building, and where they actually dug tunnels through the snow and ice to work on the road-bed; down from the summit around cliffs, along the edge of precipices, through miles of snow-sheds, through tunnels and deep rock-cuts, across chasms where you shudder as you look down into the rushing torrent far below; and all this, until you reach the plain of the Sacramento, through a country even yet almost uninhabited, believed ten years ago to be uninhabitable, presenting at every step the most tremendous difficulties to the engineer as well as to the capitalist.

The story of the building of the Central Pacific Railroad is one of the most remarkable examples of the dauntless spirit of American enterprise. The men who built it were merchants, who probably knew no more about building railroads when they had passed middle age and attained a respectable competence by trade, than a Colusa Pike knows about Greek. Huntington and Hopkins were, and are, hardware merchants. Stanford was at one time a wholesale dealer in groceries, though later Governor of the State; the two Crockers were dry-goods men. These five, all at or past middle age, all living in Sacramento, then an insignificant interior town of California, believing in each other, believing that the railroad must be built, and finding no one else ready to undertake it, put their hands and heads and their means to the great work, and carried it through.

---

* There is a story of Huntington, which is so characteristic of him and of the spirit of Yankee boys, that I venture to relate it here. He was one of a large family, I have been told—children of a poor and hard-working Connecticut man. The children knew that they would have to fight their own way in the world, and young Huntington's first dollar was earned when he was less than twelve years of age. A well-to-do neighbor employed the boy to pile up in the wood-shed a quantity of fire-wood which had been sawed for the winter. He piled it neatly and smoothly, and this done, with that spirit of thoroughness with which, in middle age, he built railroads, he picked up all the chips in the wood-yard, and swept it clean with an old broom. His employer was much pleased with the boy's work, and, patting him on the head, gave him a dollar, and said, "You have done this so well, that I guess I'll have to give you the job next year again." "My mind was divided," said Huntington, later in life, when he related this incident, "between delight at the dollar and the praise, and contempt for the man who thought that I should be at no better work than piling wood in a year from then."

Every body knows what is the common fate in this country of railroad project- ors. A few san- guine and public- spirited men pro- cure a charter, make up a com- pany, subscribe for the stock, drag all their friends in, get the pre- liminary surveys made, begin the work—and then break down; and two or three cap- italists, who have been quietly wait-

FLUME AND RAILROAD AT GOLD RUN, SIXTY-FOUR MILES FROM SACRAMENTO.

ing for this foreseen conclusion— foreseen by them, I mean — there- upon step in, buy the valuable wreck for a song, and build and run and own the road. This is a business in itself. Dozens of men have made millions apiece by this process, which is per- fectly legitimate; for, as the French say, in order to succeed you must be successful; or, as we say in this country, to the victors belong the spoils.

Now the projectors of the Central Pacific Railroad completed it, and to- day control and manage it; they did not let it slip out of their fingers; and, what is more, being only merchants, totally inexperienced in railroad building and railroad managing, they did their work so well that, in the opinion of the best engineers, their road is to-day one of the most thoroughly built and equipped and best-managed in the United States. Their bonds sell in Europe but little if any below United States Government bonds, and their credit as a company, in London, Frankfort, and Paris, is as high as that of the Govern- ment itself.

Moreover, you are to remember that these five Sacramento merchants, who undertook to build a railroad through eight hundred miles of an almost unin-

habited country, over mountains and across an alkali desert, were totally unknown to the great money world; that their project was pronounced impracticable by engineers of reputation testifying before legislative committees; that
it was opposed and ridiculed at every step by the moneyed men of San Francisco; that even in their own neighborhood they were thought sure to fail;
and the "Dutch Flat Swindle," as their project was called, was caricatured,
written down in pamphlets, abused in newspapers, spoken against by politicians, denounced by capitalists, and for a long time held in such ill repute that
it was more than a banker's character for prudence was worth to connect himself with it, even by subscribing for its stock.

Nor was this all. Not only had credit to be created for the enterprise
against all these difficulties, but when money was raised, the material for the
road—the iron, the spikes, the tools to dig, the powder to blast, the locomotives, the cars, the machinery, every thing—had to be shipped from New York
around Cape Horn, to make an expensive and hazardous eight months' voyage,
before it could be landed in San Francisco, and had then to be reshipped one
hundred and twenty miles to Sacramento by water. Not a foot of iron was
laid on the road on all the eight hundred miles to Ogden, not a spike was driv-
en, not a dirt-car was moved, nor a powder-blast set off, that was not first
brought around Cape Horn; and at every step of its progress the work depended upon the promptness with which all this material was shipped for a
sea-voyage of thousands of miles around Cape Horn.

Men, too, as well as material had to be obtained from a great distance.
California, thinly populated, with wages very high at that time, could not supply the force needed. Laborers were obtained from New York, from the lower country, and finally ten thousand Chinese were brought over the Pacific
Ocean, and their patient toil completed the work.

When you get to Sacramento, if you have a quarter of an hour to spare,
ask somebody to show you No. 54 K Street. It is not far from the railroad
dépôt, and it is the place where the Central Pacific Railroad was nursed, and
from which it grew. You will see over the plain frame store a weather-beaten
old sign, "Huntington and Hopkins," and if you walk in you will find a tolerably complete assortment of hardware. Here C. P. Huntington and Mark
Hopkins, the first from Connecticut, the last from the hill country of Massa-
chusetts, gathered, by diligence, shrewdness, and honest dealing, a respectable
fortune. They were so cautious that they never owned a dollar of stock in a
mine, never had a branch house, never sent out a "drummer" to get business,
and never sued a man for a debt. It is still related in Sacramento that the
cardinal rule of the firm was to ask a high price for every thing, but to sell
only a good article—the best in the market.

In fact, Huntington and Hopkins were merchants, and nothing else, in business. They sold hardware. But in politics they were Free-soilers, and later

EAGLE GAP, ON THE TRUCKEE RIVER.

Republicans, and they did not sell their principles. It came about that No. 54 K Street became a place where leading Republicans met to discuss the news and plan opposition to the Democratic party, which then, in 1856–'58, though probably numerically the weakest, was strongest in money, in its aggressive spirit, and in social influence in the State. In those early days, when a Pacific Railroad, though talked of, was still a dream of the far-off future, "54 K Street," which has since found room for all the various offices of the Central Pacific Company, without disturbing the hardware business—in those days it accommodated in a modest upper-story room the first Republican press of California. This was called the *Times;* it supported Fremont; and Mr. Cole, lately United States Senator from California, was its editor. Thus "54 K Street" was the head-quarters of the Republicans in the northern and central parts of the State; and here met, with Huntington and Hopkins among others, Stanford,

4

afterward the able Governor of the State, and President of the Central Pacific Company, and the Crockers, both able men, and one a judge.

Sitting around the stove on dull winter evenings in the store at 54 K Street, the two hardware merchants and their Republican allies, Stanford and the Crockers, when politics flagged, are said to have returned again and again to the project of a Pacific road. The desire for a road was in every body's mind in California; the question entered so completely into politics that no man for years could hope to be chosen to an office by either party unless he was believed to be the zealous friend of the railroad.

In 1850–'51 a wagon road was the most that was hoped for; and to this every body subscribed as he was able. Then came the telegraph; and in that all public-spirited men took stock, or to it they gave outright what they could spare. Meantime, year after year, the Pacific Railroad Bill appeared in Congress, was discussed, and laid over. The "snow-capped Sierras" were the bugbear of Senators; but Republicans in California thought they saw in this only a pretense when they heard Democratic politicians proposing to divide the State into two, and make two Pacific railroads—one for the North and one for the South.

Finally there came, to build the little Sacramento Valley Railroad, one Judah, an engineer, who, many people thought, was Pacific Railroad crazy. He begged some money among the most sanguine railroad men, and made a reconnaissance of two or three gaps in the Sierra. After some time he proclaimed that he had discovered what every body wished for—a possible passage for a railroad. By way of Dutch Flat, he asserted, there was a long, easy ascent, practicable for a road. Judah, sanguine and restless, personally solicited subscriptions from the people of Dutch Flat, Auburn, Grass Valley, and Sacramento, to help him to make a more thorough exploration. Public meetings were held, and men gave, according to their means, ten, fifty, a hundred dollars for this object. A law of the State, which made every stockholder individually liable for the debts of a company, made people cautious about subscribing to new projects, and Judah got his support chiefly in gifts; and among his leading supporters in this way were the five merchants I have named.

About this time came the rumble of war, and the San Francisco capitalists, mostly at that time Southern men, would not have any thing more to do with the scheme; and once more it seemed to be crushed.

Working under the State laws, which provided that before a company could have a charter $1000 must be paid in for every mile of its proposed road, it was not easy to raise the capital—about $135,000—needed to obtain a charter; and yet affairs had now come to such a pass that it was no longer worth while, or even possible, to go on without organization. Sacramento was canvassed, but with too little success; San Francisco had buttoned up its pockets; and at last Huntington, who had refused to give any more money for mere reconnaissances, proposed to half a dozen others to undertake the enterprise among themselves of making a regular and careful survey. "I'll be one of ten, or one of eight, to bear the whole expense, if Hopkins will consent," he said, at a meeting called at Governor Stanford's house; and thus the great work was at last begun, seven men binding themselves in a compact for three years to pay all needful expenses of a thorough survey out of their own pockets. Of these seven, one, Judah, had no means, and shortly afterward died, and another presently dropped out. There were a few outside subscriptions; but it is curious to remember that when a prominent banker friendly to the project, and having faith in it, was asked to take some stock, he declined on the plea that the credit of his bank would suffer if he were known to be connected with so wild a scheme. This was in 1860, twelve years ago.

The Central Pacific Railroad Company was thus at last organized, with Leland Stanford as president, C. P. Huntington as vice-president, and Mark Hopkins as secretary and treasurer; and the same men hold the same places to-day.

Affairs now began to look, to the prudent hardware dealers at No. 54 K Street, as though they were likely to have more railroad presently than would be good for the hardware business. While the explorations and surveys were going on in the winter of 1860–'61, and while a Pacific Railroad Bill was getting drawn in Congress, business details began to be examined; and at 54 K Street they asked themselves why it was that so few railroads in this country had been successful in first hands. The answer was that, first, they were not prudently and economically managed in the beginning; and second, that American railroads are built largely on cred-it: thus it almost always happens that the interest account begins to run before the road can earn money; and to pay interest when no business is done would ruin almost any undertaking, even the hardware business, thought these shrewd merchants.

FIRST OFFICE OF THE CENTRAL PACIFIC RAILROAD.

As to the first fault—on this page you may see a picture of the first building erected by the Central Pacific Railroad Company. You will notice, perhaps, that "C. P. Huntington"— *Central Pacific* Huntington he began to be called in those days—was its "architect." The engineer had designed what to his professional eye seemed a proper building for the Sacramento business. It was large, elaborate, complete, and would have cost $12,000. Huntington approved of the plan, which he said was *admirable for by-and-by;* "For the present," said he, "we are not doing much business, and *this* would do better:" and with a piece of chalk he drew the outline, on one of the iron doors of 54 K Street, of such a board structure as he thought sufficient; the four sides were nailed together in an afternoon; it was roofed the next day; it cost $150; and when it grew too small for its original uses, it was removed and used as a paint shop. There was no nonsense or flummery about 54 K Street. And I may add that the same spirit still prevails there. Of course the company now owns and occupies an extensive river frontage in Sacramento, as well as in Oakland, at Vallejo, and in San Francisco, for its business; its real estate is worth many millions of dollars; but the business offices you will still find in the very plain frame house, 54 K Street, over the old hardware store; and if you visit the New York office, you will find there an equally plain establishment.

As to the second point—Huntington was, after consultation, sent to Washington, strictly enjoined to see that in the Pacific Railroad Bill it should be provided that the company should pay no interest on the bonds it received of the Government for at least ten years; and if this condition was refused, to abandon the whole matter, and sell the wreck for what it would bring.

Another and more notable thing these five men did. When they sent Huntington to Washington, they gave him a power of attorney authorizing him to do for them and in their name any thing whatever—to buy, sell, bargain, convey, borrow, or lend, without any *if* or *but*, let or hinderance whatever, except that he should fare alike with them, in all that concerned their great project. It is not often that five middle-aged business men are found to place such entire confidence in each other as this; but it was vital to their success that they should feel and act just thus.

At last, one day, Huntington telegraphed from Washington: " The bill has passed, and we have drawn the elephant." Thereupon the company accepted the conditions, and opened books for stock subscriptions to the amount of eight and a half millions to carry the road to the State line. The beginning was not hopeful. The rich men of San Francisco did not subscribe a cent. One man in Nevada took one share. Others elsewhere took five one-hundred-dollar shares more. Six hundred dollars in all were subscribed at the first rush to build the Central Pacific Railroad! Later, mechanics, working-women, and others in Sacramento and other small towns—homesick people who wanted to get back to the Atlantic States without the perils of the sea, it was said—took up about one hundred and fifty shares more. It was a long time before more than a million and a half of stock was taken.

Meantime, in the summer of 1861 a considerable traffic had sprung up between Nevada and Sacramento. This was done over the Placerville Turnpike, and Mark Hopkins took pains to ascertain the amount and value of this commerce, which the Pacific Railroad would do, of course, as soon as it was sufficiently completed. He caused the number of teams on the turnpike and the number of passengers to be counted; and this gave a certain promise of local business. Next it was necessary to cause well-known bankers to certify to the world the good standing and pecuniary responsibility of the principal subscribers to the stock. The California Legislature then merged the State charter in the Federal charter; all the statutes of the State bearing upon the company were gathered together; and thus armed with facts and credentials, Huntington went to New York—to raise a great many millions of dollars.

He was promptly told by capitalists that the bonds of the company had no value in their eyes until some part of the road had been built. The Government bonds, of course, were not to be given until a certain part of the road was completed. The stock subscriptions came in too slowly for practical purposes. Huntington, courageous, full of resources, and of faith in what he had undertaken to do, announced that he would not sell his bonds except for money, and that he would not sell any unless a million and a half were taken; and finally, when that amount was bid for, he called all the bidders together, explained in detail the full importance and value of the enterprise, and thereupon the bonds were taken, on the condition that Huntington and his four partners—Hopkins, Stanford, and the two Crockers—should make themselves personally responsible for the money received, until the bonds could be exchanged for Government bonds. Huntington did not hesitate a moment to pledge his own moderate fortune and those of his associates to this effect. These bonds built thirty-one miles of the road—the easiest part of it, fortunately.

And now came the severest test of the courage and endurance of the men at 54 K Street. Eleven months passed over before they could get the Government bonds for the completed and accepted part of the line; these bonds in the mean time had gone down from one and a half per cent. premium in gold, where they stood when the charter was accepted, to thirty-nine cents for the dollar. Railroad iron in the same period went up from $50 to $135 per ton. All other materials, locomotives, etc., rose in the same proportion; insurance for the eight or nine months' voyage around Cape Horn, which every pound of the material of the road-bed and running stock had to make, rose from two and a half to ten per cent.; freights from $18 to $45 per ton.

Intent on keeping down their interest account, the five men at 54 K Street asked the State to pay for twenty years the interest on a million and a half of bonds, in exchange for which they gave a valuable granite quarry, guarantied free transportation of all stone from it for the public buildings of the State, and also free transportation over their line of all State troops, criminals, lunatics, and paupers. This was done. Then Sacramento and some of the counties were asked to exchange their bonds for the stock of the company, and this was done by a popular vote. But most of these contracts had to be enforced afterward in the courts, the Democratic financial ring opposing every step.

Meantime the money was used up.   The business was from the first kept rigidly under control; every contract was made terminable at the option of the company; every hand employed was paid off monthly; and in reading over some old contracts I came upon a clause specially obliging the contractors to keep liquor out of the camps.   When Huntington, after long and trying labors in New York, returned to Sacramento, he found the treasure chest so low that it was necessary to diminish the laboring force, or at once raise more means. "Huntington and Hopkins," said he, "can, out of their own means, pay 500 men during a year; how many can each of you keep on the line?"   The five men agreed in council at 54 K Street that out of their own private fortunes they would maintain and pay 800 men during a year on the road.

SNOW-SHEDS ON THE CENTRAL PACIFIC RAILROAD.

That resolution ended their troubles.   Before the year was over they had received their Government bonds.   They still had the worst and most costly part of the line to build; they still had to transport all their material around Cape Horn; they had many trials, difficulties, and obstacles before them, for nearly four years were consumed in crossing the Sierra; they had to encounter lawsuits, opposition, ridicule, evil prophecies, losses; had to organize a vast laboring force, drill long tunnels, shovel away in one spring sixty feet of snow over seven miles of the line, merely to get at the road-bed; had to set up saw-mills by the dozen in the mountains to saw ties; haul half a dozen locomotives and twenty tons of iron twenty-six miles over the mountains by ox teams; haul water forty and wood twenty miles for the construction trains on the alkali plains; but it seems to me that this brave resolution was the turning-point in their enterprise. Surely there is something admirable in the courage of five country merchants, ignorant of railroad building, and unknown to the world, assuming such a load as the support of eight hundred men for a year out of their own pockets for an enterprise in the success of which, in their hands, very few of their own friends believed.

The secret of their success was that these five country merchants meant in good faith to build a railroad. They did not expect to get money out of an enterprise before they had put money of their own into it. They managed all the details as carefully and prudently as they were accustomed to manage the hardware or dry goods business. They were honest men. When Huntington began to buy iron and machinery in New York, people flocked to him to sell, and there is a story of some one who came with an offer of a handsome commission to Huntington if he would deal with him. "I want all the commissions I can get," was the reply; "*but I want them put in the bill. This* road has got to be built without any stealings."

" Don't keep a man at work whom you can't pay regularly at the end of the month: we won't stop work, but if we can pay only one man, we will employ only one," was their rule. Therefore every contract was made terminable at the will of the company. In New York, where the money was to be raised on the bonds, and the material had to be bought and shipped, the bonds were sold only for money, and the iron bought for cash. And all this time the interest was kept down by every possible care and prevision. " If there is any money to be made in building this road," said Huntington, " I mean that the company shall make it." When somebody tells you that " the Central Pacific people were close," you will understand that they were honest.

Nor were they satisfied merely to complete their road. They have busied themselves in establishing feeders for it in California, and already own and manage almost the whole railroad system of that State. North toward Oregon, and southward, through the great San Joaquin Valley, toward Los Angeles, San Bernardino, and the Colorado River, engineers are busy laying tracks or completing surveys. The California and Oregon Railroad, which will be completed this year, opens the whole of the great Sacramento Valley and the northern part of the State, and connects with the Oregon Railroad system. The Southern Pacific Railroad, with the Visalia branch, in like manner opens up the still richer San Joaquin Valley, as well as the series of smaller valleys lying west of the Coast Range, which already produce enormous crops of grain. The Western Pacific and California Pacific Railroads complete connections between Sacramento and San Francisco; and the Napa Valley, the Copperopolis, the Watsonville, and other branch roads gather in the products of fertile regions, and carry them to the main lines. About fifteen hundred miles of railroad will be completed this year under the management of the Central and Southern Pacific Companies; and the enormous area brought into profitable culture by these roads may be guessed from the fact that the company owns in all about twelve millions of acres of land, in alternate sections granted it by Congress; much of which is now rapidly settling up.

SNOW-PLOUGH ON THE CENTRAL PACIFIC RAILROAD.

The Central Pacific Railroad was one of the most expensive to build in the world. Its engineers, Montague and Grey, would have been famous all over the world had they constructed a road half as difficult in Europe.* They had

---

* S. S. Montague, still chief engineer of the Central Pacific Railroad, was the active and working head of the engineer corps which built the road. He was born in New Hampshire, but was brought to Illinois by his parents when he was but six years old, in the year 1836. He attended the country schools in his neighborhood, and at the age of twenty-two, having shown readiness in mathematical studies, joined a corps of railroad engineers and learned his profession in the field, in the States of Illinois and Iowa. He lived on his father's farm until he was twenty years of age, attending school during the winter, and taught school for one year, after he was twenty. In 1859 he left home to seek his fortune at Pike's Peak; but the company with which he traveled broke up, and he joined another going across the plains to California, and there found work on the Folsom and Sacramento Railroad, which was then building. In 1862 he joined Theodore Judah, as his first assistant on the Central Pacific. Judah died in 1863, and Montague succeeded him as chief engineer in this great undertaking. He had to locate the greater part of the line, and to organize and command the force which built the road; and though the difficulties he had to contend with are apparent even to laymen, only professional engineers, conversant with the history of the work, can, I suspect, appreciate its magnitude, and the many novel questions which presented themselves in its execution.

Colonel George E. Grey, consulting engineer during the progress of the work, was born in Oneida County, New York, began his career as an engineer on the State canals in 1839, and was engaged on different railroads in New York till 1853. In that year he became chief engineer of

not only to build a road through an almost inaccessible country, but when it was completed they had the further problem of running trains over it at all seasons. You will see little of the costly and solid snow-sheds, through which you pass mostly by night, and which are now being roofed with iron; you will not see at all, perhaps, the ponderous snow-ploughs, of various patterns, some to push the snow off on one side, some on the other, down a precipice; others made merely to fling it off the track on the plains; and behind which, during the past winter, often eight heavy engines were harnessed to "buck" the snow, and throw it from twenty to sixty feet away.

CENTRAL PACIFIC RAILROAD HOSPITAL.

Nor will you see, unless you inquire for it, in Sacramento, an admirable institution, the Central Pacific Railroad Hospital, a fine building which stands in an open square, cost $60,000, and is supported by a monthly contribution of fifty cents from every man engaged with the company, from the president down. One of the ablest physicians of Sacramento has charge of this hospital, and he too was one of eight men who, in 1856, originated the Republican party in California. In the report of the State Board of Health this hospital is spoken of as "first in the order of salubrity and successful results in the world," and it is in every way a complete and carefully managed institution.

The company, which, as I have told you, has still its head-quarters at 54 K Street, Sacramento, now employs more men than all the other manufacturers in

---

the New York Central Railroad, where he remained till May, 1865, when he came to California as consulting engineer of the Central Pacific Company. Colonel Grey built the first wrought-iron bridge on the New York Central Railway.

Mr. Montague is still chief engineer of the Central Pacific, and has built or is building the California and Oregon, the San Joaquin Valley, the San Francisco and North Pacific, and the San Pablo and Tulare Railways—having the general superintendence of the engineering work on all these roads. Colonel Grey is at present chief engineer of the Southern Pacific Railroad.

California; its pay-roll in the State alone contains nearly seven thousand names. It manufactures within the State every article and material used in building or running its roads; it is spending half a million dollars per month in building new roads, and it has, still at 54 K Street, Sacramento, the most complete land-office in the United States, not excepting that at Washington— a place where you may select on maps, locate, and pay for, any quantity of the company's lands you wish for, and where you may obtain in a few minutes detailed and specific information concerning lands in any part of California.

One incident of the building of the road will conclude what I have to say of it. In April, 1869, ten miles of road were built in one day. This is probably the greatest feat of railroad building on record. What is most remarkable about it is that eight men handled all the iron on this ten miles. These eight giants walked ten miles that day, and lifted and handled one thousand tons of rail bars each.

A BIRD'S-EYE VIEW OF THE TRANS-CONTINENTAL ROUTE.

ROUNDING CAPE HORN.

CHAPTER IV.

THE TOURIST IN CALIFORNIA.—WHAT TO SEE, AND HOW TO SEE IT.

THE tourist will find San Francisco one of the pleasantest and most novel of all the sights of California. The hotels are admirably kept; the streets are full of strange sights; the Cliff House will make one of your pleasantest experiences; at Woodward's Gardens a good collection of grizzly bears, and other wild beasts native to California, will amuse and instruct children from fifteen to fifty years of age; the Chinese and Japanese shops have curiosities at all prices, from twenty-five cents to five hundred dollars; and the Chinese quarter will occupy your leisure several days, if you are at all curious.

Your first drive in San Francisco is likely to be to the Cliff House. You may breakfast there if you like; and as all outdoor amusements in this place are controlled by the climate during the spring and summer months, the cold sea-breeze making the afternoons uncomfortable, it is a pretty and sensible thing to rise at six some morning, and see the sea-lions while it is yet warm and still.   Moreover, you are sure of a good breakfast at the Cliff House, and you take it on the verandah, with all China, and Japan, and the King of the Cannibal Islands, looking at you across the broad Pacific.

If you have children in your party, they will not tire of watching the sea-lions, no matter how long you stay.   And if you have any fancy yourself in wild beasts, you will be both amazed and amused at the huge strange creatures which cover the rocks two hundred yards from you, and look, with their pointed heads and shiny bodies, like monstrous maggots crawling and squirming; who lie like dead things upon the rocks; whose howls and hoarse, discordant roars cross to you and make a strange music for your meal.   A seal in Barnum's Museum was a strange beast—but these monstrous misshapen creatures, furious, wild, free, yawning in your face, pushing each other aside, quarreling, suckling their young, rolling off the precipitous rocks into the sea, make the strangest sight my eyes ever beheld.   If Gustave Doré could see them, he would add another weird picture to his chamber of horrors.

The greater part of San Francisco is smoothly laid with wooden pavement; and the city is approached from every side over admirable roads.   A New Yorker boasts of Central Park roads till he has driven thirty miles in a brief forenoon, forty or fifty miles in a day here, over the best ways I ever saw. Go where you will, within fifty miles of the city, and you find smooth, hard roads, broad avenues, often, as at Santa Clara, lined with long, double rows of fine shade-trees—roads over which you may drive at the rate of ten or twelve miles per hour and do no harm to your horses nor tire yourself.

A prominent and wealthy citizen of San Francisco drives into town daily from his country place, twenty-four miles distant, and does it in one hour and fifty minutes.   I wondered at his endurance, until I saw the road he drives over —then I only wondered that he is the only one who does it.

" How do you get such roads?" I asked; and discovered that, like almost every thing that is well done, it was achieved by private enterprise.   The Cliff House road is a toll road; the fine avenues which you ride over about Belmont, Menlo Park, and Fair Oaks, in the San José Valley, were built by private enterprise, the country road-masters only stepping in when a beginning had been made and a model set them.   Outside of Oakland we drove for three or four miles over an admirable road, built through a difficult piece of country by a company only to make a new watering-place accessible.

Most of these roads are macadamized; private enterprise provides steam stone-crushers and steam rollers; and you see constantly, near Oakland, heavy wagons laden with crushed stone, which is brought from a distance of three or four miles. We in and about New York have got into such a habit of expecting the town or county or State government to do every thing for us, that all private effort and enterprise is crippled. Here in this newer country they do not wait for the slow-moving Government, but do things themselves, which we, to our own discomfort, leave undone.

You will easily find the streets in San Francisco devoted to the Chinese. They occupy a considerable part of the heart of the city; and their shops, in Sacramento, Dupont, and other streets, are open to visitors, though you will not find much to buy in them, nor many of the merchants and clerks able to speak or understand English. Ladies and children may safely and properly walk in the main streets in the Chinese quarter by day. The tourist who wishes to investigate farther should get a policeman stationed among the Chinese to show him around after dark. He will see some strange and unpleasant sights; and ladies and children must be excluded from this tour. But all may go to the Chinese theatre. If you have a party of ladies and children, you should apply the day before to the manager of the theatre, a Chinaman, whom you will find on the premises, for a box. This will cost you two dollars, and fifty cents additional for every person in your party. Go about half-past eight, and stay until ten or eleven. The boxes are up stairs, at one end of the gallery; opposite you will see the Chinese women huddled together in a place by themselves: the audience below vehemently resents the indecorum of a woman appearing in the pit. The play usually contains some admirable feats of tumbling; but the whole performance you will find most strange and extraordinary.

You should also, during the day, visit the Chinese temples, or joss-houses, to which a policeman will guide you. They are in the shabby style of the theatre, decorated with cheap tinsel; but you will see the Chinese manner of worship, and in one of the temples some curious carving in wood.

The Chinese quarter is perfectly safe and orderly; and you need no protection, even for ladies and children, in going to the theatre or elsewhere.

Among the sights in California most attractive to the tourist, the groves of Big Trees and the wonderful Yosemite Valley are, of course, the chief.

Travelers who come for but a hurried stay will economize time by seeing first San Francisco and its neighborhood, in which I include the San José Valley, the Almaden mine, and Santa Cruz; and on the north the Geysers, Clear Lake if you have time, the Napa Valley, Santa Rosa, and the Sonoma country. Having "done" the coast, you can turn your face eastward, and, leaving your luggage at the hotel at Stockton or Merced, begin the tour of the Trees and the Valley.

Those who mean to see Los Angeles, San Diego, San Bernardino, or Santa Barbara should, of course, take the steamer trip also before leaving for the interior.

In a previous chapter I have given details of the time needed for, and the

INTERIOR OF SNOW-SHED, CENTRAL PACIFIC RAILROAD.

cost of, various excursions in the State.   Here I mean to give a few hints to those contemplating these journeys.   And first as to the coast trips.

To the Geysers you may go by way of Healdsburg or Calistoga.   At either place you remain overnight, and reach the Geyser Hotel the following fore-noon.   The Healdsburg route is the best; but it is well to go by one way and return by the other.

In going to the Geysers you have an exciting but not dangerous ride through a fine country.   The horses are well trained, and the drivers are ex-perienced men.   Foss, who is the great whip on this route, usually drives six-in-hand; and if you sit with him on the box you will find yourself whirled around turns so short that sometimes you lose sight of the ears of the leaders. The road, which for miles skirts a precipice, is well built and carefully looked after; no accident has ever happened, and you may safely trust yourself to either Foss or any of his subordinates. At the Geysers, where there is a comfortable hotel, you arrive about eleven o'clock, and you leave the next morning. Do not omit to take a soda bath. It is very refreshing, and itself worth the journey.

You buy your tickets for the round trip in San Francisco. It should be understood that the so-called Geysers are not spouting springs. A narrow valley, or cañon, as it is called in California, is filled with flowing hot springs, and the whole soil is covered with a crust of sulphur, iron-rust, and other mineral deposits, and filled with steam from the boiling water. The surface of the ground is so hot that you will be uncomfortable in walking over it if you wear thin-soled shoes.

If you have time, you should see, on the northern side of the bay, San Rafael, which you reach by steamboat, making a pleasant day's excursion, and passing on the way San Quentin and the State Prison; also see the Napa Valley, which contains some of the finest agricultural land and vineyards in the State.

South of San Francisco, the San José Valley contains the finest country places on the Pacific slope. The best way to see it is to telegraph beforehand for a carriage to await you at San Mateo, and tell the driver to show you the best parts of the country, and set you off at Mayfield in time to catch the evening train for San José. There you will find the Auzeray House very comfortable. Engage a team overnight to convey you the next morning to the New Almaden quicksilver mines. Set off at half-past seven, and you will have time to see the works, return to dinner, and drive after dinner to Santa Clara over the beautiful road called the Almeda, which is shaded for two or three miles by the finest trees of their kind in California.

From Santa Clara, or San José if you return thither, the train will take you, by way of Gilroy, to Watsonville, where you may see wheat growing luxuriantly almost to the sea-shore; and by stage through a charming country to Santa Cruz, one of the pleasantest watering-places of California, and, if you wish to see it, to Monterey, the old capital of California. You can not do better than to ride up the coast, through lovely scenery and pleasant villages, to the famous beach of Pescadero, and back to San Mateo, where you take the railroad to San Francisco. This is one of the most delightful of the excursions to be made around San Francisco, and it will give you an excellent example of the agricultural wealth of California, as well as of the picturesque beauty of its scenery. In May and June the whole country is covered with lovely flowers. The brilliant yellow and orange of the eschscholtzia, or California poppy, and the tender blue and white of the lupine, line the road and cover the fields in broad masses, which give a perpetual delight to the eye.

The oak groves, too, will excite your admiration. The California oak is a low-branching and far-spreading tree, disposed in irregular masses, which give a lovely, park-like effect to the landscape, and add very much to the rural beauty of this part of the country. The roses, too, grow in masses, free from disease, and of a size and depth of color not found with us in the East; and in the highly cultivated places in the San José Valley you will meet with the pomegranate, the fig, the almond, and a great variety of flowering shrubs, and some evergreens, unknown to us in the East, many of the former brought from Japan, China, and Australia. The eucalyptus, or Australian gum, is deservedly a favorite tree in all parts of California'; it has made, in favorable places, a growth of fifteen feet in a single season, is evergreen, and its bluish-green foliage contrasts finely with such trees as the lovely Monterey cypress, which is also a rapid grower.

The camellia here remains out-of-doors all winter; the heliotrope is a stout, woody shrub; the gladiolus is already past its bloom in June, and is planted in the fall; and you find it difficult to recognize in the massive eight foot high shrub, whose brilliant bloom almost hides its foliage, and which is used as a hedge or screen, the scarlet geranium. Even the humble little sweet alyssum which with us creeps along the ground, here rears its flower spikes two feet high.

The windmills are a peculiar feature of the Californian landscape. You see them even in San Francisco, on the tops of houses; but in the suburbs every place has one. Everywhere ample provision is made for water; and on one fine place near Menlo Park I was told at least half a mile of water-pipes was laid.

Field irrigation is not practiced near San Francisco except in special cases; but during the long dry season, which lasts from April to October, when it does not rain at all, they preserve their lawns by sprinkling, and new plantations are also freely watered. Artesian wells are common; and the windmill stands usually on top of a tank, from which the water is distributed to the house, the stables, and all over the grounds, hydrants being placed at frequent intervals. From the hydrant a hose is led to a sprinkler, which stands on the lawn, on a tripod, and sends out constantly a thin and finely divided spray. The gardener removes this from time to time, and thus the whole spacious lawn is watered and kept as green and lovely as though it were in the White Mountains.

With such help, I need not tell you that the strawberry grows to perfection. It is larger and I think much sweeter than with us. I am not, at home, a strawberry lover, but here I have relished them without sugar. On one place, near Santa Clara, I noticed an ingenious arrangement for irrigating a strawberry bed of about three acres. A large shallow tank stood near one end of this "patch," with its bottom nearly on a level with the upper end of the rows. From this was led a main, which was connected with a pipe running across the whole upper end of the great field. Between every two of the rows a hole was made in this pipe, and this hole was stopped with a wooden plug.

SUMMIT OF THE SIERRAS, FROM CENTRAL PACIFIC RAILROAD.

Thus we saw only a long row of wooden plugs; pull out any one of these, and the water began immediately to run down the depression between the two rows.

Of course all this appliance of windmills, water-pipes, tanks, and fountains is possible only in a country where they have steady winds and no severe frosts. With us the tanks would burst, the pipes would have to be deeply buried in the ground; and the whole machinery would be continually getting out of order. Yet I could not help seeing that our common complaint of rusty and unpleasing lawns during July and August could be prevented, on the fine places near New York, by the help of a windmill, and a tank which might be emptied in the fall and housed over.

The Californians seem to me to enjoy all the advantages of a tropical climate with but a few of its disadvantages. They have about here no malarious fevers, no musquitoes, no poisonous reptiles; yet their roses bloom all the year round: "I do not know the day in the whole year when I can not gather a bouquet in my garden," said a San Francisco lady to me; in one place in Oakland, I saw the gas-meter out-of-doors near the stable; dwellings need no furnaces to warm them in winter; and the whole cumbrous machinery by which we guard ourselves and our animals and tender plants against cold is here unknown. The greenhouse and conservatory are only affectations; the oleander remains in the ground the winter through; and the fan palm flourishes everywhere.

The people of San Francisco complain of their climate, which is, in truth, somewhat harsh. Every day at ten o'clock during the summer they get a stiff and cool sea-breeze. If you go out in the morning, no matter how warm it is, you are warned to take with you a shawl or overcoat. But on the other hand, for seven months in the year you may lock up your umbrella; and we, too, have dusty roads, but no constant alleviation of cool breezes.

Moreover, a journey of thirty miles puts you into an entirely different climate. The San José Valley, the Napa Valley, and others, lie behind the Coast Range, and are thus sheltered from the ocean breezes; and here there is no afternoon gale, and all the winds are gentle. We came up from San José on a brilliant, warm day, which we had enjoyed by driving early to the quicksilver mines, and later over the lovely Almeda, to Santa Clara. As the train neared the city, we closed the windows; presently the ladies drew shawls about them; and when we got out of the cars at San Francisco, I drew on my overcoat, and was glad to close the carriage windows; and we sat by a fire in the evening. Thus it is all summer; and as there is no rain, the country, of course, gets dusty; and in the country houses you find wraps for the neck, and other appliances to keep out the dust when you drive out, and in your room a queer sprinkler over the wash-basin, wherewith conveniently to wash the dust out of your hair when you return from a drive.

If you make the voyage to the southern counties, you will see at Los Angeles and its neighboring settlement, the mission San Gabriel, a number of fine orange orchards in full bearing—surely one of the most beautiful objects in nature; at Santa Barbara groves of the olive and almond, as well as some bearing and finely grown English walnuts; and near San Diego, at the old mission, several date-palms, and the oldest olive grove in the State. You must not expect to find at these places or in San Bernardino the evidences of wealth and high culture which are abundant nearer San Francisco; but the short sea-voyage is a pleasure in itself, and the sights you will see will show you how various are the capacities of California. If you go by steamer, secure a state-room on the shore side, as you sail all the way in sight of the coast, which has a great deal of fine scenery.

Santa Barbara and San Diego have become, within two years, favorite winter resorts for invalids from the colder Eastern States. The climate of both places is remarkably equal and warm all winter. Observation, as well as the experience of consumptives, shows that it is far superior to Mentone, Nice, or even Aiken in South Carolina.

I come next to the Yosemite and the Big Trees, and give you the following hints :

Give as much time as you can spare to this part of your tour. At the Calaveras grove there is a comfortable hotel, from which you can, and will want to, make short excursions on horseback or in wagons to a larger and recently discovered grove; and if you are fond of hunting, small game abounds in the forests.—N.B. Do not attempt to hunt for grizzly bears. The man who declared that *he* had lost no grizzlies was a wise fellow. You can see the Calaveras *sequoias* in one day, remaining two nights at the grove; but if you take three days you will be better satisfied.

Go into Yosemite Valley by way of Merced and Inspiration Point, and leave it by way of the Coulterville or Chinese Camp routes, either of which will carry you through a country of extraordinary interest—the great exhausted placer mining district of California—to the Calaveras grove.

Give ten days, if you can, to the Valley itself. You can "do" it in three, but you will be sorry you had not arranged to stay longer, and every additional day will give you greater enjoyments and pleasanter recollections. Read all you can get hold of about it before you enter it—Hutchings's book, Whitney's book, and whatever else there may be accessible to you, and do not fear disappointment.

Take a clear day to ride into the Valley, and rather lie over outside one or two days than allow the guides to hurry you in on a cloudy day. Almost every day is clear and bright in the traveling season.

Take with you from Stockton or Merced a spare suit of clothing and extra stockings, wear stout shoes and a broad-leafed hat, carry a duster or light overcoat, and leave all finery behind. People do not stand upon ceremony in the Valley.

Do not let timid or silly people alarm you on the way. We met persons last year who gave the most dolorous and terrible accounts of their fears and sufferings in going into the Valley; but I took in with me at that time a weakly girl of ten years, who enjoyed every foot of the ride, and was benefited by it ; and no lady who is not physically or mentally incapable of walking a mile, or sitting on a very gentle and sure-footed horse, need have the slightest apprehension. People sometimes go in such haste as to exhaust themselves by lack of rest. They make a hardship of what ought to be a pleasure. Take it easy on the road; and especially, if you are not accustomed to a horse's back, do not let yourself be hurried. You are taking a pleasure trip, and need not spoil it. If you are timid, do not go with a large party, which will hurry you, but take a guide for yourself, and make him lead your horse at a walk. All the horses are trained, and are very careful, gentle, and sure-footed; and you will be amazed to find how rapidly you yourself pick up confidence, and become accustomed to ways which are certainly not smooth or level.

Within the Valley you can not walk very far, because in many places the ground is boggy. At whatever hotel you may stop, you have the privilege of retaining your horse and guide during your stay at the regular charge, which is five dollars per day for both. A party of four or six requires but one guide.

ALKALI DESERT, CENTRAL PACIFIC RAILROAD.

The finest excursion within the Valley is to the Nevada Falls, which requires a whole day, especially if you climb up to the top of this magnificent fall, which any healthy person can do, and which ladies and children are sure to enjoy. You leave the hotel as soon after breakfast as is convenient, dine at Snow's, at the top of the Vernal Fall, at half-past eleven or twelve o'clock, and Mrs. Snow will give you an excellent and abundant dinner; then climb up to the top of the Nevada Fall, or ride up if the new bridle-path is opened, peep into the singular ravine called the Little Yosemite, wander about on the rocky crags over which the Nevada tumbles, return to Snow's, go down the ladders past the Vernal Fall—a very easy and safe descent—and find your horses waiting for you below for a pleasant canter back to the hotel.

Take with you into the Valley, above all books, Whitney's "Yosemite Guide-Book." The author is the State geologist of California. His little work, published by Little, Brown, and Co., Boston, will fit your coat pocket, and will interest you more than any novel; and you will be encouraged by it to do what ladies and children can do with perfect safety and convenience, what every body ought to do, but very few do—make the tour of the *rim* of the Valley. A party of four or a dozen can make this journey in four or five days, carrying with them provisions, shelter and covers, on animals, and gaining an enjoyment unique in every way, and views of the Valley which can not in any other manner be obtained.

If you travel by stage toward the Valley from Merced or Copperopolis, you will naturally wish to sit outside. Every body has this desire; unfortunately some must sit inside. If you can secure your right by purchase, do so; otherwise you must take your chance in an unpleasant scramble. The pleasantest way for a party of three, four, or five to travel is in a private conveyance; this you can secure at Stockton or Merced, at the stage-office, and carriage and driver will cost a party of four no more than their fare by stage. It is well enough, therefore, not to buy your tickets in San Francisco, if you have a party to fill a carriage. But for one or two it is better to go by stage; you can lie over at any point as long as you like; you will make rather quicker time on the journey; and if you mean to stay in the Valley more than four days, you will save money, as the private carriage would be a charge to you while waiting outside for your return.

Do not expect all the "modern conveniences" in the Valley hotels. A very comfortable bath-house was set up last year near Hutchings's, and there is now a telegraph line into the Valley. The hotels are all slightly built, but the food is abundant, and the accommodations good enough for tired travelers. If you know beforehand the day on which you will enter the Valley, you will do well to telegraph from Merced to some one of the hotels for rooms to be reserved for you. It will save you ten or fifteen minutes of irksome waiting when you arrive, tired and dusty, at the place.

Finally, make up your mind before you start to suffer some inconveniences. You can not carry the Grand Hotel with you into the mountains. But on the whole journey you will find every one, stage-drivers and tavern-keepers, civil and obliging. The wayside inns are clean, though often very much crowded, the food is plain but abundant, the service polite, and the charges reasonable. At some part of the journey you will have to rise very early, but this is only on one morning; and as it is impossible for most people to eat breakfast at four or half-past four, though it is served, take a cup of coffee, and have a hearty lunch put up for you, which will be welcome to you about nine o'clock.

Pay no attention to the grumblers and croakers who abound among tourists, and you will find the whole journey a wonder and delight. The mountains which you ascend to enter the great Valley are covered with magnificent forests. The sugar-pines, through miles of which you drive in the stage, are themselves worth the journey to California to see. The forms of the mountains as you ascend are peculiar and grand, and the skies are bright in the spring and summer, and the air refreshing and exhilarating.

On your way from the Valley to the Calaveras grove you should stop a day or two at Sonora. There is an excellent hotel there, and the quaint, decaying old town, and the surrounding country, which for miles has been dug over by placer miners, is very picturesque and remarkable.

On some parts of this journey the water is not very good; even in the Valley you are apt, when riding about, to drink snow-water, which is not wholesome. In the Valley you can procure generally a mild wine, made in the neighboring foot-hills, and not sold, so far as I know, outside of Tuolumne and Mariposa counties. A little of this, taken with water, is a pleasant and wholesome drink.

BLOOMER CUT, CENTRAL PACIFIC RAILROAD.

About Murphy's, near the Big Trees, children will offer you tarantulas' nests as curiosities. You should not pay more than half a dollar for one of these singular bits of clay. At the Calaveras Grove Hotel they will sell you, for a trifle, pieces of the bark of the *sequoia*, formed into pincushions, which make an agreeable souvenir of the journey.

The hints given above will serve to prepare you for the incidents and accidents of the way, which is all that the traveler requires.

Lake Tahoe, Donner Lake, and Virginia City, you should see on your way home.   You get off at Truckee about ten o'clock at night, remain comfortably at the hotel there, and the next morning drive first to Donner Lake, two miles distant, and then, returning, to Lake Tahoe, fourteen miles away.   Crossing the beautiful lake in a steamer, you go to Virginia City, famous for its mines; and take the train again at Reno.   Before leaving San Francisco, engage your sleeping-car accommodations, making an allowance of two or three days, as you please, for the diversion on your route.   A day-car will accommodate you to Truckee, and you will need the sleeping-car only on resuming your journey eastward at Reno.

Most travelers would like to see something of gold-mining.   If you stop at Sonora on your way from the Yosemite to the Calaveras Grove, you can ride out to the Confidence mine, which is a productive and well-managed quartz mine.   In the neighborhood of Sonora, also, you may see placer mining; indeed, last year $5000 were washed out of a lot in the centre of the old town; and when the circus comes, the boys go out into the fields with a pan, and try to "pan out" as much gold as will admit them to the "show."

To see hydraulic mining you should go from Stockton, on your return from the Calaveras Grove, to Marysville, near which, at Smartsville, hydraulic or gravel mining is carried on on a scale which threatens to fill up the Yuba River.   On your way to Smartsville you will see a place made famous in the Drawer of *Harper's Magazine*—the celebrated Yuba Dam.

Marysville is on the way to Mount Shasta, which is the finest mountain in California, and eminently worth a visit.   You will need four days for this, from Sacramento and back.   There is now a comfortable hotel at the foot of the mountain, near a hot spring which affords bathing facilities.

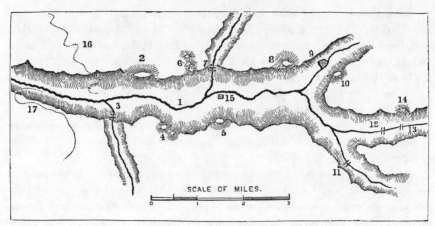

PLAN OF THE YOSEMITE VALLEY.

References.—1. Merced River.—2. El Capitan.—3. Bridal Veil Fall.—4. Cathedral Rocks.—5. Sentinel.—6. Three Brothers.—7. Yosemite Fall.—8. North Dome.—9. Mirror Lake.—10. South Dome.—11. South Fork Fall. —12. Vernal Fall.—13. Nevada Fall.—14. Bellows Butte.—15. Hutchings's Hotel.—16. Coulterville Trail.— 17. Mariposa Trail.

CHAPTER V.

THE GREAT SIGHTS OF CALIFORNIA.—HINTS TO TRAVELERS.

OF the great sights of the State which attract, year after year, an increasing number of intelligent tourists from all parts of the world, the Yosemite Valley is, of course, the chief and the most remarkable.   But the State is full of wonderful natural phenomena; and when the tourist has seen the Yosemite, the Calaveras Big Tree Grove, the Geysers, Mount Shasta, the Almaden quicksilver mine, the different methods of gold-mining, and Lakes Donner and Tahoe, he has left unseen still Mono Lake, the Dead Sea of California; the Tulare, Kern and Buena Vista Lakes, remarkable and singular sheets of water lying in the San Joaquin Valley; the magnificent scenery about the head-waters of the Kern River, which Bierstadt has gone to paint this summer, and which is said to contain more than one valley as wonderful as the Yosemite itself; the Redwood forests; and other objects, yearly becoming more accessible by good roads; and which will hereafter tempt travelers and sight-seers as much as the Yosemite does now.   In fact California has not yet shown to travelers her most remarkable or most picturesque sights.

A business man or a statistician would tell you, in a few words, that the Yosemite Valley is a floor eight miles long by two wide, with walls three quarters of a mile high.   He would give you, further, the following figures concerning the height of the precipitous mountains which form the walls, and of the water-falls which give variety to the wonderful scene:

MOUNTAINS.

Indian Name.	Signification.	American Name.	Height.
Tu-tock-a-mu-la	Great Chief of the Valley	El Capitan	3,300 feet
Poo-see-nah Chuck-ka	Large Acorn Cache	Cathedral Rocks	2,660 feet
		The Cathedral Spires	1,800 feet
Pom-pom-pasus.	Mountains Playing Leap-Frog	Three Brothers	3,830 feet
Hep-se-tuck-a-nah	Gone in	Union Rocks	3,500 feet
Loya	Signal Station	Sentinel Rock	3,043 feet
Loya	Signal Station	Sentinel Dome	4,500 feet
Ummo	Lost Arrow		3,000 feet
Patillima		Glacier Rock	3,200 feet
To-coy-æ	Shade to Indian Baby Basket	Royal Arches	1,800 feet
Hunto	The Watching Eye	Washington Column	1,875 feet
		North Dome	3,568 feet
Tis-sa-ack	Goddess of the Valley	South Dome	4,737 feet
Wayan	Pine Mountain	Mount Watkins	3,900 feet
		Cloud's Rest	6,034 feet
		Cap of Liberty	4,000 feet
		Mount Star King	5,600 feet

WATER-FALLS.

		Cataract	900 feet
Po-ho-no	Night Wind	Bridal Veil	630 feet
Yo-Semite	Large Grizzly Bear	Yosemite	2,634 feet
	First Fall		1,600 feet
	Second Fall		600 feet
	Third Fall		434 feet
Py-wy-ack	Sparkling Water	Vernal	350 feet
Yo-wy-ye		Nevada	700 feet
Illilouette	The Beautiful	South Fork	600 feet
Yo-coy-æ	Shade to Indian Baby Basket	Royal Arch Falls	1,000 feet
Loya		Sentinel Falls	3,000 feet

He would add, for purposes of comparison, that 5280 feet make a mile; that the great fall of Niagara is but 163 feet high; and that the precipitous Palisades of the Hudson River are, at their highest point, less than 600 feet high.

There the statistician would leave you; and he would be right. No man can so describe the Yosemite Valley as to give to one who has not seen it even a faint idea of its wonderful, strange, and magnificent scenery. I read, before I made the journey, Hutchings's book, Professor Whitney's book, and all the accounts of the Valley I could lay my hands on, including Horace White's in the *Chicago Tribune*, one of the best. Yet when I came to see the Valley, it was as though I had never read a line concerning it. All I had read passed out of my mind in the presence of those stupendous rocks; all I had seen was as nothing, compared with the grand, white, scarred granite face of El Capitan, which rears its precipitous side 3300 feet above the level along which you ride.

THE YOSEMITE VALLEY.

El Capitan is, to me, altogether the grandest sight in the Valley. The Sentinel Dome is 1200 feet higher; the Glacier Rock is nearly as high; and even the Three Brothers —wierd, and deserving the picturesque name of the "Jumping Frogs," which the Indians gave them—surpass El Capitan in altitude; but none of them approach in impressiveness this stupendous, solid, seamless, cream-white mass of rock, which shines with a subdued polish as though it had been carved out of ivory. It is not a mere rock or summit, but a vast wall, nearly two miles broad, which seems to dominate the Valley as you ride in on either trail, and whose grandeur grows upon you with every step your horse takes.

When you have reached your hotel in the Valley, no doubt some impatient spirits will at once gather around you and attempt to lay out for you to-morrow's and the next day's routine of sight-seeing. Drive them away, and determine in your own mind not to be hurried. After breakfast next day take a book—any book will do, but Whitney's little "Yosemite Guide" is the best for the place—sit down on the hotel verandah, in front of the Great Yosemite fall, and look at that. It will, if you are any thing better than a mere *cit,* if you have but a spark of love for fine natural scenery, repay you. You will see the wind play many fantastic tricks with the long, glittering, foaming band of water as it pours and roars down from the awful height. And as you sit there, you will get, but slowly as at Niagara also, some true conception into your mind of the grandeur of the scene.   By-and-by, after your midday meal, you may ride out; and, if you pick your way over to the foot of the Yosemite fall, you will be rewarded for your adventure by seeing what a body of water it is that tumbles down before your eyes for 2600 feet from the top of the vast precipice.

The guides will not let you miss any of the sights of the valley; and it is curious how quickly the visitor learns to recognize each of the great falls and summits.   I do not mean, therefore, to trouble the reader here with a detailed account of these.   The illustrations given herewith show all the most noteworthy objects.   The one least worth seeing is the Mirror Lake.   If you follow the bank of the roaring Merced down, on an afternoon, till you reach El Capitan, you will probably see a sight far finer than Mirror Lake affords, for the Merced has a quiet pool, large enough to reflect El Capitan himself; and it will seem to you the most magnificent shadow your eyes ever beheld.

The Yosemite Valley was given by the United States to the State of California, to be used and preserved as a park.   The State accepted the gift, and has appointed a set of managers or guardians.   These have charge of the Valley; it is their duty to prevent nuisances, and to regulate and grant leases to persons desiring to erect hotels and other improvements, "for a term not exceeding ten years," and to use the incomes of such leases "in the preservation and improvement of the property."

The Commissioners have not yet begun to "improve the property."   I saw a notice, signed " Galen Clark, guardian," that no more buildings should be put up; and as the houses so far erected are little better than shanties, this seemed to me judicious.   But it is a pity the State does not appropriate a sufficient sum of money to make the Valley as lovely artificially as it already is naturally. It is now a very rough spot; if Mr. Olmsted could be engaged to spend one hundred thousand dollars even on it, he would make it the loveliest "place of recreation" in the world.   It needs one good carriage road from one end to the other on the level plain, and a little judicious and skillful combing down of the wildness, with plantings of indigenous shrubs and flowers, and a little drainage and embankment, so that the Merced River may be kept within its bounds at all seasons.

Some day or other this will be done; but it would be most easily and cheaply done now, at once.   Under the present management it is easy to see that as travel increases more leases will be granted to hotel-keepers, and these build temporary, tasteless structures which form blots on the landscape.   They hold for only ten years, and therefore make shabby and temporary buildings; but they can not be dislodged for ten years, and are therefore serious obstacles to any substantial improvement.   No plan or place is prescribed for them; and when they have once got a lease they are independent, to a great extent, of the authorities.

But you will ask, why should the State of California, not a rich State, be burdened with such an expense as is involved in improving this Valley?   Well, the State has accepted the gift of Congress; and no private person or corporation has any rights there now.   The State can set apart a sum of money to improve and beautify the Valley; or it can do what would perhaps be better, and certainly feasible—it can ask Mr. Olmsted, the most capable man in the country for the purpose, to draw up a set of regulations for the improvement and management of the place, with plans for at least two large stone hotels, for roads, bridle-paths, baths, and other accommodations; and then offer to any responsible company a lease for twenty, or even fifty years, of the whole Valley, subject to such conditions as might be prescribed in the law or agreement to be drawn up by Mr. Olmsted.

Who goes to California will certainly visit the Yosemite; and a corporation with a lease of twenty or thirty years could very well afford to put up large and commodious hotels, and spend a hundred or even two hundred thousand dollars in beautifying this "National Park;" because their profit would be certain, and the sale of their improvements to a successor, at the end of the lease, sure. The value of their improvements would be permanent and constantly increasing.   It would be only necessary for the State to guard sufficiently their character.

The roads which give access to the Valley may be left to private enterprise. They are improving every year; and in this State—as everywhere else where they are found—toll roads made and owned by corporations are the best.

At present the Valley hotels can not accommodate more than three hundred to three hundred and fifty persons at one time, and that not without crowding.

The travel is still irregular, but it is rapidly increasing, and would be much greater now if there were more room.   Few persons stay more than three days; but if they could live comfortably many would spend a month there.

If permanent and proper improvements are not made at once, more leases for shabby and temporary structures will be demanded, and will be granted, for the traveling public will not be denied; and every new lease will be a serious injury to the Valley and an obstacle to its improvement.   I hope, therefore, that the State will either undertake the matter itself, or turn it over, under stringent and proper regulations, to a corporation.

Moreover, abuses are creeping in already.   A lease has been granted to a person who has bridged the Merced River, and charges fifty cents per head to all who choose to pass over it—which you need not do.   It will not be long before, at this rate, every point of beauty will be encumbered with a toll-gatherer. Thus, again, when I inquired for some large sugar pines of which I had heard, I was told that several of them had been cut down by enterprising leaseholders and sawed up into lumber for their buildings.   Now I believe there are not many fine trees in the Valley, and I fear that under some pretense they will all disappear.   Yet they ought to be most jealously preserved.   Not a tree of any description ought to be cut down in the Valley, except by the permission of a thorough landscape gardener.

There are two claimants to land in the Valley, Mr. Hutchings and Mr. Lamon. They claim one hundred and sixty acres each by pre-emption. The State of California has granted these rights by a very large majority of both branches of the Legislature. They ask Congress to confirm their rights as settlers. The State, it seems to me, would do wisely to buy them out, for they have some rights, and it is to their efforts, and particularly to Mr. Hutchings's,

EL CAPITAN.

that knowledge of the Valley is largely due. They can be bought out for a trifling sum now; and to dispossess them by force would be, I imagine, under all the circumstances, unjust. But I foresee that these claims will grow in value with every year, and so long as they remain will be in the way of any general improvement of the Valley, and destruction of its beauty.

THE BIG TREES

In its present condition the Valley will not remain. It must either be made more beautiful, as I have suggested, or it will become a wreck, denuded of fine trees, cumbered with enterprising toll-takers, and made nauseous by the taint of selfish and sordid speculation. California will do wisely for her own glory if she will engage Mr. Olmsted, or some other competent person, to take general charge of the improvement of the Yosemite, and allow a company, under his eye, and in accordance with such plans and restrictions as he could draw up, to make it into a truly national park and pleasure-ground.

If you go into the Valley by the Mariposa trail, from Merced, which is now the favorite route, you may ride through the Mariposa Grove. But I advise every traveler to see also the Calaveras Grove — for these sequoyas also demand time to let the visitor realize their great size; and at the Calaveras Grove there is a good hotel, where, as I have said in a previous chapter, you may spend a day or two pleasantly. You will pass the day in wandering among the sequoyas, and at every turn and look they will grow bigger to your more familiar eyes. There is one tree from which the bark has been taken for a long distance from the ground. This tree stands, happily, at the foot of a sloping hill. You should measure the tree with your eye from the bottom of the hill, then walk up the slope, and when you have risen perhaps a hundred feet, turn and look again. You will be amazed to see that the tree, from your new and higher level, looks as high as it did when you stood near its base. You will see that the high branches look bigger to you, that the bushy top is vast; and when you look once more from the summit of the hill, you perceive that the enormous height of these trees so diminishes the tops to the gazer from below as really to belittle the trees.

It is now the fashion to make a rapid run through California; and I have aimed to help the traveler to do this intelligently and to the best advantage.

But if you are a hunter or sportsman, California offers you temptations for a prolonged stay such as few other regions in this country afford. In the winter months the Tulare, Kern, and Buena Vista lakes are filled with innumerable flocks of wild geese, ducks of all kinds, swans, cranes, pelicans, and other strange birds. I have seen two square miles of geese feeding on a sheep pasture near a lagoon, and so tame that I almost rode them down before they rose. The canvass-back duck is found by thousands, yes by tens of thousands, in the lakes and lagoons of Southern California. The mallard breeds in the reeds and tules, and remains in the State during the year. I never saw in any one place so great a variety of ducks as I have seen shot here in a small lagoon. Otter and beaver abound in Kern and Buena Vista lakes, and may be shot from a boat—they are not yet trapped; and these waters have also an abundance of fish.

In the mountains which skirt the San Joaquin Valley, the grizzly and cinnamon bear, the lion—so called—the wild cat, and fox are found; and on the plains I have seen antelope by the hundred. These animals, and deer also, frequent the mountains.

This whole region is enormously rich in game; in favorable seasons the whole plain is alive with the pretty top-knotted quail; the hare, or jackass-rabbit as it is here called, is chased with hounds on the plains below Stockton, and abounds in all parts.

The mildness of the climate makes the sportsman's life in the winter months in this region charming. He needs but a slender outfit of blankets and camp equipage. The roads are everywhere good, except, perhaps, immediately after a rain; horses are cheap, and experienced guides are easily attainable.

For a hunting tour of the lakes and the Sierra, there should be a party of three or more; and it would be best to start from Visalia, which is but about thirty miles from Tulare Lake. If you follow the shores of this lake down, you will have good shooting all the way, and find yourself, at the lower end, but a short journey from Buena Vista Lake, where your sport becomes more varied and abundant than before. From Buena Vista you pass by a navigable stream into Kern Lake, and, as the season advances, a party of hunters should by all means ascend the Kern River to its head-waters, where larger game will be found in abundance. Thus three or four weeks in the early spring, or three or four months of winter and spring, can be spent delightfully, for it is possible and comfortable to camp out all winter in this region; and I know of no part in our own country which will yield such abundant and various sport, with so little trouble, cost, or hardship, or with such grand, novel, and charming scenery.

For Tulare Lake a boat can be bought at Visalia; though it is probable that boats can be hired on the lake of farmers. For Buena Vista and Kern lakes a boat can be got at Bakersfield; dogs can be got at Stockton or Visa-

6

VIEW OF YOSEMITE FROM THE MARIPOSA TRAIL.

lia. Californians have very excellent breeds of sporting dogs. Guns should
be brought from the East, though they can be bought in San Francisco. A
party of four or six sportsmen, undertaking such an adventure, should buy at
Visalia a rough, strong, covered wagon, with a span of common broncho horses,
and hire a driver, who should also be guide. This wagon would hold their
blankets—two pair of heavy blankets and a quilt for each person—and their
cooking utensils, and supplies of coffee, tea, sugar, salt, pepper, crackers, condensed milk, and pork. The members of the party should ride on horseback.
After January, your horses will get abundant food from the grass of the plains

to keep them up to their light work. When you camp you stake your animals out with long horse-ropes; and you will shoot enough game to keep your camp in meat. If you should want variety, you can buy a sheep occasionally, as you pass a sheep ranch; and the California mutton is the best in the world.

Your guide and driver should know the country well enough to bring you every day to good water, and to give you an intelligent account of the region you are passing through. You will find the people civil and ready to oblige; and will see a country which is very seldom visited by strangers, and which is almost a fresh hunting-ground, for it is very little known even to San Franciscans, who find an abundance of game nearer to their own homes.

VIEW NEAR THE STATE LINE, TRUCKEE RIVER.

CHAPTER VI.

"JOHN."

"HE is patient, docile, persevering, quick to learn, faithful, no eye-servant, the best cook or waiter you ever saw"—

"Last week he stole $600 out of my drawer, and is now in State Prison"—

"He is sober"—

"Last night you saw him smoking opium in the most horrible of dens"—

"He saves his money"—

"And takes it out of the State to spend in China"—

"He is indispensable"—

"But he is a curse to the community"—

"He will make a useful citizen"—

"His whole race are vicious and degraded."

Thus two voices run on about the Chinese in California. Nor do I wonder that there are differences of opinion.

John stands behind you at dinner, arrayed like an angel, in the most spotless and gracefully hanging white, the image—not the image, the very presence —of the best-trained and quickest-witted servant in the world; and naturally you wish your own life might be comforted by such a John; or by such another as his mate in the kitchen, who is delighting you with dish after dish cooked to perfection.

You ask his mistress, and she tells you that she has no disputes, no troubles, no worry; that John has made housekeeping a pleasure to her; if he is cook, he does not object to help with the washing and ironing—in fact, does it better and quicker than any Bridget in the world. And John's master chimes in with an assertion that, since John has reigned below, the kitchen has been the delight of his eyes, so clean and sweet is it. Moreover, John markets for his mistress; he is economical; and he does not make a fuss.

Of course, you say, every body has Johns. Well, no; people have prejudices and fears. You have two or three Johns in the house, and when you go out—if you are the lady of the house—you take the children along. There have been unpleasant occurrences.

From your friend's well-served and admirably-cooked dinner you go to Jackson Street and find Policeman Woodruff. He will take you through what is called "China-town." No doubt John is clean. There is too much evidence to doubt or dispute it. But Mr. Woodruff takes you into and through places so dismal, so wretched, so horrible, that while you are edging your way from a gambling hell into an opium hell, and from an opium hell into a worse place, nobody in the world could persuade you otherwise than that John and all his kindred are the devil's own. I can not say that, even in the worst holes I saw, John looked dirty. The thieves and jail-birds who were leaning over the gambling tables were not dirty, so far as I could see. The thieves, loafers, and other poor wretches who were lying under and on top of shelves, three deep, smoking a "bit's worth" of twice-laid opium, were many of them decently dressed; and certainly, though their surroundings were nasty, they did not look as correspondingly nasty as a similar Five Points population of whites.

Moreover, all that John does, be it virtuous or vicious, he seems to do with a certain amount of sluggish decorum. He swarms in Jackson Street and Dupont Street after night; but he makes no noise. If you accidentally elbow him, he moves gently out of the way. I passed out of the Chinese theatre in Jackson Street at eleven o'clock at night, with a lady and two children; we had to walk through a crowd of Johns, who were just then going up the long alley-way which leads to the door; and it did not even occur to my children, who walked ahead, to be afraid; and not a rude or disrespectful word or gesture was seen in the whole crowd. Now this theatre is, like the lowest of our own, the place of recreation for the vilest class. I can't say that I would have ventured into a place of the same kind, or out of it, in New York, without anxiety.

The street was crowded but quiet. The only loud voice I heard was that of a Chinaman selling soup and making himself known to his customers. John gambles, but it is with the same quiet, *blasé* air—just as a crowd of black-snakes might gamble on a rather cold day in May. In the game I saw played, the "bank" had before it a lot of "cash," the Chinese money. A handful of these was put out on the table; a brass dish covered most of them. The croupier, with a hooked stick, drew toward him four at a time of these coins. The players bet, as they chose, that at the last hand, one, two, three, or four, would remain. The policeman told me he had seen twelve hundred dollars lost at a single turn of this absurd game; and I saw poorly-dressed thieves—so I was told they were—put up ten dollars in silver and gold, and lose it; and without a wink drag out other coin from their multifarious pockets, in that painfully uncertain way in which vagabonds all over the world fish out money from their clothes, even when they have determined to spend it.

There never was a more interested or a more decorous audience in a theatre than that which watched the interminable play in the "China Theatre," as it is labeled, on Jackson Street. What the play meant I can not tell you, of course, but it was evidently well done; for it was easy to see that the audience enjoyed it. Once in a great while the clown extorted a laugh; once in a while the women, in the place set apart for them, wiped their eyes; meantime, the person who answers to the pea-nut man in our Bowery went his slow round, with a big basket of oranges and sweetmeats on his head; the audience lit its cigars and smoked; men passed silently in and out; but not a cat-call, not a noise of any kind disturbed the harmony; not a curious look even toward our private box, where sat ladies and children, who must have been objects of curiosity to them.

I am not sure but the "China Theatre" in Jackson Street is the strangest sight San Francisco has to show. The auditorium is built like that of any common theatre. It has a large pit, and above that a gallery, at one end of which are two private boxes, while at the other end is a space closed off for the Chinese women, who do not sit with the men. The whole is without ornament, and has a squalid look, as though it had been poorly done and was now poorly kept. Yet our box was clean. The chairs were very ordinary; but the place had been swept, and was not greasy.

As for the stage—attend, and I will try to describe it. In the first place, the orchestra sit at the back of the stage: they play vigorously and continuously, now on stringed instruments, which give out an ear-piercing sound like a multitude of insane bagpipes, now on cymbals, small gongs, and various other atrocious devices to make a worse and less endurable noise than the fiddles. I never heard such an outrageous collocation of sounds in my life; and how the musicians themselves endure it I don't know.

Before these gentlemen, playing in their shirt-sleeves, taking tea occasionally, and smoking when they chose—one absurd creature sawed away in his shirt-sleeves at his fiddle for dear life, sucking meanwhile the end of a very long pipe, which he had to hold out in the air by stretching his head back—before this wonderful orchestra, which kept better time than many orchestras I have heard in opera houses—the play went on. There are no curtains nor scenes. At the left side is an entrance, and at the other an exit way, each draped with a flap of cloth, through which the players dash at a trot. The properties to be used in the play stand at the sides of the stage, and the men who are to bring on or carry off these pieces of furniture lounge about among them, or pass back and forth from behind the screen which conceals the green-room. They are very dexterous in placing or removing their properties, and manage to keep out of the way of the players. At one side, in the screen, is a square hole, at which you see the nose and eyes of the stage manager occasionally, directing.

Every thing is cheap, squalid, and, to our eyes, disreputable. But the players, who came on in the cheap magnificence of players everywhere, were in earnest apparently, and shrieked, and gesticulated, and sang, with what seemed to me the careful and studied precision of men doing their best.

By-the-way, the Chinaman, who has naturally a deep and pleasant voice, no sooner appears on the stage than every utterance is in a shrill falsetto, which is more like vehement caterwauling than any other sound I remember to have heard. When we got home from the theatre one of my children made a door to creak in the room, and we all burst out laughing as we recognized the most impassioned tones of the chief actor in the play—or part of a play—we had just heard.

There is something dry and overstrained in their attitudes, gestures, and tones. It is as though they had been refining and refining for centuries, until at last they had got every natural tone and movement off their stage, and made it just what Hamlet did not want it to be. The mincing way which he counseled his players to avoid, these have made the object of their lives. Not one of the players—not even the clown—was even for an instant betrayed into a movement or tone of voice proper and natural to him or any other human being; and after we had sat for an hour, listening and looking, we could not help but admire the atrocious perfection of their unnaturalness.

The first part of the play we saw was what we should call an opera. That is to say, the dialogue was sung to the accompaniment of music. The "music" was ear-piercing, shrill, loud, and to our ears only a horrible discord. But there was evidently a method in it; the leader, whose instrument consisted of two ivory sticks, with which he beat very audible time on a block of iron, had his shirt-sleeved orchestra under full control; and the singers and the players all kept admirable time. The singing was, of course, as unnatural as the playing; and when the chief personage of the piece, a high mandarin, dressed gorgeously, and with peacock feathers a yard long sticking out of his crown, attempted a quaver or trill, we all in our box burst into uncontrollable laughter.

The action goes on continuously; the players every two or three minutes rush off the stage, only to rush on again at the other entrance; in some parts of the play there were at least twenty characters crowded on the narrow stage; and it was very droll to see the king, when he was for a moment disengaged, turn his back on the audience and take a swig of tea out of a tea-pot which stood handy; or, when he had for some stage purpose removed his crown, turn his back on the audience and carefully replace it before a small looking-glass, held up before him by one of the " supernumeraries."

In one part of the play there was some excellent tumbling; and in another, two of the characters took the part of the lion, being assisted by a huge pasteboard lion's head, or what in China they imagine a lion's head to be like, with a lower jaw of brass, which was made to clap noisily, to the terror of the players. The body consisted of a silk cloth, in which a small boy was hidden, who represented the lion's hinder extremities, and got a contemptuous kick on one occasion from the clown. These trappings hung on a nail at the side of the stage, and were taken down in the middle of the play by a fellow who gravely climbed up on a ladder to reach it.

There was no applause, no cheering, no noisy manifestation of displeasure or delight; there is no bar-room in the theatre; the manager and lessee sat decorously on the back of a seat among the audience, smoking his cigar; and the play was to last until two o'clock A.M., being given to a numerous audience, who, I was told, paid thirty cents per head to see it—and no free list.

If you walk through China-town on Sunday you will see a curious sight, and one which, if you are a thoughtful man, will not amuse you. Jackson Street, Sacramento Street, Dupont Street, and the streets and alleys which lie between, are the Chinese quarters of San Francisco. Here they live; here is their multitude of shops; here, in cellars, they make cigars, in shops they work at sewing-machines—the men, I mean; here, in an entry-way, the Chinese cobbler cobbles a shoe, the boy waiting at his side to put it on when it is done. Here are eating-houses, where smoked ducks, pigs' heads, livers and gizzards of fowls, whole chickens cooked in oil, sodden pork, and sausages are sold. Here is their church, or temple, with queer images of wood and tinsel, before which sandal-wood is burned, or small fire-crackers are sparkling.

Well, on Sunday it is all just as it was on Saturday—only a little more so. The shops are all open, and the grave accountants are adding up figures on the abacus, or posting up their ledgers.   The cellars are as full as ever of cigar-makers; the eating-houses are fuller than ever; and for every eating-house there are at least a dozen gambling-houses.

A Chinese gambling hell consists of a narrow whitewashed entry, at the end of which hangs a flap of cloth.   The play-room lies at right angles with the en-try, and is, of course, out of view.   In the entry sits a man, apparently asleep, or dreaming.   Near his head you will perhaps notice a rope belayed to a hook. This rope leads to a door.   If you—a white man and not a policeman—should attempt to enter the narrow passage, the watchman would pull the rope, the rope would pull to the door; and as that closes with a spring lock, you would be shut out.

LAKE TAHOE.

I counted a dozen of these places in a single block; forty-five of them were open on Sunday night; but the police say that it is not easy to prove that they are gambling dens, for no Chinaman will bear witness against them, and they take no money from a white man.

John pays no regard to Sunday.   "It is a great convenience," said a gentle-man to me, "to have servants who don't want to go to church."   Perhaps—but it is not a great convenience to have in an American community a multitude of heathen who not only prosecute their own business on Sunday, but naturally lead our people to do the same. In the Chinese quarter are numerous clothing and other shops kept by white men, whose customers are Chinese. These are all open on Sunday, which one of them told me was his best day.

There are good and bad Johns, as there are good and bad of all nations. He does not yet fit into our ways. Nor do I see, just now, how he is going to be fitted in. But he is here; John is a fact. He has "come to stay;" and it belongs to our wisest and most thoughtful men to see how he is to be made a part of us. You can not drive him out.

John now does most of the washing and ironing all over California; "Woogung," or "Ah Lee," or "Fooh Lien," "Washing and Ironing done"—with sometimes the addition "Buttons sewed on strong," is the sign you see oftenest in California towns. In the cities he collects the garbage; he is cook and waiter; he makes the cigars; he works in the woolen mills; go into any manufacturing place and you will see his face; there is a Chinaman and a half on every mile of the Central Pacific Railroad; he raises two-thirds of the vegetables consumed in the State; he makes a good shepherd; in the farming districts the commonest sight is to see John driving a wagon, or ploughing; the lonely ranch-man keeps a Chinese cook; hundreds of Chinese are going over the old mining "slum," and making money by this patient toil; he keeps his New-year's week with jollity and fire-crackers, from San Diego to Sacramento; and so far east as Denver, in Colorado, you see his sign, "Lo Wing, Washing and Ironing." Both political parties in California denounce the Chinaman on their platforms; but if you go to the houses of the men who make these platforms, you will find Chinese servants; if you visit their farms or ranches, you will find Chinese hands; and if you ask the political leader, after dinner, what he really thinks, he will tell you that he could not get on without Chinese, and that the cry against them is the most abominable demagogism; all of which is true.

Slowly, but surely as fate, he is entering one trade and calling after the other and conquering his patient way. Why? Not because he works so cheaply. A Chinese cook in a good family gets $35 per month; a waiter gets from $25 to $30. Elsewhere they work more cheaply, yet their wages keep pace with other wages, and rise from time to time.

It is not because they are cheap. Ask any one who employs them, and he will tell you it is because they do not drink, do not quarrel, are not idle or prone to change, give no eye-service, are patient, respectful, extremely quick to learn, faithful to their instructions, and make no fuss. With these qualities a workingman is cheap at almost any price; and I guess, from what I hear, that John is not slow to learn his value, and will drive his own bargain.

But with these qualities, and endurance for any labor or climate, as was proved when he worked in the snow on the Sierras and built the Central Pacific road, John will not take long to eat his way into the heart of the land. So far as he demonstrates to others, his competitors, the value—the money value —of his good qualities, so far he will be a benefit to the country. He may indeed make steady, patient, persistent toil once more fashionable among us. But in some way, not by laws, for they can do nothing, but by missionary effort, by earnest, general, conscientious training, John must be brought to a comprehension of our customs, so that, even if he does not become a Christian in name or in fact, he shall yet learn to conform his life to that of our American people, and not live among us disordering and disorganizing our own society.

The Chinese quarter of San Francisco is a blot on the city. It is worse, in some respects, than the Five Points. Yet the houses in which gambling, opium-smoking, and other vile practices are carried on are the property of men who call themselves respectable, whose children attend church, and who are not ashamed to draw their living from this vice and wretchedness. It is so with us, too; but it is not pleasant to find in a young city like San Francisco the same unconcern for the poor, the same carelessness of how your neighbor lives, the same heedless, cold, godless disregard of whatever passes outside of our own respectable doors and comfortably carpeted houses, which is the curse of an overgrown and old city like New York.

If free government is to continue among us, we can not afford to have a "lower class;" we can not afford, for our children's sakes, to suffer men, women, and children to live like beasts, for they will in time act like beasts—they will bite. If the whole Chinese quarter of San Francisco, as it is now arranged, could be blown up with gunpowder, and decent accommodations provided for the people who inhabit it, civilization and Christianity and free government on the Pacific coast would make a great gain.

John is inevitable. He has discovered America, and finds it a good country. We shall not keep him out. But it is ours, and not his, to determine whether he shall be a curse or a blessing to us. If we treat him as Christianity teaches that we ought to treat our fellow-men; if we do unto him as we would that others should do to us; if we see that he is instructed in that which we believe to be right, he may become a useful part of us. Teachable he certainly is; a far more civilized being—or, rather, a far less savage creature— than many we get from Christian Great Britain.

But if we choose to pass him by on the other side; to let him live among us as an alien from our manners, habits, customs; ignorant of what we hold as the best, highest, most sacred, and of most importance to our liberty and civilization, John may prove a more troublesome and dangerous creature than any we have yet taken on board our ship.

Just now he is poor. He lives in squalor; and even if a Chinaman is not vicious, in San Francisco his circumstances and surroundings in the Chinese quarter are all degrading.

Without Christianity, free government is impossible. But Christianity means that the ignorant shall be instructed, that the poor shall be kindly treated, that the wealthy, the powerful, the influential shall raise up the poor, ignorant, and despised; and this not by laws, but by improving public opinion, by private effort, by seeking out our neighbor, and trying, each in his own way, to make him a better and worthier man. It was remarked to me that scarcely a Chinaman comes to California who does not know how to read and write in his own language. There is an English school for them already in the city, and no doubt good work has begun; but our own city missionaries have often sadly complained that you can not make men virtuous who live on the Five Points; and so it will be found in San Francisco.

As yet, unfortunately for the Chinese problem, we get only men. There are, I am told, only about five hundred Chinese women in San Francisco, and among them but a very few wives. An important point could be gained if the Chinese emigrants could be induced to bring their wives with them. But no decent man of any nation would like to bring his wife and children to the Chinese quarter in San Francisco.

" PROSPECTING."

CHAPTER VII.

GOLD-MINING, WITH A DECAYED MINING TOWN.

IF any one tells you that the mines of California are worked out, he knows nothing about it. If any one asserts that the gold and silver have been an unmixed benefit to the people of the State, I should say he was mistaken. Mining has been followed in California, as almost every body knows, by several and different methods. Placer-mining was that in which the deposits of loose gold in the alluvial soil were washed out by cradles and other inexpensive expedients. Thus a large region of country about Sonora has been denuded, and lies still a rocky desert. Placer-mining is not now much followed in California, except by Chinese, Mexicans, and Indians, who are going over the old tailings.

Hydraulic-mining is placer-mining on a gigantic scale; and this is still a highly profitable pursuit in the State.

The first gold discoveries were made in a region where the hard-pan on which the gold was found lay from five to twenty feet below the surface. Here men could dig down to the " pay dirt," and wash that out by hand. The theory of the old miners concerning these deposits is, that ages ago, what is now California was pervaded by an enormous river, which brought down from mountains then existing and abounding in auriferous quartz immense quantities of gravel, sand, and dirt, and among this, loose gold and gold dust; and these fragments of the precious metal, being borne by the torrent, were deposited along its course, and being the heaviest substances, naturally sank to the bottom and there rested.

By subsequent convulsions of nature, this ancient river bed, of which the miners speak, was, they will tell you, in places covered over to the depth of hundreds of feet. It is supposed, for instance, that the famous Table Mountain, a mass of rock and lava, lies over a part of it; while in other parts, the bed itself was raised or thrown up; so that its traces are, they say, sometimes found high up on the side of a mountain. Old California miners speak to you with great confidence of this ancient river bed; they assure you that the signs of it are found over a considerable part of the State; and that wherever they can get at it they are sure of gold. I do not know what the geologists say about it, and, for the purposes of this chapter, I don't need to know; for it is a fact that loose gold is found; that there are signs and peculiar marks by which the experienced know where it is; and that, finally, the deposit is so certain, that given a good locality, and a mining company will invest hundreds of thousands of dollars in flumes for carrying water, or in tunnels for carrying away the earth and loose rock, and will wash away immense hills hundreds of feet high, confident that at the bottom they will find their reward.

This is hydraulic-mining, still, as I said, one of the important industries of the State.

Lastly comes quartz-mining, which is now the chief means of obtaining gold in California, and which has become and will remain for many years—so rich and abundant are the veins—one of the great legitimate industrial enterprises of the State. The discovery and the methods of working veins of gold-bearing quartz have now become a well understood business; and though, of course, there are rash and foolish ventures, and though the gambling spirit still survives, yet it is a fact that quartz-mining is now in California a legitimate enterprise, into which, if it is prudently and skillfully conducted, and with a good vein or lead, men may and do put money, with the certainty that they will reap—not sudden fortunes—but a regular and lasting return, greater or less as the mine happens to be rich or poor.

The tourist in California naturally wishes to see something of mining, and fortunately he may do so without going much off the regular and beaten road of travel. Already, on the railroad, as he swept from the summit of the Sierra down to the Sacramento Plain, he saw along the road-side long flumes or wooden channels, bearing water for the miners below. At Gold Run he may have seen the work of hydraulic-mining carried on in a deep valley below the railroad. He will hardly see placer-mining, except by Chinese in some remote parts; but on his way to and from the Yosemite Valley, he may see preparations for turning a river, which is done that the miners may get at the gold which they have reason to believe is deposited on its bottom. And at many points on his journey to the famous sights of the State, he will meet with examples of mining work, either of what has been done in the past or what is now doing. For instance, as you journey from the Big Trees—the Calaveras Grove I mean—toward the Yosemite, after you leave Murphy's, every foot almost of the soil, for mile after mile, has been at some time turned over by the gold-seekers. River beds were laid bare, and the adjoining bottoms searched; the earth all the way to the foot-hills was removed; and as you near Columbia, you see immense fields made up of nothing but rocks and boulders sticking their barren water-worn heads into the landscape, with deep pits between, showing the water-eaten sides of the rocks, which the miners searched, scraped, and polished, as a dentist does the teeth of his patient.

"PANNING OUT."

It is a strange and a wonderful sight, this of the deserted beds in which no small part of all the gold of California was found. For along this route are placed many now deserted or decaying towns or villages, once famous and busy. Along here are Dutch Flat, Mokelumne Hill (which has the accent on the second syllable), Murphy's, Columbia, Jamestown (which is more commonly called Jim Town), not to speak of Table Mountain, famous for the geological society whose violent dissolution Bret Harte has made classic.

In this comparatively deserted mining tract, where now only small parties of Chinese or Mexicans earn a precarious living, or a lonely Digger Indian indolently pans out his bit's worth of gold squatted by the river bank, you see not only the beds where lay millions of gold, but you have laid bare a part of that ancient pre-Adamite river which, millions of years ago, washed down, from quartz veins now lost, the gold which remained till our Americans came to dig it up.

You see how the swift waters of this ancient river gnawed into the rocks, until now they seem gnarled and twisted like the roots of trees—and in every corner and hole it deposited the precious gold. You can not realize how the country looked before our miners came to disturb it; for an old resident told me that where the rocks now lay bare and on a level with the road, which also had been mined out, from fifteen to thirty feet of soil, and often fifty feet, were removed before the gold was reached. They washed away hills, they shoveled away broad, elevated plains; dozens of square miles of soil disappeared, and were driven off into lower valleys that they might exhume the gold. At intervals you find a small field, a vineyard, or a garden, planted in the midst of this desolation, surrounded on all sides by rocks. Your guide—if you are so fortunate as to meet with an old miner—will explain to you that here the "slum" (as they call it), the sediment of earth with which the water is charged which has been used in "placer-mining" has been trapped and caused to deposit itself. Men have made acres and even dozens of acres of land by catching this slum. It is fine earth; all the flumes and water-courses still run red with it, for they are hydraulic-mining above; and when it dries out it makes the most fertile of gardens and vineyards. In Sonora an ingenious citizen, who had dug out his house lot to wash out the gold it bore, had filled it up again with "slum," having first laid his cellar walls; and it was laughable to see how easily he controlled the deposit.

Thus you travel toward Sonora. The stage rattles you impetuously through the one long street which makes the principal part of the town, and you notice that the stores have iron shutters and iron doors—fire-proof, but too many of them closed. You see the shops with wide-open broad doors, which tell you that there is no cold weather to be feared. You see two large, roomy hotels, which try to persuade you that Sonora is still a busy place.

It was once the most important town of this region. It is still the county town; and it has many signs of former importance; four churches, for instance, "but two of them don't go," explained an old resident to me; a jail—but it was empty; a jail built of iron bars laid across each other and bolted together, forming both walls and flat roof, and afterward built around with brick; and, as it seemed to me, with my Eastern eyes, an endless vista of barrooms or "saloons" and restaurants; all, seemingly, like the jail, empty.

The climate of Sonora is delicious; the people assert that it is the finest in the world; the water is good; there are neither fevers nor mosquitoes; the nights, even in midsummer, are always cool, as is the case all over California; the vine grows luxuriantly on all the hill-sides, and as the railroad is thirty miles away, the grapes often rot in the vineyards; the orange and the oleander grow in the streets, and roses bloom all the year round; and the people, kindly, generous, free, easily approachable, sit on their own door-steps watching the passing stage — they grow out-of-doors all the year round too; and do not grow rich.

Business is carried on with extreme moderation. Of course, as it is the county town, Sonorà has in fact a good deal of business and trade still. On Sunday, too, the Chinese gather in from the surrounding diggings, which they are going over for the second or third, or often the fourth time, to buy their supplies; other miners come also in troops or singly; the shops are open in this strange little place; the restaurants have their little tables set, with flowers on them; the bar-rooms are open; and yet so moderately is every thing conducted that, with all these temptations to indulgence, I did not see a drunken person on the streets all day, nor hear a noise louder than common conversation. There was neither fiddling nor dancing; and as the stage does not come in on Sunday, it was a day of unbroken stillness, in which, if any body "took a horn" or "irrigated," to use the phrase of this region, he did it with the decorum of a Dutch burgher of ancient New Amsterdam. As I came away from the Sunday-school which I visited in the morning, one of the most respectable gentlemen of the place politely asked me to take a drink, and so completely was I overcome by or saturated with the local atmosphere, that though I do not "drink," I came very near going in with the good man to see him take his whisky.

I ought to add that Sonora has an excellent graded public school, besides several private schools. The public school is held in a roomy brick building which is a credit to the town.

"If you stay in Sonora two weeks, you'll come back; and if you come back you will stay all your life," they say; and it seems to be true. The town contains an astonishing number of bachelors and widowers; men who came here, many of them, so long ago as 1849, most of them before 1853, and who live on with but little purpose, apparently, in their lives, except to sun themselves and to enjoy the climate. The gold has gone. In the frenzy of the earlier days, when millions were taken out every week; when the jail was as full as the mines; when on Sunday the miners formed a cue half a mile long, waiting for their letters at the post-office; when every other house in the place was a bar-room or gambling-den; when Wells-Fargo's strong box went down to 'Frisco daily with the ransom of an emperor—in the frenzy of those exciting days these elderly men spent their energies. They came to make their fortunes; those who succeeded went away to enjoy the prize; those who failed live on here, contented, thinking of the happy old days; with enough to eat,

7

for living is cheap here, and no cold winters to dread, nor prosperous people to make them unhappy.

The woeful depreciation of real estate shows both what Sonora once was, and what it now is. One citizen showed me his store, iron-shuttered, with iron doors and iron roof, solidly built of brick and stone. "It cost six thousand dollars to build, in the early days," said he; "and, if I had to sell it now, lot and all would not bring three hundred dollars." A farm or "rancho" of three hundred acres, with a vineyard of some acres in bearing, was valued at $1600. A well-placed and well-made farm of one hundred and sixty acres, with twenty acres of vines in good order, in sight of the town, could be bought for $1500.

The gold has been the curse of the town, and remains its curse still. Whoever came, came to get gold, and whoever got it, took what he got and fled. It was the single industry of the region, and it disabled men from following any other. It is strange to see how even the presence, the known existence, of gold in the soil seems to paralyze men's energies, and turn their thoughts from the active pursuit of other occupations than gold seeking.

Almost every body I met in the little town owned a quartz-claim. I asked what business was followed by the head of a colored family whose pleasant little home I noticed, and was told he was working a quartz-lead, and having a very hard time. "If he had only a little capital he would get through"—but unluckily the little capital would swallow up all his gains. What would So-and-so make, if their claim turned out fairly? I asked; and was answered that it would take two or three years for the three men to work out their claim—to take out all the gold in the vein, that is—and during that time they would make probably day's wages—no more. Even the steward of the hotel where we staid brought me out specimens of a "pocket-claim" he owned, and into the working of which I suspect the poor fellow puts all he can save from his wages. "Does every body in this town own a quartz-claim?" I asked a citizen, and he laughingly replied: "Oh no, *I* don't, for instance;" adding, after a pause, "that is to say, I *do*, but it is not worth any thing."

Before we came to the town, a merchant, unable to get the price he wished for his store, pulled it down, and we saw, in the very main street of Sonora, the singular spectacle of placer-mining for gold. The soil of his lot was taken out to the depth of fifteen or eighteen feet, and thrown into a sluice, where it was washed, and the gold—in little nuggets—taken out. He had taken out in a few weeks over four thousand dollars' worth, and was still busy. The whole operation was conducted by four or five men very inexpensively, and I believe his clerks and book-keeper were among the diggers.

The approach of a circus and menagerie excited the boys of the town while we were there, and I saw little urchins going out to the fields beyond the town with their mothers' tin kitchen-pans. They were going to pan out enough to pay their entrance-fee to the circus. "What is the use of worrying," said a stal-

CRADLE-ROCKING.

wart fellow to me; "a man can always make four bits a day with his pan, and living is cheap."

Thus the gold is still a curse, a clog; if it were all gone, men, women, and boys would cease to think of it, and the four bits and the circus money would be earned by some industry useful to the general public. But now they live on in careless ease, enjoying their delicious climate; eating in the season the finest fruit of California; careless of the future, for there is no winter, and a miner can live comfortably in the hills for ten dollars a month; and recounting to each other the past and faded glories of Sonora, and their hopes that by the success of quartz-mining and the development of agriculture its prosperity may some day be revived.

Nor is it improbable that this may come about. The soil of the hills is fertile and easily worked, and there is no doubt, as I have said, that quartz-mining, when pursued with skill and with sufficient capital, will pay regular and sufficient dividends.

Near Sonora, on top of a mountain twelve miles away, you may see a good example of quartz-mining. Here lies the Confidence Mine, whose singular story shows both how miners fail and how they succeed. It was opened and worked at a loss for several years, to the depth of nearly two hundred feet, by two successive companies. Under their management the quartz did not pay, and it was finally abandoned. The mine caved in, the machinery was removed, and all was dead, when it fell into the hands of a San Francisco capitalist. He had no desire to mine, but the present superintendent, who had worked out a mine of his own in the neighborhood, examined this quartz, studied the character of the vein, and finally proposed to the owner to reopen it, as, in his judgment, it would prove profitable. He asked for $5000 to "prospect" the lead —to investigate it, that is to say. When he had spent $2500, he was convinced that with proper economy it would pay to work. Men were engaged, and a mass of ore was taken out; and the event proved his conjecture correct— that the farther they went down the richer the ore proved. When this became certain, and then only, the machinery was put up, and was, when I saw it, working forty stamps, with ore much of which, I was told, pays about forty dollars per ton with economy. You should know that six or seven dollars a ton covers expenses, so there is a very handsome profit in the Confidence Mine. The whole capital invested in machinery and works is, I believe, less than eighty thousand dollars.

The superintendent, whose skill was thus useful, told me that he had followed quartz-mining for fourteen years. He thought—and so does every one here with whom I have spoken—that no man but a practical miner can succeed in quartz. Students and professors, however great their theoretical skill and scientific knowledge, have made no success here. Partly, and largely no doubt, this is because they do not know how to work economically, and, as a practical and successful miner and mine-owner said to me, " It is not the richness of the ore, but what it costs me to get the gold, that I think of."

If you visit Marysville, which lies on the tourist's way to Mount Shasta, drive out fifteen miles to Smartsville or Timbuctoo. You pass within sight of a classic locality—Yuba Dam; and you see and are made to understand what, until I saw it, I could not entirely comprehend—the whole practice of hydraulic-mining.

The ancient river bed from which, according to the miners, so much gold has been taken in this State, is in many places covered with earth to the depth of two or three hundred feet. Once, perhaps, they say here, it ran in a valley, but now a huge hill covers it. To dig down to it and mine it out by ordinary processes would be too expensive; therefore hydraulic-mining has been invented. Water brought from a hundred or one hundred and fifty miles away, and from a considerable height, is led from reservoirs through eight, ten, or twelve-inch iron pipes, and through what a New York fireman would call a nozzle, five or six inches in diameter, is thus forced against the side of a hill one or two or three hundred feet high. The stream when it leaves the pipe has such force that it would cut a man in two if it should hit him. Two or three and sometimes even six such streams play against the bottom of a hill, and earth and stones, often of great size, are washed away, until at last an immense slice of the hill itself gives way and tumbles down.

At Smartsville, Timbuctoo, and Rose's Bar I suppose they wash away into the sluices half a dozen acres a day, from fifty to two hundred feet deep; and in the muddy torrent, which rushes down at railroad speed through the channels prepared for it, you may see large rocks helplessly rolling along.

Not all the earth contains gold. Often there is a superincumbent layer of fifty or more feet which is worthless, before they reach the immense gravel deposit which marks the course of the ancient river; and from this gravel, water-worn, and showing all the marks of having formed once the bed of a rushing torrent, the gold is taken. Under great pressure this gravel—which contains, you must understand, rocks of large size, and is not gravel in our sense of the word at all—has been cemented together, so that even the powerful streams of water directed against it make but a feeble impression; and to hasten and cheapen the operation, a blast of from 1200 to 1500 kegs of powder is inserted in a hill-side, and exploded in such a way as to shatter and loosen a vast bulk of earth and stones, whereupon the water is brought into play against it.

You know already that the gold is saved in long sluice-boxes, through which the earth and water are run, and in the bottom of which gold is caught by quicksilver; and so far the whole operation is simple and cheap. But, in order to run off this enormous mass of earth and gravel, a rapid fall must be got into some deep valley or river; and to get this has often been the most costly and tedious part of a hydraulic-mining enterprise. At Smartsville, for instance, the bed which contains the gold lies above the present Yuba River, but a considerable hill, perhaps two hundred and fifty feet high, lies between the two, and through this hill each company must drive a tunnel before it can get an outfall for its washings. One such tunnel, driven for the most part through solid and very hard rock, was completed last year. It cost $250,000 and two years' labor, and was over three thousand feet long; and until it was completed not a cent's worth of gold could be taken out of the claim. In another tunnel, which was already thirteen hundred and fifty feet long when I saw it, and had still to be driven a considerable distance, a diamond drill was at work; and one of the proprietors of the tunnel of which I first spoke above told me that, if they had had this machine, his company would, he thought, have saved half the cost of their tunnel.

If you want to know how a part of the surface of our planet looked some thousands of years ago, here is a good opportunity; for what two or three men with torrents of water wash away into the Yuba River in a few weeks, must have taken many centuries to accumulate; and below, you see a mass of water-washed stone, rounded boulders, and large gravel, twenty or fifty or even a hundred feet deep, which was so plainly the bed of a torrent or rapidly-rushing river once, that even children recognize it.

Of course the acres washed away must go somewhere, and they are filling up the Yuba River. This was once, I am told by old residents, a swift and clear mountain torrent; it is now a turbid and not rapid stream, whose bed has been raised by the washings of the miners not less than fifty feet above its level in 1849. It once contained trout, but now I imagine a catfish would die in it.

The settlement of this country by Americans has produced many curious changes like this. General Bidwell, who lives at Chico, above Marysville, told me that fifteen years ago he had seen six grizzly bears lassoed and shot on his place by his men in one day—"and it was not a very good day for grizzlies either." So late as 1853 antelope and elk abounded on his pastures; the former, as well as deer, used to graze quietly with his cattle, and venison was a constant dish on his table. Before the gold discovery, trappers used to catch the beaver and otter on the Sacramento and Yuba rivers; but these creatures have, of course, disappeared with the elk.

All this change has taken place in little more than thirty years; and in a country which was for centuries occupied by men of another nation, who knew not either how to find out its mineral riches, to develop its agricultural wealth, or to subdue its native animals.

Forty miles above Marysville, on the California and Oregon Railroad, and on your way to Mount Shasta, lies Chico, near which place is the "rancho" of General Bidwell, formerly a member of Congress from this State. It is one of the old Spanish grants, and contains twenty thousand acres of fine land. Its possessor came to this country in 1842, and he has been farming here on a large scale for fifteen years. Twenty thousand acres of fair, smooth land, with a brook running through it, which would be called a river in New England, and which drives a flour-mill on the estate, is a property worth seeing. We saw one field of wheat of a thousand acres; a field of oats which contained, I believe, four hundred acres, and in which a man was quickly lost to sight, so high were the oats; and cattle scattered over what seemed a boundless plain. The estate has sixty miles of substantial board fence; dozens of miles of private roads; a vineyard of three hundred acres, from which General Bidwell proposes to make not wine but raisins—in which I wish him the best success; and the crops consisted, when I saw them, of twenty-five hundred acres of wheat, about seven hundred of barley, and nearly as much of oats. Over one hundred acres are, besides this, in orchard; and the almond was here as large as a good-sized apple-tree; the pomegranate was planted for screens; the fig and English walnut had grown to stately trees; and cherries, peaches, plums, apricots, and apples, all were thrifty, and so laden with fruit that they threatened to break down. The curculio is unknown here; the cherry has no knots, and in fact no fruit is yet diseased:—300 horses, 1500 head of fine cattle, 3000 sheep, and 2000 hogs make up the inventory of General Bidwell's live stock; and a hun-

THE MEXICAN ARASTRA.

dred men are fed by him daily the year round, and make up his constant working force.

In the country between Marysville and Chico a number of large farms, of from five to twelve thousand acres each, are found. In the majority of cases, I believe, such estates will not be found profitable by their owners; and I do not believe they are an advantage to the country, especially where, as is often the case, they are owned by non-residents.

Some of the illustrations in this chapter I give because, though they depict now obsolete modes of obtaining gold, they will help the reader and tourist to comprehend terms which he will frequently hear in California. The Arastra, for instance, was used in the early days to pulverize the ore. It is a Mexican contrivance, rude, but—so miners say—effective. Winnowing, or "dry-washing," was practiced also by the Mexicans. It is still used in some parts of Southern and Lower California, where the ore is found too far away from a sufficient supply of water to make any other practice possible. The wind bears away the dust and light particles of earth, and leaves the gold dust, which is heavier.

The cradle, with which so much gold was got out in the early mining days, is now disused. The flutter-wheel you may still see on some of the rivers.

The "pan" is frequently in use for trials, to test the richness of earth; but its common use has ceased.

To return, however, to mining — no year passes without the discovery of new and important veins of the precious ore in California; not to speak of its neighbor States and Territories. I do not doubt that the temptation held out by the mines has retarded the development of the agricultural wealth of the State. It is not so long since the opinion was common that California was valuable only or chiefly for its mines. But agriculture has now taken a start; the rapid growth of the railroad system of the State has brought and is bringing all its richest farming lands within cheap and quick reach of a market.

The great San Joaquin Valley, which this year has for the first time an outlet to market, by the Visalia and Southern Pacific Railroads, will double its wheat crop next year; and the whole of that vast and fertile region already begins to feel the effects of the railroad, in stimulating cultivation and enterprise, and attracting settlers from a distance.

Meantime, it is now known that quartz-mining, though a perfectly safe enterprise when prudently managed with sufficient capital, will not do for men of small capital or none. Hence will come in the future, I can see, fewer failures, and fewer adventures; but, as there is reason to believe, a constantly and steadily increasing yield of gold. We shall hear less of brilliant discoveries, or of great and sudden fortunes; but I believe the gold crop will be greater year after year.

Nor is it unworthy of notice that the California farmer and manufacturer have an important advantage from the success of mining enterprises in their State, by reason of the near and good market it gives them for their products. The mining population needs food, machinery, and clothing; and all these are supplied them to greater or less extent from their own State. Thus it may be said that the State has one more industry than any of our Eastern States—one more source of prosperity to all, of course.

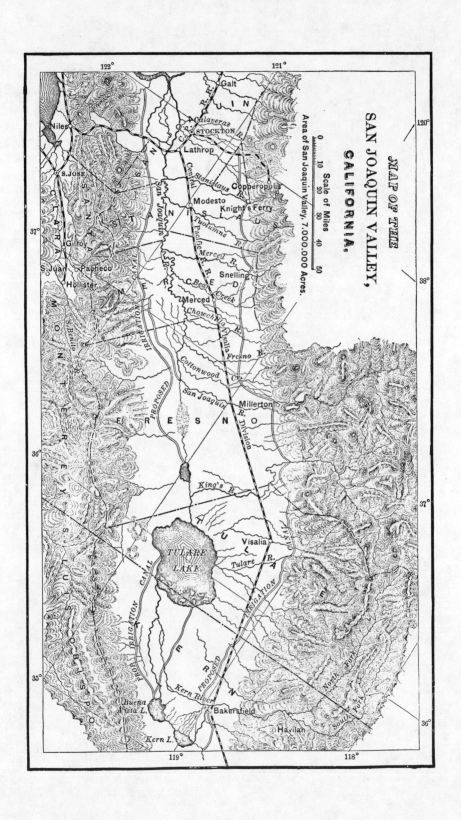

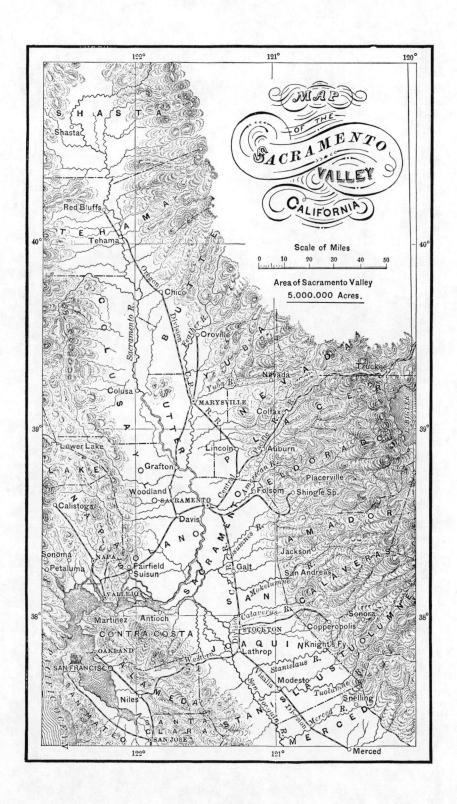

BOATING ON DONNER LAKE.

CHAPTER VIII.

SOUTHERN CALIFORNIA FOR INVALIDS.

A FRIEND and neighbor of my own, consumptive for some years, and struggling for his life in a winter residence for two years at Nice and Mentone, and during a third at Aiken, in South Carolina, came last October to Southern California.

He had been "losing ground," as he said, and as his appearance showed, for two years, and last summer suffered so severely from night sweats, sleeplessness, continual coughing, and lack of appetite, that it was doubtful whether he would live through the winter anywhere; and it was rather in desperation than with much hope of a prolonged or comfortable life that he made ready for the journey across the continent with his family.

In January I was one day standing in the door-way of a hotel at Los Angeles, when I saw a wagon drive up; the driver jumped out, held out his hand to me, and sung out in a hearty voice, "How do you do?" It was my consumptive friend, but a changed man.

He had just driven sixty miles in two days, over a rough road, from San Bernardino; he walked with me several miles on the evening we met; he ate heartily and slept well, enjoyed his life, and coughed hardly at all. It was an amazing change to come about in three months, and in a man so ill as he had been.

"I shall never be a sound man, of course," he said to me when I spent some days with him, later, at San Bernardino; "but this climate has added ten years to my life; it has given me ease and comfort; and neither Nice, nor Mentone, nor Aiken are, in my opinion, to be compared with some parts of Southern California in point of climate for consumptives."

In Santa Barbara, San Diego, and San Bernardino, one may find abundant evidence corroborative of my friend's assertion. In each of these places I have met men and women who have been restored to health and strength by residence there; and though no one whom I met had had the wide experience of my friend in other winter resorts, I found not a few people of intelligence and means who bore the strongest testimony to the kindly and healing influences of the climate of Southern California.

I think I shall be doing a service, therefore, to many invalids if I give here some details concerning the places I have named, and some others, but little known as yet in the East, which are now accessible, and whose beneficial influences upon diseases of the throat and lungs are undoubtedly remarkable.

The whole of Southern California has a very mild and equable winter climate. Stockton, for instance, which lies at the head of the San Joaquin Valley, has a temperature all the year singularly like that of Naples, as is shown by observations kept for some years by one of the most eminent and careful physicians of the place. But local peculiarities cause in some places daily extremes which are not, I think, favorable for invalids; and in other points the winds are too severe for weakly persons. At Los Angeles, for instance, the days in January are warm and genial, but as soon as the sun sets the air becomes chilly, and quickly affects tender throats. San Diego, Santa Barbara, San Bernardino, with Stockton and Visalia, are the points most favorable for consumptives and persons subject to throat difficulties.

Of these, the friend of whom I spoke above found San Bernardino the most beneficial; and a physician, who had removed from an Eastern city to the new Riverside Colony near San Bernardino, told me that he lived nowhere so comfortably as there. He could not live in New York at all, being prostrated with severe throat disease; and he enjoyed, he told me, perfect health at Riverside.

Unfortunately, San Bernardino has but a poor hotel, and is not, as I write, well fitted to accommodate invalids. But I was told that comfortable board can be obtained in several private houses, and a new hotel is now building and will be opened before next fall. The sanitary advantages of the place are little known and not much thought of by its inhabitants. My friend, who has spent there a considerable part of this winter, and who, like a genuine valetudinarian, keeps a record of the temperature with both dry and wet bulb thermometer, reports to me that the air is dryer there than at points nearer the coast; and this greater dryness, which arises from its situation, about seventy-five miles from the sea, is probably its chief sanitary advantage. At the Riverside Colony there are yet but a few small houses, and no accommodations for visitors.

San Bernardino has a fine situation; it lies in a great plain, with picturesque mountains on three sides of it. Living is cheap; horses cost from $20 to $50 each; horse-keep is very cheap; the roads are generally good; and for those who do not ride, a wagon and a pair of horses will afford the means of pleasant excursions. Oranges are grown in old San Bernardino, which is where the old mission stood, and I have an idea that there, on higher ground, and nearer the mountains, the climate is perhaps a little better even than in the town.

To reach San Bernardino you take steamer at San Francisco for Los Angeles, which place you reach from San Pedro, its port, by a short railroad. The voyage, which lasts thirty-six hours, and is made all the way in sight of land, is usually pleasant. From Los Angeles you get to San Bernardino by stage, distance sixty miles—time ten hours. The Southern Pacific Railroad Company has just completed its surveys for a railroad to connect Los Angeles with San Bernardino; and when this line is completed the journey can be made in a few hours.

San Diego seems to me to possess the mildest and sunniest winter climate on the coast. It has the advantage of a large and excellent hotel, and very good shops, and the disadvantage of an almost entire absence of shade and trees. It has pleasant society, and within thirty miles very fine and varied scenery. If I were spending a winter in California for my health, I think I should go first to San Diego, and stay there the months of December and January. It is the most southern town in the State, and presumably warmer than either Santa Barbara or San Bernardino, though the difference is but slight. It affords some simple amusements, in fishing, shell-hunting, and boat-sailing; and here, as all over Southern California, horses are cheap; and to those who are fond of driving or riding, very fair roads are open. There is less rain here than in any other part of the State; and as the so-called winter in this State is a rainy season, San Diego has the advantage over other places of less mud in December and January. In fact, I doubt if it is ever muddy there.

Santa Barbara is on many accounts the pleasantest of all the places I have named; and it has an advantage in this, that one may there choose his climate within a distance of three or four miles of the town. It has a very peculiar situation. If you will examine a map of California, you will see that, while the general "trend" of the coast-line is from north-north-west to south-south-east, at Point Conception it makes a sharp and sudden turn, and runs to Rincon Point, below Santa Barbara, nearly due east and west. Thus Santa Barbara faces directly south.

But this is not the only advantage it gains from this turn in the coast-line. The harsh and foggy north and north-west winds, which make the coast north of Point Conception disagreeable, are entirely cut off from Santa Barbara by the high coast range, which comes almost to the very shore at Point Conception, and stretches along the coast, but two or three miles back from it, to San Buenaventura. Santa Barbara lies on a narrow strip of land, with the sea and some lovely islands to the south, and a picturesque mountain range between 3000 and 4000 feet high about one and a half miles back to the north.

The town and its vicinity gain thus a remarkably equable climate. I have before me a number of reports of temperature, and could overwhelm you, if I liked, with figures, tables, and statistics concerning the whole coast; but these records are almost altogether of a mean temperature for a week, month, or year. Now what an invalid suffers most from is not recorded in such tables: I mean the daily extremes. If the day is very warm, and the evening suddenly chilly and cold, that makes a bad climate for weakly persons. Both Santa Barbara and San Diego are remarkably free from such sudden and great changes, and I think there is no doubt that Santa Barbara has the most equable climate, in this sense as well as all others, on this coast. The coldest day in 1871 was the 22d of February, when the mercury stood at 42°.

There is a good hotel there, and another one is building; but neither of them stands in a pleasant situation, and both are near the shore, where the air is less dry than in the higher parts of the town. Persons who are very sensitive to damp will do well to find lodgings in the upper part of the town, or in what is called the "Montecito"—the little mountain—a suburb, two or three miles distant, and sheltered from the sea-breeze by an intervening range of low hills. Here it is somewhat warmer—indeed it is hot in the middle of the day, and the air is, I think, a little drier. In the Montecito there is also a hot sulphur spring which has some approved medicinal virtues; but I advise people to use it only on the orders of a physician.

Stockton and Visalia lie in the San Joaquin Valley, and are, like San Bernardino, peculiarly favorable to persons who are influenced injuriously by even mild sea air. The air of Stockton and Visalia is especially dry; Stockton has, as I before remarked, a climate singularly like that of Naples, but perhaps with fewer extremes; the orange grows there; and as this place, as well as Visalia, is connected by railroad with San Francisco and with the East, both are easily reached.

Visalia, which lies in the midst of a forest of magnificent oaks, is thus sheltered from the winds which at times sweep over the great San Joaquin Plains. Both places have excellent hotels—the Yosemite House at Stockton, and the

Visalia House at Visalia. Stockton has as good shops as Sacramento; and in Visalia you can also buy any thing you need.

I do not pretend here to give any complete account of the parts of the State which invalids may visit with advantage; for there are numerous points in the foot-hills of the Sierra noted for their kindly and health-giving air, and mild and equal temperature. Sonora, in Tuolomne County, is such a place; and there are many others. If an invalid is so weakened by disease that traveling itself is dangerous or impossible, I should advise Santa Barbara, or San Diego, or Stockton, or Visalia, as a stopping-place for the winter. If locomotion is possible, I should advise, what a number of persons of my acquaintance have experienced great benefit from—a stay in San Diego or San Bernardino from November or December into January; in February, an easy overland journey in your own wagon from San Diego to Los Angeles; thence by Fort Tejon into the San Joaquin Valley; and by way of Bakersfield to Visalia. A party of two or four taking such a journey need blankets—two pair each, and a heavy quilt—and a few supplies, such as condensed milk and tea. They would find plain but clean accommodations all the way, and would make from twenty to thirty miles a day. They would see a great deal of beautiful country, and many singular manners and customs, and they would find every body civil and polite, and would have no hardships to endure which a lady who likes travel would not enjoy, even if she were not in good health. The pure air would do much for an invalid; and in April one may already safely and comfortably make excursions into the Sierra from Visalia; and May and June could be most delightfully spent on the mountains which surround the Yosemite Valley, where at that season the breezes are balmy with the fragrance of the fir, the temperature is mild, and the atmosphere exhilarating.

Such a procession from the south northward would avoid rain and mud, and insure the finest weather, and a succession of grand and lovely scenery.

Persons who come to California for the winter should bring with them their winter clothing. You do not need a shawl or overcoat if you are exercising, but in driving they are necessary. You can sit out-of-doors almost every day, either to read or write, or in any other occupation; for there are but few rainy days, and it no sooner stops raining than the sun shines out most brilliantly and kindly. I do not think there were five days, either in Santa Barbara or San Diego, in December, January, and February of this year, in which the tenderest invalid could not pass the greater part of the day out-of-doors with pleasure and benefit. In Santa Barbara there were not a dozen days during the whole winter in which a baby I know of did not play on the sea-beach. But in the evening you will sit by a wood-fire—mostly with the doors and windows open—and at night you sleep under blankets very comfortably.

The constant or almost uninterrupted brightness of the skies has, I suspect, a good deal to do with the healthful influence of the climate. The southern

8

counties have but little rain. There are no gloomy days. Occasionally there is a fog in the morning, but it is not a cold fog—rather dry and warm, like the Newport fogs.

Moreover, all winter the gardens are full of flowers, the grass is green, and Nature is in her most inviting garb.

Make them give you at the hotels a sunny room. Unless you demand this, you are as likely as not to be put into a chamber on which the sun never shines; and this not purposely, but because your hotel keeper will probably know no better.

The cost of living at the hotels is very reasonable—from $10 to $14 per week; fires are an extra charge, but you should secure a room with a fire-place or stove.

Horses can be bought in Santa Barbara and the other places I have named

DONNER LAKE, CRESTED PEAK, AND MOUNT LINCOLN.

for from $20 to $50; and for children there are donkeys, for which you pay from $5 to $10. You find at all the hotels good beds, and plain but sufficient and various food.

Santa Barbara has the advantages of pleasant society and an excellent school. It is, in fact, a cozy nest of New England and Western New York people, many of whom originally came here for their health, and remain because they are charmed with the climate. It has a number of pleasant drives, and the old Spanish part of the town is an agreeable novelty to strangers, as is old San Diego also.

But pray remember that you will not find at any of these places tasteful pleasure-grounds, or large, finely-laid-out places. Nature has done much; man has not, so far, helped her. Churches and schools are his first efforts, fortunately; peace and security and civil treatment you may depend on. I know of a family spending last winter in Santa Barbara which recklessly went to bed every night with the front door of the house wide open, and never thought of robbers. But do not expect to find yet in Southern California artistically finished pleasure resorts.

Such as they are, however, the places I have named deserve the visit of persons suffering from throat or lung disease; and it will be no small addition to their merits with many that they can be reached without a voyage across the Atlantic, and that they present for the amusement of the visitor many novel and curious phases of life.

It is an important help to invalids that the air of California makes exercise pleasant and easy, and that the climate of the southern part of the State invites to a free outdoor life at all seasons. I have known weakly women not accustomed to horseback exercise to ride, after a few weeks' practice, from five to ten miles in a day, and feel no soreness of the limbs or other unpleasant consequences; and most visitors to California are surprised to find how active a life they can lead, not only without inconvenience but with pleasure and benefit.

At Santa Barbara there is a fine beach, on which the Spanish Californians used in the old times to race their horses. It is as pleasant a stretch of three miles, for a lively canter on horseback, as you can wish for; and there are not five days in the whole winter when you may not take an exhilarating ride there, with the ocean and the islands on one side and the mountains on the other. Then numerous excursions invite you out—to Carpenteria, ten miles; to the Sulphur Springs, a rough climb on horseback, perfectly safe, and giving you lovely views and fresh mountain air, six miles; to the Big Grape-vine, three miles; to the old Mission; and, as you gain courage, westward along the shore as far as you care to go, toward Point Conception, forty miles distant. In the latter part of April and in May you may make, if you have a party, longer camping expeditions, and sleep out-of-doors not only with perfect safety but with benefit to your health, even if you are a tender invalid; for the air is pure and kindly.

At San Diego you have the bay before you, with the Coronados Islands in the blue distance. If you are fond of sailing or fishing, boats are cheaply hired, with competent men to manage them. The shore in some parts affords shells, chiefly a beautiful univalve—the *Abelona*, known to us in the East, commonly, as the " California Shell." If you prefer the shore to the sea, the Julian Mines, about forty miles distant, invite you to a novel excursion, in which you will see some fine farming lands and also fine mountains; and at or near the mines you will find the mountain air exhilarating enough to persuade you, in the spring months, to make a prolonged stay.

At San Bernardino you have a vast extent of new country, over which you may ride or drive. *Old* San Bernardino offers you a ruined mission, and some fine farms with orange groves and vineyards; and when you have gained a little courage by experience, you may ride or drive out thirty miles to the San Gorgonio Pass, and take a look at Dr. Edgar's vineyard and at the Great Yuma Desert; or you may visit the San Jacinto tin mines; the placer gold diggings nearer to the town; the saw-mills up in the mountains; and you can, without fatigue and dust, and with great pleasure and benefit, make a more prolonged excursion to San Diego, by way of the Indian settlement of Temecula, and see on the way the fine ruins of the old mission of San Luis Rey, probably the most splendid and the richest of the old missions.

Wherever you go, you need to take with you a cheerful and also an inquiring spirit.   The whole of Southern California is full of novelties and wonders to an intelligent person; but oftenest he must discover them for himself. You will not find highly cultivated and ornamented gardens; but from January onward to June, you will, if you have eyes for them, discover in your rambles a succession of beautiful, and to you new wild flowers.   Theatres and other places of amusement you will not find in the towns I have mentioned; but for all healthful open-air enjoyments you will have extraordinary facilities, because the life is free and untrammeled.   You are expected to do what you please; horses are cheap; roads are almost invariably excellent; every place has a good livery-stable; you can get competent guides; and you carry with you, wherever you go, fine mountain scenery, bright sunshine—so constant that, when I remarked to a citizen of San Diego that it was a fine day, he looked at me in amazement, and said, after a pause, "Of course it is a fine day; why not? Every day is fine here."   Moreover, at all these places you will meet pleasant, intelligent, and hospitable people, who will add somewhat to your enjoyment. Santa Barbara has even a circulating library.   There are good schools for children, if you have such with you; and with a little enterprise to plan excursions, your time will not hang heavily on your hands.

Finally, if you need them, you will find competent physicians; and I advise every invalid who settles for the winter in any one of the places I have mentioned to call in at the beginning that physician of good repute who is longest resident in the place, and get his advice as to clothing, exercise, and what precautions ought to be used in his or her special case.   Experience will show you, if the doctor does not at once tell you, whether you can bear close vicinity to the ocean, or whether you will do better two or three miles away from it, on higher ground and nearer the mountains; or farther away still, in the interior. In some cases I have known, the sea-beach seemed to be the best restorative; in others, close neighborhood to the ocean proved unwholesome, but a change of not more than a mile inland worked a speedy, indeed an almost instant improvement.   The peculiarities of constitution which lead to these differences are not always known beforehand, and only come out with trial and experience. I happened to know, last winter, persons who were much better at San Bernardino than at Santa Barbara; and others who were better at Santa Barbara or

San Diego, near the beach; at Los Angeles—which lies in a valley—it is commonly said that the Mission San Gabriel, twelve miles distant, among the foot-hills, has a better climate for consumptives than the city itself; and I believe this is true. And I have been told that there are cañons back of San Diego among the mountains, forty miles in the interior, where consumptives rapidly improved and recovered who experienced little benefit in the town itself.

VIEW FROM THE COULTERVILLE TRAIL.

CHAPTER IX.

THE AGRICULTURAL WEALTH OF CALIFORNIA.—A GENERAL VIEW.

A LADY in New York, the wife of a distinguished literary man, relates that in her younger days she met at a party the wife of a wealthy fellow-citizen, to whom, on being introduced, she incidentally remarked, "I see you every Sunday; we are members of the same church." "Ah!" was the reply; "where do you sit? I do not remember your face." "Oh, we sit in the gallery," answered the editor's wife. "Indeed! in the gallery?" echoed the fine lady, with a little shrug; then, remembering her manners, she added, "Well, some very respectable people sit in the gallery."

California has been for many years regarded by Eastern people as this lady thought of the gallery of the Reverend Mr. Phydle D.D.'s church. It is generally acknowledged that some very respectable people live in California; but we who live on the Atlantic side of the continent are sorry for them, and do not doubt in our hearts that they would be only too glad to come over to us. Very few suspect that the Californians have the best of us, and that, so far from living in a kind of rude exile, they enjoy, in fact, the finest climate, the most fertile soil, the loveliest skies, the mildest winters, the most healthful region, in the whole United States. California has long passed with us in the East as a good-enough sort of country for over-adventurous young men; it is, in fact, the best part of the American continent, either for health or for profitable and pleasant living in any industrious pursuit.

Its merits, for any thing except mining, even its own inhabitants have been slow to discover; and as the placer-mines slowly gave out, there were not wanting Californians who devoutly believed that some day their State would once more be abandoned to cattle and wild horses. In 1847, when I spent eleven months on the California coast, it was universally believed that but a small part of the soil would produce crops. "There are no trees on these great plains," said every body; "and if not a tree will grow, of course the soil must be sterile." But many of those treeless plains have since yielded from fifty to eighty bushels of wheat per acre, and there is no year in which some adventurous farmer does not discover some new product for which the climate and soil are specially adapted, and which pays better than gold-mining.

One reason for the ill repute of the State as an agricultural region is that it overturns all the habits and ideas of Eastern farmers. Our people came to the State, and attempted to plant and sow in May or June, when the rains were over, and, of course, they got no more return than if they had planted corn in Illinois in August. Then, getting no crop from their planting, they beheld the whole great plain in June turn brown and sere, the grass dry up, the clover utterly disappear, and of course they were ready to give up the country as a desert. They did not then know that the grass lies on the plain fine naturally cured hay; that the clover-seed, by a curious provision of nature, is preserved in a little bur, on which the cattle and sheep actually fatten, when to the careless eye the ground seems to be bare; and that the wild oat also holds a nutritious seed all the season; so that these brown pastures are perhaps the sweetest and best support for cattle and sheep in the world.

Moreover, they knew nothing of the different qualities of soil in California. They had to learn not only the necessity of irrigation on the lighter and drier lands, but the manner of performing that work; they had to conquer many superstitions which asserted the unproductiveness or the limited productiveness of California; and meantime mining was the chosen and favorite occupation of the majority of those who came to the State, and it was, for the most part, only those who despaired of success in the mines and in trade who turned their attention to the soil. In this year, 1872, California is still, to a great extent, a country in which mining is, as they say, "played out," while agriculture has not taken its place. In such counties as Tuolumne you will see this plainly. The people are but slowly discovering that the great source of the State's wealth is in its productive soil.

In California the rains begin late in October. The grass is green all winter; ploughing begins on the first of December; wheat, barley, oats, and other crops are sowed as soon as the land can be made fit; and sowing and planting are continued as late as March. Thus the husbandman has three or four months to put in his crops. Trees are also transplanted in this season. South of San Francisco, and in the great San Joaquin Valley, frost is rarely known; roses bloom all the winter through; the flower-garden is constantly full of flowers; and many shade-trees, like the acacias, the pepper-tree, and the live-oaks, keep their foliage green the year round.

Corn is planted from March to May, and harvested as late as December. In the southern counties, and in the San Joaquin Valley especially, many farmers take two crops from the same field—wheat or barley for the first, and corn for the second; and I have seen fields which yielded, in a good season, ninety bushels of corn for this second crop. Wheat and barley are commonly sown for hay, and in that case cut before the heads fill, in April or May. Where this is done, it is usual to plant corn on the same ground when the hay crop is cut. Thus the farmer gets two valuable crops from the same field. The harvest season for wheat, barley, and oats, is in the latter part of May and in June.

After the middle of April the rains cease, and the whole harvest season is absolutely without rain. Thus the farmer is not hurried, and the harvest proceeds with none of that haste and anxiety about the weather which trouble the Eastern farmer. The small grains are usually gathered by a machine called a "header," which clips off only the heads of the grain stalk. Wheat, oats, and barley are threshed on the field, put into bags, and left either on the field or along the railroad, for weeks often, in the open air, and until the crop is sold and shipped. The grain does not sweat, nor is it liable to injury from this exposure. Hay, too, is baled or stacked on the field, and left there until it is wanted. Potatoes are often left in the ground long after they are fit for digging. Thus it is evident the farmer has, in the long, dry California summer, an immense advantage over his Eastern competitor. He needs fewer hands, he is not hurried, and he requires no costly granaries or barns to shelter the products of his fields.

Nor does he need to put away much food for his cattle. A quarter of an acre of beets, replanted as they are used, will support two cows during the whole year. Work-horses receive barley and hay, but sheep are never fed; market cattle fatten in the pastures, and horses not at work get no food except what they pick up in the fields, in winter as well as summer. The alfalfa, or Chilian clover, which is now beginning to be largely sown, does well to feed to pigs, to cows, and even to plough-horses, and bears enormous crops. On low ground, or where it can be irrigated, as much as fifteen tons have been taken from an acre; it is not cut from December to April, but yields from six to eight cuttings in the year. Cattle and horses are more easily kept in good condition in California than elsewhere in the United States, and the farmer needs no such substantial stables as in the Eastern States.

Fruit-trees bear much earlier than in the East. The peach bears a peck in the second year from planting the pit; the apple gives a crop at five years, and begins to bear at three; the curculio is unknown; and such perishable fruits as plums and cherries keep far longer than with us. I have eaten cherries and strawberries in Colorado which had been brought from Sacramento—a four days' journey—and they were in perfect order. The growth of fruit and other trees is extraordinary. The eucalyptus, a fine Australian evergreen shade-tree, has made twenty feet in a year, and I have seen one, eight years from a small cutting, which was seventy-five feet high and two feet in diameter at the base; the apricot becomes almost a forest-tree in size; and in the southern parts of the State it is the custom to make fences of sticks of willow, sycamore, or cotton-wood, cut to the length of eight feet, and stuck into the ground in December. These strike root at once, and grow so rapidly that in the second year the farmer cuts his fire-wood from these living fences.

Moreover, the variety of fruits cultivated in the farmer's orchard, especially in Southern California, is much greater than with us. I have seen, commonly, in orchards, the apple, pear, peach, cherry, quince, plum, nectarine, pomegranate —a most lovely tree or tall shrub when in bloom; the fig, which bears two crops a year; the orange, lemon, lime, almond, olive, English walnut, and apricot; and you may eat strawberries, wherever care is bestowed upon them, in every month of the year. Fruit-trees are all free from disease, though the pear-slug has made its appearance in the San José Valley; and the finest varieties of fruit known in the East grow freely here.

When you buy a farm in California, except it be in some of the northern parts of the State or in some of the wooded foot-hills, you buy clear land. You have not to girdle trees, pull stumps, or toil among under-brush. Thousands of acres are every year bought or rented, ploughed at once, and sown to grain, without even the expense of fencing in many of the counties, which have adopted "no fence" laws. Men do here more easily what they used to do in Illinois and Indiana—buy a farm, and with their first crop clear all their expenses and the price of the land. Where there are trees, except far up on the mountain sides, they are usually the lovely oaks of this State, evergreen trees which nature has planted so that the finest park-like effects are produced. I spent the last 22d of February with a party of pleasant picnickers upon one of these oak-covered plains, green as our finest pastures are in June, with a lovely lake in the centre of a fair smooth field of about 1500 acres; with oaks scattered over the plain in irregular clumps and masses, and detached trees, as beautifully as Olmsted or Weideman could place them; with finely rounded hills, green to their summits, surrounding us on every side; with skies so bright, and the air so mild and sweet, that a baby slept on the ground, wrapped in

CALIFORNIA LIVE-OAK.

shawls and rugs, and awoke rosy and crowing. It had rained hard overnight, but we sat on the greensward to eat our luncheon; and there were New Yorkers present rash and irreverent enough to declare that even the Central Park was never so lovely as this little piece of Nature's own landscape-gardening. The California live-oak is a low-branching, wide-spreading tree; it often attains the height of seventy feet, with a width—not circumference—of foliage of one hundred and twenty feet; and where it grows the plain is usually without under-brush—as clear and clean as a highly-cultivated park.

Where nature has done and does so much, man gains a quick reward for his efforts. Our costliest and rarest greenhouse flowers grow here out-of-doors all winter, almost without care. In the vineyards are planted by the acre the grapes which at home are found only in the hot-houses of the wealthy. The soil is so fertile, that it is a common saying in the great valleys that the ground is better after it has yielded two crops than at the first ploughing; and though, as a rule, the farmers, especially in Southern California, live in small and mean houses, the climate—which permits children to play out-of-doors without overcoats or shawls for at least 330 days in the year, and which makes the piazza or the neighboring shade-tree pleasanter than a room, in winter as well as summer—is probably to blame for their carelessness. The dwelling is a less important part of the farm than with us. I am sorry that it is so; and I warn the wives of farmers who think of removing to California, to stipulate beforehand that their husbands shall build them neat and pleasant houses in the beginning. If you put it off you will never do it, for you will, like many of your predecessors, become accustomed to a small and mean-looking dwelling. The climate does not here force you to substantial building.

The dry air of California does not make a cellar necessary to health, nor need the house be of two stories. A long range of rooms, with broad and comfortable piazzas, is the best for this State. I have seen some farm-houses built in this style—which is copied after the abodes of the old Spanish Californians—which were both charming and cheap, and very convenient for the women of the household.

No doubt, the slight houses, and the constant outdoor life which the climate makes possible, do much for the health of invalids who come to the southern part of the State. But the warm and dry air has been found a great natural remedy for consumption and diseases of the throat. I have come upon some remarkable cures during the past winter — men and women who recovered strength and flesh without medicine, and very rapidly, so that they ceased to be invalids after only a few months' residence in one of the southern counties. Southern California has a better climate than Italy; and San Diego, Santa Barbara, and San Bernardino are already frequented by numbers who found no relief at Nice, or Aiken, or in Florida.

To the settler from the far-off East it is an important advantage that California has, in a remarkable degree, a well-settled, orderly, and law-abiding population. Three races—the Indians, the old Spaniards, and we "Americans"—live there harmoniously together. No man need fear for his life or his property, even in the most thinly settled parts of the State. There has been violence: stages have been robbed; highwaymen, who called themselves "road agents," have in times past waylaid travelers; in the towns and mining-camps you hear even now of lawless deeds; but the Californian has known how to build up a peaceful, lawful society better, I think, than any other man in the world. No State in the Union is better supplied with schools. In so thinly settled and far-away a district as San Bernardino County, I found country schools, attended by Spanish and American children in common, and taught by zealous and intelligent teachers. The best proof I can offer you of what I have asserted of the security of life and property is this—that I have during the past winter traveled through the most thinly-settled parts of the southern counties, over the least-frequented roads, alone or with but a single companion; have stopped to cook my dinner in the Indian huts, asked for a night's lodging at Spanish ranchos, slept sometimes on the green grass, with my horse staked out, my feet near a fire, and my body wrapped in overcoat and blanket; and journeying thus day after day, I had not even a revolver with me, and no arm larger than a pocketknife. And on one of the loneliest parts of my journey, among the mountains of San Bernardino County, I found a San Francisco lady established near a hot sulphur spring, and with but two children, the largest of them a boy of seventeen, building herself a house, employing carpenters and laborers, and "making" a place. She had found health and strength in this wilderness, and lived there without fear or danger.

For intelligent farmers—men who like to go a little out of the old ruts of farming—California seems to me the finest country conceivable. I speak now especially of the great Sacramento and San Joaquin valleys, which contain the bulk of the richest farming land in the State. Such men may establish themselves by field crops; but they will find before them an almost illimitable field for experiment, with great rewards for perseverance and skill.

Near Marysville, two years ago, a farmer, finding that his orchard of apples, pears, etc., did not pay as well as formerly, bethought him of the castor-bean. He planted several acres as an experimental crop, found that his soil was suitable for it, and last spring I saw on his place one hundred acres in castor-oil. The plant, which is with us in the East a tender ornamental shrub, was planted and hoed or ploughed like corn, and, when ripe, a press in a shed at the edge of the field made the oil. In the East his adventure would have needed a solid brick building for his machinery, as well as costly drying and bleaching rooms. Here the oil was bleached under a rainless sky, and a shed which could not have cost fifty dollars sufficiently protected his engine and press.

In the Napa Valley a farmer thought hops would pay. He planted ten acres, and two crops gave him a handsome little fortune. Some years ago farmers within reach of the San Francisco market planted cherries; and I know a man whose cherry orchard, wherein Chinese pick the fruit at a trifling expense, has netted him for several years past thirty dollars a tree. Several persons in different parts of the State have succeeded in making first-class raisins, and it needs only that the right kind of grape shall be planted to make the manufacture of raisins a highly profitable industry in Southern California.

Beet sugar has been successfully and very profitably manufactured for two years in several parts of the State, and the sugar-beet, which is found to yield a larger percentage of sugar in this climate than in France, is a very profitable crop wherever machinery for reducing it is at hand.

Cotton is already produced, and of excellent quality, in the San Joaquin and Tulare valleys; twenty acres can be planted and kept in order by one man, and a crop averaged last year seventy-five dollars per acre. Colonel Strong, a Mississippi planter, reports that the whole cost of making and marketing the crop is twenty-eight dollars per acre, leaving a net profit of forty-seven dollars per acre, or nine hundred and forty dollars on twenty acres, which is the quantity per man. The silk culture is successfully carried on in several parts of the State, and it would be more generally successful as an adjunct to other farming operations, where there are women and children to attend to this branch. Hops, of which I spoke above, obtain a higher price than those raised in the East, being stronger, and, owing to the dry summer, more sure to be gathered in good order. Rice, flax, and hemp are all, on suitable soils, sure crops; and the culture of the ramie promises to be more profitable and successful in Southern California than anywhere else in this country. I have seen several plantations in Santa Barbara and other counties which promise well.

The vine, of course, grows well almost everywhere, and the best vineyardists are now planting German and French varieties, and trying to make light wines. But I believe in the San Joaquin and Tulare valleys the raisin grape will be found more profitable than even wine-making or brandy-distilling.

As an adjunct to farming, or where men come with capital enough to attempt it as a business, wool-growing and cattle-raising yield handsome profits. Sheep are neither fed nor housed in this State; they are herded all the year round, and the wool-grower counts upon doubling the number of his sheep every year—that is to say, he raises as many lambs of both sexes as he has ewes. Many men who keep sheep do not own lands, but hire the pastures at so much per head—usually ten cents a year for each sheep; and, as a rule, it is reckoned that the wool pays all the expenses, and the sheep, for which there is always a ready sale—are clear profit. Colonel Hollister, one of the largest sheep-owners in the State, came here, in 1853, with three hundred American sheep; and he has said that each one of these sheep earned him one thousand dollars before it died. He is now a millionaire, and the owner of over one hundred thousand acres of land; and he was in debt when he came to this State from Ohio.

One cause of Colonel Hollister's success is that he "stood by his sheep." He kept sheep year after year, giving to that business all the ability he possessed. The curse of farming in California has been that men took it up too often as a mere whim, or as a speculation. I met last winter a young man on his way to the Arizona mines, who told me that he was tired of farming in California. In reply to some questions, he related that he had rented the previous winter a thousand acres of land, had it ploughed and sown to wheat, and as last summer was very dry, and as the land he hired was upland, his crop did not return him his original investment, which amounted to several thousand dollars. This man thought farming would not pay. But neither does gambling pay; and his kind of farming was merely a gambling or speculative transaction. He was not an experienced or trained farmer, and what he really did was to bet so many thousand dollars that it would be a wet season. It happened to be a dry season, and he lost. This year there is a wet season, and the high land which he sowed last year will, no doubt, yield forty, and perhaps sixty, bushels of wheat to the acre.

A blunder too often made by farmers in this State is that they try to own too much land.   In the southern part of California a man does not need more than one hundred and sixty acres, and he can live comfortably and secure an independence after some years on eighty acres.   Indeed, I know shrewd men who are planting forty, and even twenty, acres with almonds, or olives, or oranges, or English walnuts, all of which grow in proper situations in Southern California, and who hope to secure in six or eight years a handsome and permanent income.   And every farmer in the region which bears the culture of these fruits ought to set apart ten or twenty acres for them.

In the East a prudent farmer plants an orchard of apples, pears, peaches, plums, or all of these, as a source of income when they come to bear.   All these fruits, except, perhaps, apples, are perishable, and need to be marketed at once, and of apples it is found already that the area on which they can be raised is so great that the price is low.   Now Southern California bears not only all our Eastern fruits, as I have said before, but also these six: the orange, lemon, almond, olive, citron, and English walnut, for which the market extends over the whole country, while the area in which they can be successfully grown is limited.

Concerning the range and the profitableness of these fruits, I give detailed and carefully gathered information in another chapter.   The facts and figures there given surprised me as much as they will my readers; but I have been careful to give only well-ascertained facts.

THE SENTINEL, YOSEMITE VALLEY.

CHAPTER X.

THE AGRICULTURAL LANDS OF CALIFORNIA.—HINTS TO SETTLERS.

THE greater part of the farming lands of California lies in the two large valleys of the Sacramento and the San Joaquin, including the Tulare. The Sacramento Valley is forty miles wide, bounded on the west by the Coast Range, and on the east by the Sierra Nevada. It is an immense fertile plain, containing about five millions of acres, becoming mountainous in its northern part, but having a vast area of fertile land, much of which never needs irrigation, and produces fine crops in the driest years. In the spring of 1871, when a drought prevailed all over California, I saw a field of oats of one thousand acres at Chico, on the California and Oregon Railroad, so high that I could and did tie the oats over my head.

Northern California—namely, the Sacramento Valley, and the counties which lie on the same parallel with it—has a climate mild compared with that of our Eastern States; but it has frosts and some light snows, and the semi-tropical fruits do not flourish there, except in certain favored localities. Southern California, which includes the San Joaquin Valley and its extensions, the Tulare and Kern valleys, as well as the sea-coast counties parallel with these, is the real garden of the State.

At Stockton begins the great San Joaquin Valley, which has an area of about seven millions of acres. This stretches from Stockton to the Tejon Pass, a length, north and south, of three hundred miles. It has, without including the foot-hills, an average width of forty miles, or with the foot-hills, which contain excellent land, fifty miles. With the foot-hills on each side, and the smaller mountain valleys, this region has over eighteen million acres of land, of which not less than ten millions are susceptible of highly profitable cultivation. The plains alone contain nearly seven million acres of land, of which less than seven hundred thousand were cultivated last year.

The whole valley has at this time a population of less than fifty thousand persons.

The San Joaquin, Tulare, and Kern valleys, included in the general term of the San Joaquin, form the "new country" of the State. Its soil is the richest, its plains are the broadest, its climate is semi-tropical, and in it already the orange, cotton, ramie, the sugar-beet, as well as corn and wheat and the other cereals, have been grown. At present two railroads, the Southern Pacific and the San Joaquin Valley (a branch of the Consolidated Central Pacific), are rapidly building, which will open the whole of this immense territory to settlement; and already its natural wealth is drawing thither not only farmers, but capitalists with schemes for irrigation upon an extensive scale. Shrewd men in San Francisco begin to see that if it was profitable for companies to build canals and flumes, sometimes a hundred miles long, to facilitate mining operations, it will be more permanently profitable to build flumes, canals, ditches, and reservoirs for irrigation.

One irrigation company is already at work in the San Joaquin country upon a large scale; it has forty miles of canal dug, and a large force of men is now at work extending this canal. The plan of this company contemplates not only irrigation, but incidentally the reclamation of a million of acres of swamp and overflowed lands. An able engineer, Mr. R. M. Brereton, long experienced in extensive irrigation works in India, made during the summer and fall of 1871 a reconnaissance of the valley, and his report to the company proposes the construction of canals and ditches, at a cost eventually of $7,660,000, which would irrigate 2,806,000 acres of land, every acre of which will, with water, produce two crops a year. Mr. Brereton writes me: "Irrigation can only grow with the increase of population. It must be small at first; and my object has been to design such a system as would be capable of future enlargement, as population increased the demand for water. Therefore, under my plan, canals that in the next fifty years may cost $10,000 per mile will not at first cost $1500 per mile."

During the season of 1872 not less than 100,000 acres will be irrigated in the San Joaquin Valley. The cost to the farmer for water is about one dollar and a quarter per acre for each crop, and two crops are taken off in the year Mr. Brereton writes: "I saw in Bakersfield and its environs magnificent crops of Indian corn growing, which had been planted about the end of June and beginning of July, after a crop of wheat had been obtained off the same land. The corn in one field averaged from 16 to 18 feet in height; the cobs were of immense size, and about a span in length. This was the result of irrigation. I was also shown fields of alfalfa (a kind of lucern) which had already yielded under irrigation three crops, averaging from six to eight tons to the acre."

Meantime the people in this valley have already constructed between forty and fifty irrigating ditches of different lengths, of one of which, near Visalia, I shall give some details in another chapter; and on the fields which have been thus watered corn, wheat, cotton, flax, barley, and a number of other products have been raised. At present the San Joaquin Valley is largely used for grazing. The immense quantity of government and railroad lands which it contains were reserved from sale until the railroad companies should locate their grants. This work was completed during the summer of 1872, and the whole great valley is now open to settlement, while the two railroads, which are being energetically prosecuted by wealthy companies, will give to farmers a quick and certain access to market.

It is my belief that in the San Joaquin Valley farmers coming into the State from the East will find the most eligible locations for some years to come. The soil is rich and very easily cultivated; the climate is such that not only the cereals, but cotton, and the sub-tropical fruits, can be safely and profitably cultivated there; irrigation has now been so far advanced that it will keep pace with the needs of settlers; as soon as the railroad companies locate their grants it will be possible to buy the best land of them or of the Government at two dollars and a half per acre, in quantities of from forty to six hundred and forty acres; two railroads will give access to markets; two crops a year from irrigated land will make less land necessary to the farmer, who can do as much with eighty acres here as with one hundred and sixty elsewhere, even in the cereal crops only; where land is irrigated the farmer can plant live fences of willow, sycamore, and cotton-wood, which, after the second year, will yield him all the fire-wood he needs without further trouble; and it is an incidental advantage of this region that farmers will for some years to come be able to graze stock freely upon the unappropriated government and railroad lands near them.

The government and railroad lands are the cheapest, and probably the best, in the State. They are the most easily selected and located, for the Government land-offices have accurate maps, and the railroad land-office in Sacramento has an organization so perfect that a farmer searching for land can obtain there, without delay, the most precise and detailed information, not only as to location, but as to quality and distance from the railroad and from settlements. Moreover, the titles are perfect, which is not always true of lands held under the old Spanish grants. The railroad companies give five years' credit on their lands; the Government also deals very easily with purchasers, and a farmer may preempt eighty acres, and by specified improvements secure it from the Government for nothing, under the Homestead Act.

One immense advantage the farmer has who settles on such land as that in the San Joaquin Valley — his land is ready for the plough as soon as he has bought it. It has no shrubbery or under-brush; it does not need to be cleared; and as the next State Legislature is almost certain to enact a "no fence" law for the whole State — many counties have it already — he will not even need to fence.

Cattle can be more easily and profitably "soiled" in this climate than elsewhere. A quarter of an acre of beets, replanted as the beets are used, will keep two cows; and the beet grows in Southern California not only the whole year, but for two years if it is left in the ground. Corn and other fodder may be sown in every month; and a wise farmer can stall-feed stock of all kinds here more cheaply and easily than in any other State. Of alfalfa, the Chilian clover, a quarter of an acre will keep a cow in hay, by successive cuttings, for nine months in the year.

After a thorough examination of this region, I believe Southern California to be the finest part of the State, and the best region in the whole United States for farmers. I have visited within twelve months almost every part of the State; and while the climate is mild and the soil rich everywhere, the bright skies and the great variety of valuable products in the southern counties make that region, in my judgment, the most eligible. But I advise farmers from the East to be content with small farms of from eighty to at most two hundred acres. The rage for large possessions has been a curse to the farmers of this State. I have seen a wheat field of forty thousand acres in the San Joaquin Valley; fields of wheat of from one thousand to five thousand acres are not uncommon; nor is it rare for their owners to be ruined by losing a crop. I am certain that an industrious farmer who cultivates one hundred and sixty acres in the San Joaquin Valley, who plants orange and almond and olive orchards on twenty acres, who soils his stock, who keeps a good vegetable garden for his family, and attends to his crops with care and thoroughness, will be worth more money at the end of ten years, and have a more valuable place besides, than his neighbor who has ten times as much land and has raised wheat only. The small farmer will require less capital, he will run fewer risks of loss, his income will be greater on the average, his living will be more comfortable, and, in the end, his small farm will be worth more money than his neighbor's exhausted and carelessly kept large farm.

There are hundreds of farmers in California, men who would be thought wealthy in any farming community in the East, who own several thousand acres, and who do not raise even a potato for their families. Wheat, wheat, wheat, is their only crop, and for this every thing else is neglected. Their families live on canned fruits and vegetables; all their house supplies are bought in the nearest town, of the groceryman; in a good season they sell their wheat for a large sum, and either buy more land or spend the money in high living; and when a dry year comes they fall into debt, with interest at one per cent. a month; and when the next dry year comes it brings the sheriff.

What is the best and easiest way, you will perhaps ask, for an Eastern farmer to settle himself properly and safely in so far distant a State as California? The best and pleasantest way would be for four, six, or eight families to unite together, with the design to live on adjoining farms. Such a little association could send out one of their number as a pioneer to seek a suitable location. For four families a section of land would be sufficient. It would give each 160 acres of land. But if more is required, and if, for instance, it was desired to settle upon Government or railroad land in the Sacramento or San Joaquin Valley, it should be remembered that these are held in alternate sections (see diagram).

Now so complete is the railroad land-office in Sacramento, that a stranger, coming to the State upon such an errand as I have supposed, would do best to go first to that office, look over its maps and descriptions of railroad "sections," which can be purchased on five years' credit, with one-fifth paid down, and there, surveying the whole field at once, make up his mind what parts of it are best worth a more particular examination. A day or two in the Sacramento railroad land-office would give him more information about the disposable land in California than a more tedious and costly search among the three or four Government land-offices located at different points, and each concerned with only a part of the State.

Having thus generally determined upon the part of the State which he thinks it best to examine, he will find it easy to make choice of some particular section or sections among those on his minutes.

In making his selection, he should bear in mind these things, among others:

1. California is subject to droughts. Experience shows, so far, that there are about seven good years out of ten; that is to say, in ten years the farmer may, in almost any part of the State fit for agriculture, expect to get seven good field crops without irrigation. This is the general testimony of careful and experienced farmers to whom I put the question. There are bottoms, as in the Pajaro Valley, and there are tracts of land in the northern part of the State and elsewhere, which are never affected by drought. But of the great bulk of the arable land in California what I have said above is true.

2. Moreover, the farmer in Southern California, as in the San Joaquin Valley, who should plant the orange, lemon, almond, and other sub-tropical fruits, needs water to irrigate these.

3. Water is also needed, except in seasons when the rain-fall is above the average, to get two good crops from the same land in a year. With water this is easy and certain, and you may follow your crop of wheat or barley, sown in December and reaped in May, with a crop of corn planted in May or June on the same land.

4. For all these reasons, it is a very great advantage to have a water supply on your place, or at least within reach. "Be more careful to buy water than land," said an experienced and successful California farmer to me—a man who, beginning with but a small capital fifteen years ago, has now an income of fifteen thousand dollars a year from his farm and orchards. Water is not scarce in California; but there are tracts of land which have it not, and these it is best to avoid. It is astonishing how small a stream answers every purpose; and to an Eastern man few things are more surprising than the ease, skill, and cheapness with which a small stream is tapped by half a dozen Californian farmers according to a plan matured at a "ditch-meeting," led into a reservoir, and made available for irrigation.

5. If there is a proper irrigating canal or ditch available to the land you prefer, that is sufficient. You have only to ascertain the price of the water. The company which has now built forty miles of canal in the San Joaquin Valley, and whose extensive plans I spoke of above, charges one dollar and a quarter per acre per crop, which is a very light burden; far cheaper than manure on an Eastern farm.

6. On the eastern side of the San Joaquin Valley, in the San Bernardino Valley, and in other parts also, artesian wells are easily and cheaply made. A flowing well, wherever it can be got at moderate cost, answers admirably for irrigating purposes; and a well of seven-inch bore will water a considerable piece of land. Gardens and pleasure-grounds are commonly irrigated in this State by means of windmills, which pump water into small tanks. The windmill is universal in California; the constant breezes make it useful; and as there is no frost to break pipes, water is led from the tank into the house and stable, which is a very great convenience, at a small cost.

7. The level or plain land is probably the richest; it is certainly the most easily cultivated, and it comes first into use. But the foot-hills have a peculiar value of their own, which has been overlooked by the eager California farmers. The vine, and, I believe, most of the sub-tropical fruits, grow best in the foot-hills. The soil is somewhat lighter; it will probably not bear such heavy crops of grain; but a homestead on the hills has a fine look-out; water is probably more easily obtainable; the air is fresher than on the plains; and, for my own part, I have seen, in the more settled parts of the State, that the cheapest lands —the foot-hill lands, namely—were, on many accounts, preferable. Vine-growers begin to perceive that the best wine comes from these higher lands; and ten or fifteen years hence it is believed that the principal and most profitable vineyards in the State will be in the foot-hills.

8. California is a breezy State; the winds from the sea draw with considerable force through the cañons or gorges in the mountains, and sweep over the plains. This is no doubt one of the chief causes of its remarkable healthfulness; and it gives to the workman, in the summer, the great boon of cool nights. No matter how warm the day has been in any part of the State, the night is always cool, and a heavy blanket is needed for comfort. Now there are places where the wind is too severe, where a constant gale sweeps through some cañon, and is an injury to the farmer. Such places should be avoided, and are easily avoidable. In many parts of the State farms would be benefited by trees, planted as wind-breaks; and, fortunately, the willow or sycamore forms, in two years, in this climate, a sufficient shelter, besides furnishing fire-wood to the farmer.

9. Where one man has selected land for himself and several friends, he can easily and quickly prepare the way for them. Fences and houses can be built by contract in every part of the State. Men make it their business to do this; and at the nearest town the intending settler can always have all his necessary "improvements" done by contract, even to ploughing his land and putting in his first crop. In this respect labor is admirably organized in California. You will see, then, that your pioneer may make ready for those who are to come after, so as to save them much delay and inconvenience.

10. In some parts of the State Indians hire themselves out as farm laborers. They usually live on the place where they work, and they are a harmless and often a skillful laboring population, though somewhat slow. They understand the management of horses, are ploughmen, and know how to irrigate land. The Chinese also make useful farm laborers, and are every year more used for this purpose. They learn very quickly, are accurate, painstaking, and trustworthy, and especially as gardeners and for all hand-labor they are excellent. White laborers are—as in every thinly-settled country—unsteady, and hard to keep.

11. If you have a little ready money beyond what you need to make your

place and live on till your crop is harvested and sold, you can invest it very well in your neighborhood. In many parts of the State men lend money at two per cent. per month by the year, interest payable semi-annually or quarterly, and on good security. This seems monstrous to an Eastern man, but there are many industries which yield a profit large enough to bear this drain without suffering. Sheep, for instance, where they are well managed, return forty-eight per cent. per annum on the cost of the herd. Ten per cent. is the common rate of interest in the State, and large sums are constantly lent at twelve; while in the thinly settled and rapidly improving sections sums of one, two, or three thousand dollars are easily and securely lent at two per cent. a month. I think this not a slight advantage to a farmer who comes to California with a little ready money ahead.

12. Several land colonies are at this time formed, or forming, in California. They are all, I believe, in the hands of honorable men, and they offer some advantages to settlers. They put, however, too high a price on their lands; and where four or five, or even two or three, families known to each other come out here together, they can do better than join a colony. The success of the Anaheim Colony, of which I give the history in another chapter, shows that these experiments are meritorious. At Anaheim each colonist bought only twenty acres of land and a town lot; the ground was planted in vines for the most part; and though the people had for a while a severe struggle, they are now independent. "We are all worth from $5000 to $10,000 apiece," said one to me, "and we are happy and comfortable." This colony is now twelve years old.

13. To settlers of limited means it is an advantage to be near one of the lines of railroad now building, as the Southern Pacific or the San Joaquin road; for the companies give steady employment, at good wages, to all able-bodied men, and a stout man may easily earn a farm by a summer's work.

14. As the winter in the Northern States is said to be the best time to see the country if you mean to buy, so the summer and fall are the best seasons for a farmer to visit California if he thinks of settling there. After May there is no rain until November. This makes a long dry season, in which many of the smaller streams dry up, the pastures become brown and look bare, the roads are dusty, and whatever is disagreeable in climate or country comes out to the surface. Fortunately, during this period also, the harvest takes place and the fruits are ripening, so that not only the dust and dryness, but the fruitfulness and wealth of the land, are seen. Moreover, if you select your land in summer or fall, you are just in time to have your crop put in when the rains begin.

15. Thus it is possible and easy for one person coming out during the summer or fall to not only select land for a party of friends or neighbors, but to have their houses and stables built, their fences—if they need any—made, and their first crops put in, by contract, so that when the families come out in No-

vember or December all would be prepared for them, and they would have only to move in, and during the first winter to make vegetable gardens, put in beets and corn fodder for their cattle, and set out their orchards. In Southern California the roads are generally good all winter; the rains do not last long, and the bright sun quickly dries up the mud; and there is no "freeze and thaw" to break up the roads, as in our Northern States.

16. The California Immigrant Union, at San Francisco, gives information to all who write to it concerning farming and other industrial enterprises in the State. Its officers are careful and responsible men, who are salaried by the State, and have no private interests to further.

It is of course not necessary that several families should remove from the East together. The people of California are eminently friendly and hospitable to new-comers. They have, as a rule, a strong love for their old homes; and being themselves comparatively new-comers, they are helpful, and glad to have neighbors.

In subsequent chapters I give details concerning California life and industry, especially in the southern part of the State, which will, I believe, answer most of the questions which the preceding general sketch leaves untouched.

NORTH DOME, YOSEMITE VALLEY.

CHAPTER XI.

A JANUARY DAY IN LOS ANGELES.

AS I drove out from Los Angeles into the country on a January morning with a friend, we met a farmer coming into town with a market-wagon of produce.

It was a cloudless, warm, sunny day, and the plain where we met him was covered with sheep suckling their lambs, for in January it is already lambing-time here. The farmer's little girl sat on the seat with him, a chubby, blue-eyed little tot, with her sun-bonnet half hiding her curls, and a shawl, which her careful mother had wrapped about her shoulders, carelessly flung aside. To me, fresh from the snowy Plains and Sierras, and with the chill breath of winter still on me, this was a pleasing and novel sight; but the contents of the man's wagon were still more startling to my Northern eyes. He was carrying to market oranges, pumpkins, a lamb, corn, green peas in their pods, sugar-cane, lemons, and strawberries. What a mixture of Northern and Southern products! what an odd and wonderful January gathering in a farmer's wagon!

Around us the air was musical with the sweet sound of the baa-ing of young lambs. Surely there is no prettier or kindlier sight in the world than a great flock of peaceful, full-fed ewes, with their lambs, covering a plain of soft green, as far as the eye can reach. All the fence corners, where there were fences, were crowded with the castor-oil plant, which is here a perennial, twenty feet high—a weed whose brilliant crimson seed-pods shine like jewels in the sunlight. Below us, as we looked off a hill-top, lay the suburbs of Los Angeles, green with the deep green of orange-groves, and golden to the nearer view with their abundant fruit. Twenty-one different kinds of flowers were blooming in the open air in a friend's garden in the town this January day; among them the tuberose, the jessamine, and the fragrant stock or gillyflower, which has here a woody stalk, often four inches in diameter, and is of course a perennial. The heliotrope is trained over piazzas to the height of twenty feet, and though the apple and pear orchards, as well as those of the almond and English walnut, will continue bare for some time, and the vineyards, just getting pruned, look dreary, the vegetable gardens are green as with us in June, and men and boys are gathering the orange crop.

The Puebla de Los Angeles—the town of the angels—is not, in its present state, a very angelic place. It is irregularly built, the older part having but one principal street, at one end of which, however, stands a building which is, both for size and excellence of architecture, worthy of San Francisco or New York. If you walk down this street, you will be surprised at the excellence of the shops and the extent of some of the warehouses, and will see abundant signs of a real and well-founded prosperity, which will surprise you if you have listened to the opinion of San Franciscans about this metropolis of Southern California.

In fact Los Angeles has many of the signs of a prosperous business centre; it has excellent shops, and a number of well-built private residences; it sends its exports to the sea by a well-managed and prosperous railroad, and expects to be connected within a year with San Francisco by the Southern Pacific Railroad, by way of Bakersfield. It is chiefly noted for the production of wine and oranges; but in its neighborhood there is a large tract of fine corn land, El Monte, where large crops are raised every year. Los Angeles is the trade centre of a considerable region, which includes San Bernardino to the east, and reaches to the Inyo and Owen's River mines to the north-east.

The old Spanish town, nicknamed Sonora, lies at one end near the mission church, the somewhat discordant clangor of whose bells startles you out of your sleep early in the morning as they summon the faithful to prayers. Next to this come the business streets, and beyond these the American part of the town. Orange-groves surround the town almost, and vineyards are numerous.

The population consists of Americans, Spaniards, Chinese, and Indians. Los Angeles became, during and after the late war, a stronghold of Southern men; and it attracted a considerable number of a class known all over California as "Pikes." These are, in fact, the migratory Southern poor whites. They received their name here, I suppose, from a fancy that they came from Pike County, Missouri; but the term, which once denoted Missourians, has come to have a more general significance here, for you are told of Texas Pikes, etc. The better class of these people are settled, and often own valuable farms, and are thrifty and money-making. They are frequently rough in their speech; but I have found them kind and hospitable, making the traveler welcome to substantial fare, among which the "bacon and greens" will remind him, if he has been in Missouri, of that land of plenty, the home of the "Pikes."

The true "Pike," however, in the Californian sense of the word, is the wandering gypsy-like Southern poor white. This person often lives with his family in a wagon; he rarely follows any steady industry; he is frequently a squatter on other people's lands; "he owns a rifle, a lot of children and dogs, a wife, and, if he can read, a law-book," said a lawyer describing this character to me; "he moves from place to place, as the humor seizes him, and is generally an injury to his neighbors. He will not work regularly; but he has great tenacity of life, and is always ready for a lawsuit."

"I found a Pike the other day killing and salting hogs, and actually hauling the salt pork off to sell it," said a gentleman in whose company we were discussing these people.

"Certainly that was an industrious Pike," said I.

"Yes, but, confound it, they were *my* hogs," he replied, with natural wrath.

Near San Diego a Pike family were pointed out to me, who had removed from Texas to California, and back to Texas, four times. They were now going back home again to please "the old woman," who, it seems, had had a fit of home-sickness. They traveled in an old wagon drawn by a pair of broncho or native horses, and would probably be six or eight months on the road. Of course they lived off the country, and probably lived as well on their travels as when they were settled.

You are told endless droll stories about these Pikes. In one county in this State, which contains a large number of them, some San Franciscans who own property there desired to help the people make certain improvements. They called a meeting by public printed notice, to be held at the school-house, in a district containing about 2000 inhabitants. A few days after this notice was put up, one of its signers received a note from a lawyer telling him that a mistake had been made in the call, as the district had no school-house.

"Very well," said the amazed San Franciscan, "we will build them a school-house; it will improve our property." You must know that California is as well supplied with schools as a New England State.

But to this the leading Pikes objected when it was proposed, on the ground that the ringing of a school-house bell scares all the deer away.

"As soon as he hears a piano," said an old resident to me, "the Pike sells out and moves away."

Well, the Pike is the Chinaman's enemy. He does little work himself, and naturally he hates the patient industry of the Chinese. Of course, if you ask him, he tells you that he is "ruined by Chinese cheap labor." "You could no more get these fellows to work than you could get grasshoppers out of a vineyard," said a farmer to me; "but they sit in the saloons, and growl about the unfair competition of the Chinese. One Chinaman is worth a regiment of them."

But while the politicians of the baser sort cry out against the Chinese, sensible men, whether Democrats or Republicans, employ them; not because they work cheaper than white men, for they do not; they exact just as high wages as any body else; but they work steadily, and do not go off at five minutes' notice, or get drunk two or three times a week. "Drive the Chinese out of the State, as these vagabonds demand, and you would put California twenty years back in her prosperity," said an intelligent Democrat to me.

The respectable classes, though too often silent, are utterly opposed to the cry against the Chinese; and Governor Booth signalized his entrance upon office by appointing as district judge, to fill a vacancy in this Southern country, Judge Widney, an able lawyer, who had the courage to go out pistol in hand among the Los Angeles mob, and save the life of one Chinaman who had already a rope about his neck.

The architecture of this region will remind you that you are in a land where it is never very cold. The dwelling is a secondary matter here, and it results that many people are satisfied to live in very small and slight houses. Muslin and paper inside walls are common; a barn is like Jack Straw's house, neither wind-tight nor water-tight. In the Pico House, at Los Angeles, you must walk across an open, brick-paved court, containing a fountain and flowers, to get from your room to the dining-room; at San Bernardino, most of the rooms in the hotel have no entrance from within at all; you go on to an open corridor, and enter your chamber from that; and, as the stores and shops are mostly without chimneys, at San Bernardino I saw clerks and shop-keepers on a cool day warming their coat-tails by a fire built in the middle of the broad business street. I should say that what a farmer from the East would spend in bringing his family out here he would more than save in the cost of his farm buildings.

The price of land at first strikes the stranger as high. Near Los Angeles they ask from thirty to a hundred dollars per acre for unimproved farming land. I thought they were already discounting the railroad which is coming to them, and which will no doubt cause this part of the country to increase rapidly in population and wealth. Every body was "talking railroad." A corps of engineers of the Southern Pacific Company was near the town completing surveys for the road; and as I had seen in the East the rise in prices following the mere announcement of a new railroad, it was natural for me to think that prices here had been affected by the same cause. But I am satisfied that they are, on the whole, not too high.

"If I can make an acre of ground produce me, after seven or even six years, with a comparatively slight expenditure of money, five hundred dollars per annum for a long term of years, ought I to hesitate to pay one hundred dollars for it?" asked a farmer to whom I told my impressions.

"If I can get two crops a year from farming land which I buy already cleared, and can plough in December; if I can raise from ten to fifteen tons of alfalfa hay by successive cuttings in a year; if I can support two cows from a quarter of an acre of beets; if my peach-trees bear a peck to a tree in the second year from the pit; my apple-trees give a full crop in five years; my vines yield grapes the second year after I plant them; and if my kitchen garden is green and productive all the year round, and I need not provide shelter for stock or fire-wood for my house, why am I foolish to pay one hundred dollars per acre?" said another.

I reserve for another place some detailed and trustworthy statements regarding the profitableness of the culture of such fruits as the almond, the orange, olive, and English walnut, in Southern California. These are now deservedly attracting attention in this and other of the Southern counties of the State. In the mean time I may say that the rapidity and certainty with which trees grow in this region is amazing. This paragraph is written in January, in the open air, under the shade of an acacia-tree which is six inches in diameter at the base, and comes from a seed planted three years ago, and never watered.

The pepper-tree, an evergreen, and one of the most beautiful shade-trees, can be transplanted safely and easily when nine inches in diameter, and being closely trimmed will make a grateful shade the first season. Vines do actually bear at two years from the first cutting. Strawberries ripen abundantly in January. Mr. Rose, at the Mission San Gabriel, has a eucalyptus-tree (the Australian blue-gum), which in eight years from the cutting which he planted has made a sound and stately growth of seventy-five feet, with a trunk proportioned to its height. I accepted the invitation of a farmer to see a field of mangel-wurzels, half an acre, which he said were "as big round as a nail-keg, and mostly two feet and a half long," and I saw them. I should add that they had been eighteen months growing.

It is the universal testimony that corn yields from fifty to one hundred bushels an acre on moist land, and wheat—this county is not a wheat country —from thirty-five to fifty bushels. It is the habit of farmers to put in barley when the winter rains begin, cut that down for hay in April or May, and plant a crop of corn on the same field without manure, with a certainty, if the season is good, of forty or fifty bushels to the acre for this second crop.

Of course, when men ask fifty or a hundred dollars per acre for land, it is "with water." Land which has little water is sold for from one to three dollars per acre, in large quantities, for herding sheep or cattle. "If you buy in our county, be more particular about how much water than how much land you get," said a shrewd and successful farmer to me.

Grain crops are not yet irrigated here; but they might be with advantage, I am told. It is usual to plant corn only on low ground. Fruits and vegetables are all irrigated; and though at a distance this seemed to me a troublesome thing, now that I have seen it practiced, it appears to me, as it does to the farmers hereabout, a very great convenience and benefit. In the first place, the testimony is universal, and strongest from the most intelligent and oldest farmers, that if you irrigate land you need not manure it. The water, they say, restores to the soil in some way its fertility, and I have actually seen fields whereon grain was raised for a dozen years without any decrease from the yield after the second crop. They do not pretend to manure the olive and orange orchards or the vineyards.

Next, irrigation means a dry summer, which is one of the greatest possible conveniences to the farmer. From the first of May till November the skies are serene, and there is no rain. Crops are put in here in December and January. The barley is already sprouting in some fields. When grain ripens and is harvested, the farmer has no rain-storm to fear. He does not cut in haste, or at the wrong time, for fear of a storm; he need not hire an extraordinary force to get his crop into barns. In the Sacramento and San Joaquin valleys, as well as here, the grain is thrashed on the field, put into bags, and lies there in the open air until it is sold. Hay, in the same way, when it is cut in spring, is stacked in the field or barn-yard, and rests, without even a shed, until November. The harvest may last a month or six weeks.

Nor is irrigation difficult or troublesome. Lazy people have complained to me that it necessitates frequent ploughing; but when you consider that an orange orchard is irrigated once in five or six weeks, and ploughed only after every irrigation, and when I tell you that, according to the best accounts I have from experienced men, one ploughman can irrigate and plough from fifteen to twenty acres of such an orchard without haste or difficulty, you will not, I think, care for the lazy man's complaint.

The Congress land which remains unoccupied in this and the adjoining counties has been reserved from sale until the Southern Pacific Railroad line is determined, and that company, which works, I believe, with the help of a land grant, shall have located its alternate sections. There is, I am told, a great deal of good land in this part of the public domain—how much I am unable to tell. The soil in this county is mostly a rich, loose, sandy loam, with patches of adobe, which is a stiff black clay, and forms, with proper cultivation, the very richest grain land of California. It is on the adobe soil about Watsonville and Santa Cruz that the enormous crops of wheat have grown, some farms averaging for several years in succession from seventy to eighty bushels of wheat per acre.

MIRROR LAKE, YOSEMITE VALLEY.

CHAPTER XII.

FARMING IN SAN BERNARDINO.

SAN BERNARDINO, which is a point seldom visited by tourists, and but little known to the Eastern settler or farmer, lies sixty miles east from Los Angeles, under the mountain range from which it takes its name. It has a climate more charming and healthful in winter than Los Angeles, and no hotter in summer; but there have been cases here, in the low grounds, of a mild type of intermittent fever. This is not prevalent, however, and occurs, I was told by an intelligent physician of the place, chiefly among the class who drink the strong grape brandy of the region and live otherwise carelessly.

The San Bernardino Valley, which contains 36,000 acres, was bought many years ago by the Mormons. In 1861 Brigham Young recalled his disciples to Salt Lake, but a large number refused to go from here, and are still living here in peace. They call themselves Josephites, I believe, and are an industrious, quiet people. The valley they bought is abundantly watered, and appears to me one of the most fruitful parts of the Southern country. All the fruits and grains which are raised in Los Angeles grow here as well, some even better. I have not seen anywhere more thrifty orange and olive trees than at one or two farms near this town.

The valley has not only abundance of running water, constant the year round, but a large number of spouting artesian wells have been bored; they get flowing water of very good quality at from one hundred and fifty to three hundred feet, and it is usual to make a seven-inch bore, which gives water enough to irrigate a large space of ground.

The country between Los Angeles and San Bernardino varies greatly in quality. Some parts are very fine. About Ruebottom's, where stage passengers stop to dine, there is first-class farming land; ten miles beyond you reach the famous Cocamungo vineyard, which produces a great deal of what seems to me a poor and very spirituous wine, and also a good deal of brandy. Beyond that you cross for ten miles a tract which was once, I believe, fertile, but has been covered by a wash of boulders, stones, and gravel from the mountains. Then you enter the valley after which San Bernardino is named, which, with the adjoining foot-hills, contains a great tract of first-class farming and orchard land—perhaps as much as half a million of acres, most of it easily watered. A part of this is in private hands, some in considerable tracts; but a large part of it is Congress land, now reserved from entry until the Southern Pacific Railroad shall have located its alternate sections, but likely to be open to entry at the double minimum rate within the year 1872.

In the mean time I noticed that farmers are ploughing (early in February) large spaces of this Congress land, and sowing it with wheat and barley, intending to get a crop off before it is open to entry, and to buy the land of Government or of the railroad company by-and-by. Unimproved farming land near the town, with water easily accessible, is sold for from three to ten dollars per acre, in tracts of from fifty to one hundred and sixty acres. Improved farms are not readily bought, as there are but a few, and they are too valuable to sell. A company of Costa Ricans have recently bought 2600 acres near the town, and intend, I believe, to raise sugar-cane as well as sub-tropical fruits; and, as they have capital, they will, no doubt, succeed.

Fencing costs one dollar and fifty cents per rod, for a proper board fence; lumber, such as is used for houses and fencing, twenty-five dollars per thousand. Common farm-horses cost from twenty-five to fifty dollars, and cows thirty dollars. One of the oldest settlers in the place, a very intelligent practical farmer, told me that irrigation was not necessary for grain crops. They sow barley here on the first of January, and, after taking off a crop of from forty to sixty bushels to the acre, plant corn on the same land, and get their second crop fully ripened, and often as much as sixty or seventy bushels per acre. On new land, one hundred bushels of corn or seventy bushels of barley is not an uncommon crop; and I was shown a large field which for seven successive years has given a crop of barley and one of corn every year. Alfalfa is cut seven times in the year, and yields from ten to fifteen tons per acre; it is fed to milch cows and to plough horses, and hogs keep fat on it in this climate.

Where nature has done so much, you would perhaps expect to find that man had made a beautiful garden of this valley. You would be grievously disappointed. Cultivation is too often careless; men live for years on a place without planting the most valuable fruit-trees; and there is a lack of neatness in the farm surroundings, and an air of shabby thriftlessness about the houses, which disappoint an Eastern man. I supposed at first that the people were sluggish and thriftless because they lay out of the way of a market; but this is not true. San Bernardino has an important traffic with Arizona. I found a miller who has to buy wheat in San Francisco to keep his mill running; oats, which grow perfectly here, were brought from the upper country, for this place, in the same boat in which I came to San Pedro; barley brings two cents a pound here, and only one cent and a half in San Francisco; and I believe there is but one market garden near the town, though a man might make a small fortune in a year from vegetables and strawberries. "There is no market for a man who has nothing to sell," is an old adage.

Of course this unthrift is not universal. I found several well-kept farms near the town; and their owners were all doing well and making a good deal of money. In fact, wherever I found a farmer with produce to sell, he amazed me by telling me how readily he found a profitable market. Wine, from its bulky nature, is perhaps the most difficult article to sell in such a place as this; but a farmer who makes 2500 gallons a year assured me that he sold it all, on the ground, for fifty cents per gallon; and he had not even a barrel left over a year old.

As you drive over the uncultivated part of the plain you see occasionally the white floury efflorescence of alkali. Frequently a farm would extend into the midst of this alkali land; and I was assured by the farmers that with proper handling it became, after the first crop, their best land. They plough in barley-straw, which rots quickly, and, they say, so ameliorates the soil, or decomposes the alkali, that the following winter they may put in barley, wheat, or corn.

Of course, where irrigation is practiced, the farmer is tolerably independent of droughts; but much of the farm land in this valley is not irrigated; and farmers told me that on such land they counted upon seven good seasons in ten years. The grasshopper, which did some damage last year in all this Southern country, comes, it is said, after a dry season. Some farmers thought that grasshoppers could not breed on ploughed land; I do not know how this may be, and they spoke from but a limited experience; but it seems probable, from what I was told, that the scourge is lessened when the soil is frequently and thoroughly cultivated.

The neighborhood of San Bernardino appears to me an admirable country for thrifty farmers. Land is cheaper than near Los Angeles; water is abundant; there is still much valuable Congress and railroad land; there is a good market for all products; the soil is almost universally excellent, and I do not doubt that a thrifty New England or New York farmer would here raise a large family in comfort and independence on forty or at most eighty acres of land; and if he planted ten or twelve acres in oranges and walnuts, would, in ten years, have a handsome income with trifling labor for the rest of his life. By the time the valley is settled, the Southern Pacific Railroad, whose engineers are already working this way, will run through or near it, and the Arizona trade, which it already possesses, it will not lose.

It struck me here, as elsewhere in this lower country, that the foot-hills contain the best lands for thrifty farmers. The soil is usually loose, though probably of less lasting fertility; water comes from the mountains; the views are enchanting; and the orange will certainly do better there than on the plain. The old Mission of San Bernardino, now a shapeless ruin, lies high up among the foot-hills; and 2000 feet above San Bernardino, in the San Gorgonio Pass, lies Dr. Edgar's vineyard, which produces the best light wine I have tasted in California—proving once more, what is now generally suspected by the thoughtful vine-growers of this State, that the hill and mountain sides will produce the best wine here.

Farmers in this country make two mistakes not uncommon to American farmers, but less excusable here than elsewhere. They try to own too much land, and they are content with shabby houses. Eighty acres will make an industrious farmer rich in this climate; his living ought to cost him very little money after the first year, for he may have fresh vegetables out of his garden every month in the year; of potatoes, one hundred bushels to the acre is but a moderate crop; the tomato-vine bears for two or three years in succession; every fruit-tree of the temperate zone bears here far more quickly than with us in the East; and when the pepper-tree and the acacia and eucalyptus grow from ten to twenty feet in a single season, there is no excuse for a lack of shade about the house.

As to the house itself, the family lives so much out-of-doors, and the weather is so fine all the year round, that a dwelling appears, no doubt, a secondary consideration. But it is abominable to see well-to-do farmers living, as they do hereabout, in shabby little shanties, and to find the rarest and loveliest flowers adorning what looks to an Eastern man more like a pig-pen than like a house. No doubt many of the people of whom I complain came hither poor, and have become accustomed to live as they continue to do; but half a dozen thrifty, neat, New England families would make such a change in the appearance of San Bernardino as would amaze the old settlers—unless, indeed, they too fell into the ways of their predecessors.

Fences and houses are best built by contract. Ploughing can also be done by contract. The common farm laborers are Indians. They are docile, know how to handle horses, and are used for every kind of labor. They receive from fifty cents to one dollar and twenty-five cents per day, and are a useful people; their only faults being a propensity to get drunk on Saturday night—not ir-regulary during the week, however—and to wander from place to place. There are but few Chinese at San Bernardino.

San Bernardino has a Methodist, Presbyterian, and a Mormon, as well as a Catholic Church. It has also, what you would hardly find in a town of its size and character outside of California, a large, well-built, and well-kept school-house. The school-houses in this State are a constant surprise to an Eastern traveler. You find them everywhere; and if you are interested in education, you will easily discover that the people take great interest and pride in their public schools. The school building at San Bernardino would be creditable to an Eastern town of 10,000 inhabitants.

Artesian wells are made here by the simple pressure of a lever upon a wrought-iron tube. The double sheet-iron tube, seven inches in diameter, costs one dollar per foot here; and for boring, in which a sand pump is used to bring up the contents of the pipe, the charge is one dollar per foot for the first hun-dred feet, and fifty cents per foot additional for every hundred feet lower. The water usually flows with force enough to carry it through a two-story house, and in such abundance that it is used for irrigation.

Near San Bernardino lies the land of the Riverside Colony. The Company owns 8000 acres; it has brought water down in a flume, at considerable cost, enough to irrigate not only this tract, but 15,000 acres more of a plain lying somewhat lower down. The land has been but lately open to settlement; and as it is a large, open, treeless plain, with but a few small houses scattered over it, it does not look very inviting. The company offer land for from twenty to forty dollars per acre; and the charge for water would, the agent told me, be about two dollars per annum per acre. The land is good, though I think a little less kindly than that of the valley and foot-hills of San Bernardino. I have no doubt that it is good wheat and fruit land, and it offers some advan-tages to persons who desire to settle in a colony. There is already a school-house, a post-office, and, of course, an abundant supply of water. But the price asked for land is high for this region, and the company propose no restric-tions about liquor-selling, nor conditions for the planting of shade-trees, or the style of improvements—nor, indeed, do they stipulate that a purchaser shall improve at all.

I was not surprised to be told that several of the settlers had bought ten or twenty acres of the company lands, but were raising a crop from two or three hundred acres of the adjoining government and railroad land. The agent as-sured me that ten acres would support a family, and that more than twenty acres were not necessary to a farmer. But he is mistaken; no man should come out to this part of the country to make his living from the land and get less than forty, or, better yet, eighty acres. It is true that when his orange, or olive, or walnut, or almond orchard comes into bearing, he will have a handsome income from ten acres; but for this he must wait at least eight or ten years, and he must live in the mean time.

There is no doubt that Riverside has, in common with the surrounding country, uncommon advantages for consumptives and persons subject to bronchial troubles. The air is dry and bracing, and the temperature uniform and equal. One may live out-of-doors almost every day of the year in this Southern California, and I have seen, on my journey, dozens of people deeply gone in consumption when they came here, who had been restored to health by residence in some one of the southern counties, or in sheltered spots like San Rafael, north even of San Francisco.

It will, perhaps, occur to you, as it did to me, to ask what people do on such a great plain for fire-wood. They plant live fences of willow or cotton-wood, which grow so rapidly that after two years a man may cut from his cottonwood fence not only fire-wood, but poles to support the overladen fruit-trees. This is the common custom about San Bernardino, where several thousand acres have been newly inclosed this winter—how droll it seems to call it winter, while I am writing in an open porch, and in the shade! You may see everywhere long rows of gaunt poles, from three to six inches in diameter, stuck into the ground, which will presently take root, throw out leaves, and become substantial trees; and these are at once fence and fire-wood.

THE THREE BROTHERS, YOSEMITE VALLEY.

CHAPTER XIII.

AN OLD CALIFORNIAN RANCHO.

ON my way from San Bernardino, I stopped overnight at a large Mexican rancho, the Laguna. *Laguna* means lake; the house stands, in fact, at one end of a large fresh-water lake, with mountains towering up on all sides. The sheet is about four miles long and three wide; it has a border of perhaps half a mile of arable land on the side which I passed over.

We got to Señor M.'s house an hour before sunset, and received at once a grave permission to unsaddle our horses and remain overnight. An Indian came up to take away the horses, which were turned into a pasture lot to shift for themselves; receiving a little barley in the evening and next morning. As for myself, I looked around with some curiosity, for this was the first time I had had an opportunity to see how the old Californians of wealth live.

Señor M. is reputed to possess 40,000 acres of land. He told me that he had sold last fall 1800 young colts at six dollars per head. He owns several thousand sheep; as to cattle, he could not tell till after the *rodeo* how many there were. The *rodeo* is the annual gathering of cattle, when the owners in a large district drive all the stock into one great plain, and each with his vacqueros, picks out his own cows, withdraws them into a separate herd, brands the calves which innocently follow their mothers, and then turns the whole mass adrift again, or in some cases drives them home to his own land.

Señor M. is therefore a person of substance; he is a man above middle height, a little corpulent, forty-five years of age, a little grizzled, and grave with all the gravity of the Spaniard. He politely invited us into the house; but seeing my inclination to remain out-of-doors, where a magnificent sunset was making rosy the western mountain tops, he gravely and silently brought out chairs for us. As for himself, he leaned up against the house, and looked at my curiosity with mild contempt.

I offered him a rather good cigar, whereupon he became a little communicative. He had worked hard, he said, but he was now getting old, and took it easy.

"Could he find a grizzly bear for me in the mountains?"

"Well, yes, he could; but he was not fond of grizzly bears; one had come down among a flock of his sheep, a mile off, the night before, but the herder had driven it off; it was a bad beast; he used to hunt them when he was younger; but now"—and he shrugged his shoulders.

"Yes, he had Indians"—seeing me look at several who were skylarking about the place, catching each other with lassos—"they are useful people; not good for much;" he added, "but quiet;" he paid them fifteen dollars a month; and they bought what they needed at his store.

You must understand that in California parlance a man "has" Indians, but he "is in" sheep, or cattle, or horses.

I remarked that the Laguna was a lovely piece of water.

"Yes," he said, "it will do," with another shrug. He had had a boat, but nobody took care of it, and it rotted away. A flock of wild ducks took advantage of this circumstance to sail about under our noses, at such a prudent distance from the shore as made it mere murder for me to shoot them, for I should have had to swim out to get what I had shot.

I looked into his garden, where he had half an acre of young grape-vines, two or three dozen young apple and orange trees, and a small orchard of young English walnuts, set out much too close together. I undertook to admire this moderate collection in horticulture, whereupon at last the grave Spaniard relented a little.

"Yes," he said, with a mild shrug, "it is very well; the garden is growing; it is not much; but I am *muy contente*"—well satisfied. "What do I want more?" he asked, with a kind of grave scorn; "I am well; I have enough; I owe nobody money; if any body comes to buy of me he must bring me the money in his hand;" here Don M.'s countenance looked a little implacable. "I am not afraid to die," he added; "only I don't want to be sick. *Muy contente*," he repeated, in his gentle and careless voice, several times, to impress it upon my ears, which are unaccustomed to Spanish.

Presently, a fire being made upon the hearth in the sitting-room, and night falling upon us in that noiseless way with which the dark comes on in this country, where no chirruping or humming insects are heard, we walked in and sat down.

And now you shall hear how this contented man of great wealth lived. The house was of adobe, which, as you know, is a sun-dried brick. It was an oblong, and contained three rooms. The front room was the store or shop, where he dealt out calicoes, sugar, coffee, and other dry goods and groceries, besides grape-brandy, to his Indians and any others who chose to come. The next room, which had no windows, contained two beds, in which his three young boys slept. It contained, also, the materials for the family sewing and a closet. The third room, which held Señor M.'s bed and a fire-place, was also our dining-room; and here, presently, a coarse but clean cloth was spread, and three women and a little girl began to lay the table and serve the supper.

At one side of the house a small room had been built on for a kitchen; opposite to that was a capacious store-room, in which hung " carne seco," jerked beef, from the rafters—bloody sheets of meat which looked unfit to eat, but which make a savory stew; while on the floor two or three young lambs were confined, which by-and-by succeeded in getting out, and came bleating into the dining-room—a quite startling spectacle to us, but evidently indulged playthings.

Beyond the house itself, about fifteen feet distant, was a clay oven for baking bread, covered over with raw bull's hide, the hairy side downward, intended to keep the top dry in case it should rain; and beyond this, a few feet farther off, marking the boundary of what Western people call their " yard," was a range of open shanties, which, on riding up, I had innocently taken for cattle sheds. Here, close to the house, the Indians lived.

Later in the evening, hearing singing and the droning *tum-ti tum-ti* of a stringed instrument, I walked out, and saw how they live. Half a dozen men were sitting around a wood fire, which had been made in the centre of the open shed. They sat on wooden blocks or lounged on the earthen floor; they talked in Indian or in Spanish, as it happened, and at intervals one broke in with a snatch of song, which was taken up by the rest, and swept, not unmusically, through the air, slowly rising and falling away, until there remained only the *tum-ti tum-ti* of the musician, whose instrument was composed of a corn-stalk about thirty inches long, stretching a single string made of lambs' entrails.

"They are poor creatures," said Señor M., with a shrug of his shoulders; "poor creatures, but quiet; not good for much, but useful."

"But where do they sleep?" I asked.

He pointed to a door, which opened into a lightly inclosed shed, which I had imagined to be the chicken-house. In the farther end, truly, the chickens were at roost, but the larger part was floored with poles, on which barley-straw was spread, and here the Indians slept—if they slept—of which, later, I had occasion to entertain some doubts.

Outside of the yard near the house was the wood-heap; near it lay a beef's head, skinned and gory; everywhere except immediately about the house was what we should call careless disorder and litter.

When supper was served, two benches were drawn up to the table, and we three men sat down and helped ourselves to the stew of meat and onions, to excellent bread—but no butter—to a dish of black and red beans, to some fried potatoes, and to coffee or tea as we preferred. Presently came in two boys of thirteen and eleven, and to them was added, in a few minutes more, their mother, stout and healthy-looking, as is the habit of the Californian Spanish women. She took one end of the table and drew a chair to her side for a lad of eight years, her youngest, who ate out of her plate, drank coffee out of her cup, and was indulged with sundry hugs and kisses during the meal. Later dropped in a young woman—a poor relation, probably—and a little girl who held the same situation. After the manner of poor relations, they spoke in whispers, sat uneasily on their chairs, and finished their meal sooner than the rest of us.

I presently discovered that two of the lads could speak a little English; and after supper they got out their reading-books and slates, and astonished and pleased me by their precision in reading and the readiness of their ciphering. They had, I found, a teacher or tutor, a young Spaniard, to whom our host paid seventeen dollars a month—"and of course a horse and whatever he needs here," he added. This young man had been educated in one of the public schools in this part of the country; and he told me that the youngsters, his pupils, were very quick with their lessons. What is odd, is that while they could read in English with perfect readiness and correctness, they did not understand more than half the words which they pronounced, and could give me but a broken account of their lesson. A very intelligent young teacher, whose school near San Bernardino I visited, told me that it was too often the custom in the public schools to teach the Spanish children to spell and read merely by rote, and that they are so quick at learning as to satisfy an indolent or careless teacher, without understanding much English.

I find that the Spaniards very generally in this Southern country send their children to the public schools; and they have everywhere the reputation of being very quick to learn. In several schools which I have visited, American and Mexican children attend together, but, for the most part, while the American children acquire Spanish, the others retain only their own tongue. In many cases it is necessary to carry on the school in Spanish; the teacher very commonly, in these Southern counties, understands both languages; and it is not unusual for the children to talk at play in Spanish during the recess, and returning to the school-room to sing together, and with surprising readiness, "My Country, 'tis of Thee," or some other American song.

To return to our supper: my host lit his cigar before he left the table; and, indeed, he did not wait until I had done with my own supper; and we smoked while the table was cleared away. The principal vacquero, a Sonoranian, as they here call the natives of the Mexican province of Sonora—they call a person from Texas a Texanian—came later for his supper; and meanwhile we talked about the schooling of the boys, who were very ingenuous and kindly though evidently much-indulged youngsters.

"Yes," their father said, "they shall be taught; they learn well; I have enough for them; they shall not work with their hands, as I did; they shall labor with their heads. When they are larger I shall send them to a school; and when they are young men I mean to put them into a Jew store, where they will quickly learn how to trade. I mean to make men of them," he said, with pride.

You will laugh at his way of making men of them; but, after all, he had reason for it. Twenty years ago the countrymen of this man owned the whole of California; the land, the cattle, the horses, and sheep were theirs. To-day the majority of them are poor; in fact, very few retain even a part of their old possessions. They were not business men; they liked to live free of care; and they found it easy to borrow money, or to obtain any thing else on credit. They know nothing of interest; even Señor M. to-day probably buries his coin or hides it away in some secure place. As for the most of his fellow-land-owners in the old time, they squandered their money; they borrowed at two, three, and five per cent. a month; they were ready to have their notes renewed when they fell due, and to borrow more on top of them; and it is said of them that it was perfectly safe to lend them money, for they would pay, if to pay ruined them.

Of course it did ruin them. One great land-holder in Los Angeles County, when his settling day came, was confronted, among a multitude of other accounts, with a baker s bill (with interest) for $18,000. He paid all, but his children are poor people to-day.

On the other hand, the country merchants with whom they chiefly deal are Jews. They abound all over California, and are justly respected as a highly honorable, fair-dealing, and public-spirited class; and their thrift and prosperity strikes men like Señor M. as something very admirable and enviable.

The style of living I have described, poor and simple as it looks to us, is that usual among the old Spanish or Californian population. Their food is chiefly beef, "carné seco" or dried beef, beans, tortillas, which are wheaten or corn cakes, in shape like Scotch scones, and coffee. Señor M. being a careful man, had a cow—I mean a milch cow. His house had a wooden floor; but in Santa Barbara the last Mexican lieutenant-governor lived in an adobe house with an earthen floor, and he was a man of wealth and intelligence. Earthen floors were almost universal in the old times, and are still quite common.

Curious tales are told of the improvidence of the old Californians in their last days. When the Americans from the East rushed into the country on the discovery of gold, cattle suddenly became valuable for their meat; before then only their hides were sold; and I have myself, in 1847, in Monterey, seen a fat steer sold for three dollars to the ship's butcher, who later sold the hide for a dollar, thus receiving the whole carcass for only two dollars. The Yankee demand for beef made the cattle owners suddenly rich, and they made haste to spend what they so easily got. Saddles trimmed with solid silver, spurs of gold, bridles with silver chains, were among the fancies of the men; and a lady in Santa Barbara amused me by describing the old adobe houses, with earthen floors covered with costly rugs; four-post bedsteads with the costliest lace curtains, and these looped up with lace again; and the señora and señoritas dragging trains of massive silk and satin over the earthen floors. It must have been an odd mixture of squalor and splendor.

An adobe house, no matter what is the wealth or condition of the Californian who lives in it, is simply a long range of rooms. It is one story high, has a piazza roof in front, an earthen floor, usually no ceiling, a tile roof, and each room, or all but one in houses where there are grown and unmarried daughters, has a door opening on the verandah.

One room, at the end of the long row, has no outward door, and only a narrow window. In this room it was customary for respectable people in a town like Los Angeles to lock up their unmarried but marriageable daughters about sunset, to preserve them from the temptation of young men—a custom which, curiously enough, did not prevent weddings.

To return to the Laguna: outside of the palings which inclosed the house, the Indian quarters, the little orchard, and a pasture-field, roamed cattle and horses at their own sweet will. At night twenty or thirty horses were driven into a large corral, from which the vacqueros chose their riding-beasts the next morning. We smoked and talked until nearly nine o'clock, by which time this excellent family gaped so fearfully that I proposed to retire, and was immediately shown into the store, where a mattress was spread for each of us on the floor, our own blankets and overcoats serving us for covers. Ventilation, I found, the roof afforded; and it was nearly twelve before the Indians, our neighbors, ceased their chattering and singing. They began again at four; and by five—before daylight—I arose and found these uneasy spirits sitting around the fire talking.

We breakfasted a little before seven, and then went out on the great common to see two vacqueros lasso a wild bull. They very neatly separated the animal from the herd, drove it at full tilt toward us, and, when it threatened to run us down, whizz went the riata, and, though I looked with all my eyes, I saw nothing except that the animal stopped in mid-career, and tumbled over as though it was shot. Thereupon the vacquero coolly got off his horse, first winding the end of the riata about the pommel of his saddle, and then I saw the most curious part of the whole business. The horse, a mere pony, stood with his fore legs planted firmly, and a very knowing look in his eyes. Presently the bull began to struggle; he managed by a sudden motion to raise himself half erect; but the horse quietly took a step backward, tightened the rope, and down went the bull, helpless. This was repeated several times, till I did not know which most to admire, the horse, or the man who had so thoroughly taught it.

PIUTE SQUAW AND PAPOOSE.

CHAPTER XIV.

THE INDIANS AS LABORERS.

ABOUT San Bernardino the farm laborers are chiefly Indians. These people, of whom California has still several thousand, are a very useful class. They trim the vines; they plough; they do the household "chores;" they are shepherds, and trusty ones too, vacqueros, and helpers generally. Mostly, they live among the whites, and are their humble and, I judge, tolerably efficient ministers. Near San Bernardino, at any rate, I found that it was thought a great advantage for a man to "have" Indians.

At Temecula, twelve miles from the Laguna, we came upon an Indian settlement. You know already that these California Indians were, in the old times, gathered by pious priests into missions, where they were taught various useful industries and the habit of labor. The old missions of California, now mere shells and ruins, show yet abundant evidence, in aqueducts, buildings, mills, reservoirs, and orange and olive orchards, of the skill and perseverance which the Dominican friars brought to their task of civilizing the savages. "Those old fellows knew better how to manage the Indians than we do," said a rough man, who had walked with me through one of the old missions. They did a good work, for they found the Indians savages, and left them at least thoroughly tamed. The Indian of these southern counties is not a very respectable being, but he is of some use in the world; he works. It is true that he loves strong grape-brandy; that he gets drunk; that he lives poorly; that he does not acquire money; and has even fewer notions of what we call comfort than his Spanish, half Spanish, Pike, and American neighbors. But he does not assassinate like the brutal Apache, and he has wants enough to make him labor for money. "I do not think my Indians would stay with me if they could not get drunk every Saturday night," said one who had just praised them as tolerably steady, and very useful and indispensable laborers.

I have already described how the Indians on an old California rancho live. In Temecula they are to a large extent the employers of their own labor. They hold small farms, plant corn and wheat, and own some sheep and cattle. Horses they have as a matter of course, and on Sunday morning they rode up to the store, and about it they were riding all day, taking a frequent "drink" of *aguardiente*, discussing various matters, and doing a little shopping in company with their wives, who dropped in neatly dressed, and usually with their faces muffled in a shawl in that curious and not ungraceful Spanish way which leaves the eyes and nose only exposed, and needs a quick eye to tell whether you are looking at a young or an old face. In spite of the frequent "drinks," they were not noisy; and only a few became tipsy later in the afternoon.

Seeing so large an assemblage, I asked the store-keeper if they had no church. No, they had no church; they had a grave-yard, walled in with adobe, on the outskirts of the little village, and full of graves, each with a cross over it. They had a *padre pro tempore*, an Indian authorized to act in certain emergencies, as baptism, if no proper priest were at hand; but when the Indian padre was pointed out to me I found him to be the tipsiest man on the ground, and a little disposed to hector his parish, who paid not the slightest attention to him.

The houses in which they live are mostly constructed of reeds and barley-straw, laced with long poles. You will see, if you enter, a single dark room, without windows or chimney; the fire planted at one end, and smoke escaping by the door; the stone on which grain is ground for tortillas, near the door; the beds on the floor occupying half the space within; the women and children, and on Sunday the men, sitting around the fire waiting for the mess which is boiling in the pot, and which seemed to me to be generally mush, with no trace of meat; and without the door a few pots, pans, chickens, ducks, and dogs.

This house is planted seemingly by chance, anywhere, without relations to any thing except usually another house just like it. It has a flap door, made of an old apron or dress; but under the same roof you will generally find another room, with a door, which is fastened. At first I thought this an apartment to let, but it is a store-house, and seems to be a sort of genteel sham, for every one into which I got a peep was empty, or very nearly so. It had prob-ably the same relation to the dignity and good standing of a family that a her-metically sealed parlor has to a respectable countryman's house in New En-gland.

If you can tell the difference between mere squalor and filth, you would see that these Indian houses and their inhabitants are not dirty. I think it likely that they learned cleanliness from the old Spanish Californians, who, it should be known, are an eminently cleanly people. At one of these houses, at a little distance from Temecula, I begged some hot water to prepare myself a little lunch, and while this was getting ready took an inventory of the interior. It contained three children; a very old blind man, who bent over the fire and mut-tered to himself; three women; a girl who was rubbing wheat on the tortilla stone; a man sleeping on the beds, with his head covered and his feet sticking out near the fire; a baby tied into a wooden frame, in which the little ones are held, carried, and rocked; a fire, a few baskets—which are beautifully made by these people, and are water-tight; two saddles, an ox-yoke, a table, a sieve, two earthen oyas in which water is kept cool in this country; a stone mortar and pestle, a gridiron, a coffee-pot, an axe, a sun-bonnet, a pair of laced shoes care-fully hung up and evidently not often used, and a small picture of some saint. Outside stood two very respectable-looking wooden wash-tubs, several pots— and for the rest, dogs.

Now here was an outfit, in fact, superior to that which I noted in several Pike shanties on the way. Here were preparations for living simply, but, after all, not uncleanly. Beyond this the Indian does not get. As you ride through the country, you can tell at a distance the character of the inhabitants of a house you are approaching. If the house is of reeds and straw, the owner is an Indian; if it is of adobe, it is a Spaniard who lives there; if it is of frame, be sure it is an "American," as we of the old States proudly call ourselves. Often the wooden house is a mere box, smaller and less comfortable than the Indian's straw hut, but it is of wood.

The Indian, in this part of the State, is harmless. Being white, and of the superior race therefore, you have the privilege of entering any Indian's house, and you will be kindly received, and if you want water out of his oya, or wish to cook your own dinner at his fire, you are welcome. You will prefer to camp out beside your own fire, in the open, rather than take lodgings in his house.

The land cultivated by the Indians about Temecula is of good quality, and in some parts is well watered. They get from twenty-five to thirty bushels of wheat and forty to forty-five bushels of corn to the acre, which are small crops in this rich State. Oranges, almonds, and other semi-tropical fruits are grown here in small numbers, but sufficient to show that the climate and soil are adapted to them. Horses cost from ten to fifty dollars per head, the last being a common price for what is called an "American" horse, or half-blood. For an Indian pony, well broken, you pay twenty-five to thirty dollars, and they are very serviceable beasts. The land not inclosed is used in common for grazing, and every body keeps some stock.

During the evening I went to a dance, or fandango. These Indians count it an evidence of their civilization to dance only Spanish and other common dances. The women were plainly and becomingly dressed; the men in their every-day clothing. The floor was of clay, a fiddle furnished the music, and a floor manager ordered the dances, while the spectators sat around along the walls. Altogether it was an extremely decorous and common-place affair, every body conducting himself with the gravity of a Spaniard; and the only novel incident was that during the dance men went about selling egg-shells, decorated with colored paper. When a young man bought one of these empty eggs, he rose, and, watching his chance, dexterously broke it over the head of some girl he admired. Then I saw that it had been filled with very finely-cut small pieces of colored and gilt paper, which fell all over the girl's head, and shone like spangles. When the dance closed the girl returned the compliment with another *cascarone*, as these things are called. The store-keeper at Temecula told me that the Indians around him were not thrifty, but well-meaning, easily influenced, and in their way industrious. They have credit with him within the limits of their property, and he seemed to be certain that if a man had property he would pay his debts—another good quality which these people have caught from their Spanish instructors.

These Temecula Indians are, I am told, descendants of those who formerly lived around the missions of San Luis Rey and San Diego. A thoughtful man can not visit these and other old missions in this part of the State without feeling a deep respect for the good men who erected these now ruined churches, gathered around them communities of savages, and patiently taught them not only to worship in a Christian church, but also the habit of labor, the arts of agriculture, and some useful trades. They used the labor of the Indians to bring water in solidly-built aqueducts, often for a distance of miles, and to store it in tanks built of stone and cement, which still stand empty, and some with trees growing out of their depths. They introduced in this State the olive, the orange, the date palm, the almond, as well as the cereals; and the olive orchards at the San Diego Mission, the earliest planted in the State, still bear heavy crops, and are a source of profit.

Moreover, when you have seen two or three of these old missions, it will dawn upon you that the good old padres had an excellent eye for country. What they sought, apparently, was a fine view, shelter from rude winds, good soil, and the vicinity of water; and so well did they secure their objects that a mission site is without exception, so far as I know, the very best spot for residence and for agriculture in its district. At Santa Barbara, for instance, the white mission buildings can be seen for a dozen miles in almost every direction; they are completely sheltered from rough winds; and the adjoining mission lands are notoriously among the most fertile in the region. About San Diego the country, which gets but little rain, has an arid look, until you drive into the Mission Valley; but even in this dry year the view from the old mission church, now a sad ruin, is lovely. You have a broad expanse of green before you, with the beautiful grayish green of the old olive-orchard for a foreground, and stately palms rearing their heads above the olive-trees.

The history of the missions of California has been compiled by a well-known Roman Catholic writer; but his work gives too little information concerning the character and objects of the old Dominican friars, to whose patience and perseverance in a noble work Southern California is to-day indebted for a valuable laboring force. Their views were, no doubt, limited and narrow; they had not enough faith in the Indian character to try to found, with their help, an empire, or a self-subsisting community; it was a race pre-ordained to subjection, which they aimed to make useful to the ruling race, and no doubt, as they piously thought, fit for heaven. Perhaps they discussed for many, many weary hours their work, their aims and objects, in those pleasant shady walks bounded by olive-trees on one side and pomegranates on the other, traces of which you may still discover in some of the old mission grounds. What a pleasant, sunny nook of the world they occupied! What wonder that they forgot, in this land of plenty and ease, of eternal summer, of the orange, the almond, and olive, to inculcate upon their dusky disciples that love of wealth and ownership which might have secured them a future in the land. No doubt they made happy communities; but the children of the missions never grew under their hands to the stature of men of our century.

THE BRIDAL VEIL FALL, YOSEMITE VALLEY.

CHAPTER XV.

THE COAST COUNTIES IN FEBRUARY.

CALIFORNIA has certainly the finest climate in the world. At Santa Barbara I left my horse, on the twentieth of February, and rode in the stage through parts of Santa Barbara, San Luis Obispo, and Monterey counties, over the mountains and through the long and magnificent valley of the Salinas.

The route is so arranged that you travel all day and almost all night for the whole journey, which lasts nearly sixty hours. I slept three hours at the little town of San Luis Obispo, and three more at the crossing of the Salinas. I need not say that the perpetual rumble and tilting of the stage ceased to be amusing before we got through, and that I hailed the sight of the railroad at Hollister with a great joy.

Nevertheless the whole drive is through so fine a country, and under such brilliant skies, that the pleasure is greater than the inconvenience. The country, at this season, is clothed in the loveliest green which I have ever seen, I do not remember ever to have read of the peculiar tint which the *alfilleria*, the native grass of this region, gives to the pastures. It is a light green, with a tinge of yellow, soft to the eye, rich beyond any thing I have ever seen in pastures at home, and reflecting, with a peculiar loveliness, the light of the sun.

In many parts the *alfilleria* is quite high; but it gives everywhere a smooth-shaven, lawn-like appearance to the vast fields in which it grows, which is helped, no doubt, by the freedom of these pastures from weeds.

How it comes about I do not know, but the grazing lands of California are almost universally free from weeds. The wild mustard is often found, and grows in some places as high as a man's head; and just now the valleys are full of flowers growing in masses, and of brilliant tints of crimson or blue, or —on the mountain slopes—yellow. You may imagine the effect—I can not describe it to you — of great blotches of crimson, or the deepest and most brilliant blue, acres in extent, upon the immense carpet of green over which your stage carries you.

Each color is massed by itself as the most skillful gardener would do it; and you pass now a broad patch of red, and again one of blue or yellow or orange, for the *eschscholtzia* is just beginning to flower; and when you happen to face the mountain, you see the sides covered with yellow bloom. Over a large part of our journey—until we reached the great Salinas plain, which is a real prairie—the ground was rolling and diversified; the plain was broken by gently undulating hills, and little valleys green and fair broke on either side into the mountains.

Now all this landscape was beautified by interminable groves of live and white oaks, growing as these do in California, low-branching, gnarled, huge, and as artistically disposed in groups and single trees as though the most skillful landscape gardener had planted them, and finer, so far as individual trees are concerned, than any oaks you can find outside of an old English park.

No doubt the freedom from weeds and under-brush adds much to the beauty of this park-like scene, but many individual trees are indescribably grand; and the way in which they are massed, and in which single trees stand out from the groups, and vistas are open between them, is something quite wonderful, and a sufficient defense of the natural school of landscape gardening, if that needed any defense.

Through this long, lovely, magnificent park I rode in company with one of a class of people not very numerous in California at this day—a pioneer. I am not sure but he gave himself some different title, for he was not a "forty-niner," but one of the original settlers. He had come to the State as a young man, in 1830; he was very talkative; he owned a large rancho in the northern part of the State; and he had married a Mexican woman.

I mention him chiefly to repeat to you his opinion that the country has been

11

going to the dogs ever since 1849. The adobe house he thought the most convenient and sufficient that man could build in this climate; and there he was not altogether wrong. "We had no crime before the Americans came," he said; "there was not a prison in the whole province. The first solid building which the Americans erected was a jail; and almost the first thing we knew of them was by the taxes they laid on us, the thieves who stole our cattle and horses, and the prisons and sheriffs they introduced into the country."

I suggested that the value of real estate had improved since the Americans came; but he had none to sell. In fact, if the Americans had not come, he could have had a rancho for each of his eighteen children, so that you will see why my suggestion made him indignant.

It is probably true that the old Californians were, so far as merely material existence is concerned, perhaps the happiest people who ever lived upon the face of the earth. They were few in number in a country of inexhaustible natural wealth; the climate enabled them to live out-of-doors all the year round, and made exercise a pleasure, for it is neither too warm nor too cold at any season. The cattle, horses, and sheep fed on the richest pastures, and were never cared for as we care for our beasts in the East. If they needed more land, they could get it for the asking; and a man portioned his daughters from the public domain, and had only to take the trouble to select what he thought the best.

Poverty was unknown, for he who was poor lived on his rich relations; their houses were always open to every one; and at their tables sat uncles, cousins, and nieces, to the farthest degree removed, welcome with them to the *carné con chilé*, the beans and tortillas, which made their sufficient meals.

Indians were their servants, and cheaply did their drudgery. Illness they did not know, nor doctors' bills; and when the ranchero traveled he found a free hotel at every house; and when his horse was tired, he simply lassoed a fresh horse out of the first pasture he came to, turned his own adrift, and went on.

Their few wants were mostly supplied from their own lands, and for the luxuries of coffee, tea, sugar, or bright calicoes for the women, they sold hides and horns to the Boston traders.

But they had none of the energy and ingenuity of civilized life. They merely lived; they planted no trees; they ploughed few fields; and a soil which is the richest in the world, and a climate in which the orange, the vine, the almond, and olive flourish, served them merely for pasture. But I do not wonder that the old Californians regret the change.

Santa Barbara, San Luis, and Monterey counties are largely held in Spanish grants. In San Luis County we drove through an estate of eighteen leagues— a league of land is 4440 acres—and there are many of from four to eleven leagues.

It is easy to see that these great places injure and retard the prosperity of this region, for while almost the whole of it is sparsely inhabited, you no sooner come to Hollister than you find a numerous and active population, excellent farm-houses, and a thriving, busy country.   Here some great ranchos were subdivided into small tracts.

Salinas City, San Juan, Hollister, Watsonville, and Santa Cruz are the chief towns of a region which the Southern Pacific Railroad has but recently brought to public attention—a country of almost unexampled fertility.   Fortunately, to a considerable extent it is owned by small farmers, in tracts of from seventy-five to one hundred and sixty acres, and a more prosperous population it would be difficult to find.

In the Pajaro and adjoining valleys wheat has been grown on the same fields for twenty years in succession, and these still produce heavy crops.   The soil is a deep sandy loam, with frequent patches of stiff adobe.   Irrigation is not needed in most places, and at any rate is practiced only in gardens and nurseries.   Wheat, barley, and oats are the principal crops.

I saw oat straw which, hung up and dry, measured eight and a half feet, was as big round at the base as my middle finger, and which yielded, on one piece of fourteen acres, the enormous crop of one hundred and two and a half bushels per acre.

During the last season, which was a dry year, one wheat field yielded ninety bushels per acre.   Flax-seed, which is also grown, yields from twelve to fifteen sacks per acre, of one hundred pounds to the sack.

The average yield of wheat over the whole tract is, I was assured by men in whom I have confidence, and whose testimony I compared, between forty and fifty bushels to the acre; the average yield of barley from fifty-five to sixty-five bushels, and of oats over fifty bushels per acre; sixty bushels of wheat to the acre is so far from an uncommon crop that a dozen farmers were shown me who had got that by measurement.   Of potatoes the average crop is from two hundred to three hundred bushels.

There are several hop farms, some of which, with skillful management, have paid well; but I think the sea lies too near for successful hop culture.   Wheat and barley grow here in fields down to the very edge of the sea; and no doubt the fog and moisture from the ocean help this fertile country in dry seasons. Last year nearly the whole of California suffered from drought, but in the Pajaro Valley the crops were good.

Farms are sold for from thirty to one hundred dollars per acre, within three miles of Watsonville, in the valley; and the hill lands, which seemed to me just as fertile and as available, bring from ten to twenty-five dollars.   I was sorry to hear that much land is rented from great holders, who get, for farms which are fenced and furnished with rather poor houses, from four to twelve dollars per acre per annum.

YOSEMITE FALL, YOSEMITE VALLEY.

But where a tenant is thrifty he is soon able to buy. I saw one man, an energetic Dane, who began here with $1000; bought on credit a farm for $8000; and in five years was out of debt. I ought to add that he had a very thrifty, energetic wife, without whose help he could not have achieved this.

The peach does not do well in the valleys, but flourishes on the hill-sides; of apples, the Jonathan and White Winter Pearmain begin to bear in two years from the graft; others in three. The plum yields an abundant crop in four years from budding; the vine does not do well; but the strawberry is here in its glory; and the curculio does not trouble the plum. In this and the San José Valley, however, the slug begins, I hear, to be seen on the pear-trees.

These valleys have two great advantages besides their fertile soil and fine climate. Lumber is very cheap, this being the famous redwood region; and the Southern Pacific Railroad gives them ready and quick access to market, San Francisco being less than one hundred miles by rail from Watsonville.

The redwood makes an excellent lumber for houses and fences, and in fact, for all uses. It is sold in Watsonville for from fifteen to twenty dollars per thousand at retail, and the saw-mills employ a considerable force of men.

The people are petitioning Congress to change the route of the railroad, which—through ignorance of the country, I suppose—was laid so as to cross the Coast Range near Hollister; whereas it ought certainly to have run the whole length of the Salinas Valley, thus developing a very rich region nearly one hundred miles in length, and from ten to fourteen wide. It may be, for aught I know, that there are engineering difficulties in the way of crossing the mountains lower down; for it is no joke to run a line through a country so embarrassed with mountains as this State. But the great Salinas Plains need only a railroad to make of them very quickly one of the richest parts of the State.

At present a large part of this fertile region is given over to cattle, and miles of land are fenced in for pastures, on which would grow magnificent crops of grain, and which would furnish pleasant homes for a large rural population. The people begin, in this State, to see their way to making the great land-owners sell out, by forcing them to bear their fair share of the burden of taxation. When this is done the great estates will be rapidly broken up. But in the mean time there is no scarcity of land here.

SECRET TOWN—TRESTLE FROM THE EAST, 1100 FEET LONG, 90 FEET HIGH.

CHAPTER XVI.

SEMI-TROPICAL FRUITS IN SOUTHERN CALIFORNIA.

I PROMISED, in a previous chapter, to give a particular account of the culture of what are called semi-tropical fruits in Southern California. The facts and figures which are given below will surprise many persons, as they did me. I was at first incredulous as to the brilliant pecuniary returns of this culture, and was the more careful to make a thorough investigation of the facts. The details which I present are in every case rather under than over-stated, and may, I believe, be depended on.

The orange, almond, olive, lemon, citron, lime, and English walnut, are the fruits to which attention has been for some years specially directed in the counties of Santa Barbara, Los Angeles, San Bernardino, and San Diego. They will and do grow in many other parts of the State. There are considerable almond orchards in the Napa Valley, and in Alameda County, near San Francisco; General Vallejo has an orange orchard in bearing in Sonoma; the orange grows well in Marysville, in Yuba County; and in several parts of the San Joaquin Valley. Wherever it has been tried, it, as well as all the other trees I have named, succeeds perfectly, with the exception, perhaps, of the almond, which would, in some of the northern parts of the San Joaquin plains, be a little uncertain, unless it were protected by other trees. But even the almond will do well in most parts of that valley. There is thus a great area of land in California on which these fruits can be grown with safety and profit; and much of this land, that in the San Joaquin Valley, is still very cheap, and is easily prepared.

Most of these fruits were cultivated at the old missions for many years, but they appear not to have attracted the attention of their Spanish neighbors, nor even of the Americans, who were, in their devotion to gold and silver mining, slow to see the advantages of this State for agriculture and horticulture.

Santa Barbara County has a long, narrow strip of sea-coast, fronting south, as you will see on the map, which is believed to be peculiarly fitted for the culture of the almond, which in Los Angeles is found to be sometimes hurt by a late frost, as the peach is with us. Of course, frosts anywhere in Southern California are slight, but the almond-tree, when in full bloom, is tender. Santa Barbara County is thought to be less fitted, for some reason, for the orange, which grows finely in Los Angeles and San Bernardino.

There are several varieties of the almond; and Mr. Heath, living near Santa Barbara, and Judge Fernald, of that town, and no doubt others, have originated seedlings of their own, of which many planters think highly. But the variety most planted here is called the Languedoc, and comes from several trees imported from France some years ago. Its good points are, I am told, that it blossoms late, the nut has a tolerably soft shell, and the tree is said to be a prolific bearer.

The almond does best in a sandy loam, will grow without irrigation—though I believe it does best with water, unless on low ground—and the custom is to plant one hundred and eight trees to the acre. They begin to bear at three years from the bud; and at five years may be expected to yield twelve pounds to the tree, or say 1200 pounds per acre, which, at twenty cents per pound, would give two hundred and forty dollars per acre. They bear for a number of years; at eight years they may, I am told, be counted on for twenty pounds to the tree, which would give four hundred dollars to the acre.

No disease troubles the tree here; but the squirrel and gopher destroy it when it is young, and the former sometimes robs the tree. These, however, are easily driven out by poison and perseverance; and one man's labor suffices to keep in order twenty or even thirty acres of trees, and extirpate the gophers and squirrels.

When they are ripe, the almonds fall to the ground; the husk falls off of itself, or is easily picked off, and as the harvest-time here is always dry, the shells are usually bright and clean. Some persons, however, improve their appearance by the use of a sulphur vapor bath—a harmless device.

The native seedlings are mostly hard-shell; these, of course, bear a lower price in the market, but they are said to have an advantage in being exempt from the attacks of a little bird, the linnet, which occasionally appears in large numbers and does mischief.

The olive, of which the oldest and one of the finest groves in the State is at the San Diego Mission, while the finest young olive orchards are, I think, those of Judge Fernald and Mr. Packer, of Santa Barbara, is propagated by cuttings. It grows slowly at first, begins to bear at four years, under favorable circumstances, but does not yield a full crop until the tenth, or even the twelfth year. It should then return an average, for the orchard, of twenty-five gallons of olives per tree. Sixty trees are planted to the acre, here, by the most experienced men.

The olives are sold here, at this time, I am told, for sixty cents per gallon in the orchard, and the few olive groves now in full bearing in Southern California, at that rate, are worth, gross, nine hundred dollars per acre per annum. No doubt, as new groves come to bear, the price will go down; but there is here an immense margin, as you will perceive.

The finest olives I have ever tasted I ate at the San Diego Mission; and the olives of this State, when carefully pickled, are far superior to those we get from France or Spain. They are of moderate size, but very plump, juicy, and full-flavored. Pickled olives fetch here seventy-five cents per gallon.

I am told by proprietors of olive orchards that it is more profitable to make the fruit into oil than to pickle it. From five to seven gallons of ripe olives go to one gallon of oil. The machinery for pressing the oil is very simple, and usually stands under a shed in the orchard; the pulp is crushed from the pits, and stuffed into strong rope nets, which are then pressed, the oil running down into a tub of clean water, on the surface of which it collects.

The refuse and the crushed seeds, on pressure, yield a quantity of oil of a lower quality, which is boiled to clarify it. The first oil needs not even bleaching here.

The olive-tree, with its curious grayish-green foliage, does not at first seem beautiful to you; but it grows on the sight, and I think there is no finer object than a grove of these healthful, finely-grown trees. Santa Barbara is likely to become the centre of this culture. The olive is not particular as to soil, and it does not, here, need irrigation. The gopher eats the roots of the young tree, but this is its only enemy.

That you may not think I have exaggerated the olive-tree's productiveness, I will add that one tree in Santa Barbara, now thirty years old, bore forty-eight dollars' worth of olives for three years in succession; another, at twelve years, bore over two barrels of olives. At San Diego, a tree reputed to be seventy years old bore this year over one hundred gallons; but in that old orchard, which has been shamefully abused, some trees did not bear at all this year; and this one tree may have had a rest for years past.

I do not know the cost of working an olive orchard; the cultivation should not cost more than that of the almond; but the picking is probably expensive, as it would employ a number of hands.   Children, however, are used in this labor.   The fruit does not ripen all at once; and for pickling it must be picked by hand.   For making oil, the ripe olives are sometimes whipped off the tree with switches.

The English walnut in the extensive orchards of Mr. Rose, near Los Angeles, in Mr. Childs's in that place, and in a few other cases in San Bernardino and Santa Barbara, shows itself as a stately, magnificent tree, with clean, grayish bark, and wide-spreading branches.   It is, like our own black walnut, a tree of slow growth, and does not begin to bear until it is seven or eight years of age.

At twelve years, with thorough culture and irrigation, it bears from fifty to seventy-five pounds of nuts; at fifteen years, from one hundred to one hundred and fifty pounds.   Thirty trees may stand on an acre; and it is customary here to plant almond-trees between the rows of walnuts, which pay the cost of cultivation and a handsome profit, and are cut down when the walnuts begin to cover the ground.

The nuts sold this year for twelve and a half cents per pound in Los Angeles.   A little arithmetic will tell you that, at one hundred pounds to the tree, which for an orchard fifteen years old would be, every body tells me, an underestimate, the yield would be three hundred and seventy-five dollars per acre. The only expense is the cost of cultivating and irrigating; one man could easily care for thirty acres.   The nuts fall when ripe, and are picked up and sacked, as hickory-nuts with us.

It is asserted that the tree is absolutely free from disease or enemies in the State; it needs no pruning, and it may be safely transplanted when three years old, so that the planter would get a crop in seven years.   At twenty years, trees have borne two hundred and fifty pounds of nuts.   Two English walnut-trees near Santa Barbara, thirty years old, have yielded fifty dollars' worth of nuts each per annum for several years past.

In Los Angeles there are several fine Spanish chestnuts, noble trees, which at fifteen years of age bore one hundred pounds of nuts each.   There are some young orchards of these, also.

The citron, which bears in four or five years, is also a profitable plant.   It is a straggling, tall shrub; three of them in Los Angeles bore, at four years, without special care, this year, forty-five dollars' worth of fruit.

The lemon, which becomes a stately, far-spreading tree, bears in ten years a valuable crop.   It is not yet planted in orchards to a great extent; one tree, ten years old, which I saw in Los Angeles, yielded six hundred lemons; one, fifteen years old, bore two thousand lemons.   They fetch in San Francisco thirty dollars per thousand.

Last, I come to the orange. "All these trees do well, and are profitable," said an orange cultivator to me; "but they don't compare with the orange; when you have a bearing orange orchard, it is like finding money in the street."

Los Angeles is, at present, the centre of the orange culture in this State. The tree grows well in all Southern California, wherever water can be had for irrigation. It does best nearest the mountains, among the foot-hills, probably because it there gets a more uniform temperature; and I think I have noticed in orchards at Los Angeles, San Gabriel, and near San Bernardino, that it is grateful for such protection as house, out-buildings, or hedges give it from severe winds. At Los Angeles the frosts are sometimes severe enough to nip the tender leaves of the young plants, and on the plain near San Bernardino I found that year-old plants were protected with some slight covering during the past winter, which every body tells me has been uncommonly hard.

Sixty orange-trees are commonly planted to the acre. They may be safely transplanted at three or even four years, if care is used to keep the air from the roots. They grow from seed; and it is believed in California that grafting does not change or improve the fruit. It begins to bear in from six to eight years from the seed, and yields a crop for market at ten years. With good thorough culture and irrigation, it is a healthy tree; if it is neglected, or if the gopher has gnawed its roots, the scale-insect appears; but a diseased tree is very rarely seen in the orchards.

It is in California, as elsewhere, a tremendous bearer. At Los Angeles I saw two trees in an orchard, one seventeen years old, from which 2800 oranges had been picked, and it still contained a few; the other, three years younger, had yielded 2000 oranges.

At from ten to twelve years from the seed the tree usually bears 1000 oranges, and they are selling now in San Francisco for from fifteen to thirty-five dollars per thousand.

I have satisfied myself, by examination of nearly all the bearing orchards in the southern counties, and by comparing the evidence of their owners, that at fifteen years from the seed, or twelve years from the planting of three-year old trees, an orange orchard which has been faithfully cared for, and is favorably situated, will bear an average of 1000 oranges to the tree. This would give, at twenty dollars per 1000—a low average—a product of $1200 per acre.

One man can care for twenty acres of such an orchard; and every other expense, including picking, boxes, shipping, and commissions in San Francisco, is covered by five dollars per 1000. The net profit per acre would, therefore, be a trifle less than nine hundred dollars.

To show you that this is not an overstatement, I will tell you that I have been in an orchard of less than nine acres, which has produced for its owner for several years in succession a clear profit of over $8000. An orchard of forty acres in Los Angeles is reported to me to bring a clear rent of $15,000 per annum; and the lessee is believed to have made a fortune for himself. You will probably believe, after all, that I have exaggerated the profits of this business, but the orange-growers of Los Angeles will smile at the extreme moderation of my statement. "People tell large stories about oranges," said one such man to me; "but the truth is big enough—at ten or twelve years trees may be safely counted on to average ten dollars each clear profit, with sixty trees to an acre, and that is big enough for any body." And thereupon this orange-grower proceeded to show me the accounts of one little orchard of his own, which so greatly exceeded his moderate statement that I shall not give you the figures.

After ten years the tree rapidly and steadily increases in fruitfulness; the older trees in the orchards are now bearing, so every owner assured me, very little less than 2000 oranges to the tree. The best cultivators do not prune the tree at all; but in all the orchards willow poles are used to prop up the overladen branches. It lives to be over one hundred years old.

Near Los Angeles, at the Mission San Gabriel, you will find two large and fine places, those of Mr. Wilson, State Senator from this district, and Mr. Rose. Both are able men, and careful horticulturists. Of Mr. Rose's place, as a model of its kind, I will give you a few particulars, which will bring before your eyes the manner and extent to which fruit culture is practiced here.

Mr. Rose has 2000 acres of fine, fair-lying land, well watered, so that he can irrigate the whole of it. Twelve hundred acres are under fence, and in cultivation and pasture. He raises, as field crops, barley, wheat, and oats, and keeps a large range for a valuable herd of mares and colts, the latter from three stallions which he has imported from the East.

His orchard consists of 400 young but bearing orange-trees, 4000 not bearing, and 2000 more now being planted; 500 lemons, of which fifty are in bearing; 135,000 vines, from which he made 100,000 gallons of white wine, and 3000 gallons of brandy, last year; 350 English walnuts, 150 almonds; and the place contains besides, in considerable quantities, apples, pears, peaches, apricots, nectarines, pomegranates, figs, Spanish chestnuts, and olives.

He mentioned to me, as part of his last year's crop, 250,000 oranges, 50,000 lemons, 25,000 pounds of walnuts, etc., etc.

He thinks his success due to deep and thorough cultivation, and regular irrigation. He irrigates all his trees once in six weeks, and ploughs or hoes after every irrigation. I did not see a single weed or bunch of grass in all his orchards, and such clean culture is very pleasant to the eye. He has on his place wine-presses, and a still-house for making brandy. One man on his place, and with his system, can care for twenty acres of orchard, and one man can pick 5000 oranges in a day. He buys the shooks and makes his own boxes, and also makes his own wine-casks. His regular force consists of fifteen men, of whom the ploughmen are Indians; some others are Chinese.

The orange ripens in December, when they begin to pick. It hangs on the tree, and gets sweeter, until the next fall, but is in perfection in April; and it increases in size as long as it remains on the tree. This circumstance, and the other that it bears transportation so well, give it great value. The orange-grower has at least five months in which he may market his crop. And Los Angeles oranges have been sent to Boston overland, and arrived in good order.

Of course there are not many places in the State like those of Messrs. Rose and Wilson. There are, in fact, but few bearing orange or nut orchards in California. I was told in Los Angeles that Mr. Rose had this spring refused $150,000 cash for his farm; and I doubt if any reasonable sum of money would buy a bearing nut or orange orchard. But a large number of trees are set out every year, mostly on small places of ten or twenty acres.

It has been proved beyond doubt, by thoroughly practical experiment, that the orange, lemon, lime, citron, English walnut, olive, and almond, thrive in Southern California. There are orange-trees in the State twenty years old, olives seventy years planted, English walnuts thirty years old, and almond orchards which have borne full crops for a number of years. The fact, therefore, that the climate and soil are adapted to these products is settled beyond a doubt, and the enormous productiveness of the orchards is as certain.

But the whole of California has at this time less than thirty thousand orange-trees planted, less than twenty thousand olives, less than twenty thousand English walnuts, and not five thousand lemons. This industry is yet in its cradle. "How, then, shall we be certain that it will not be overdone by the time orchards, to be planted in two or three years, shall come into bearing?" some one will ask.

I asked the same question of a shrewd farmer who, having four thousand young orange-trees planted, was this spring putting out two thousand more. I asked it of a gentleman who is planting a large area in these fruits. I asked it of a number of planters who have bearing orchards; and I will tell you their reply.

They say, first, that it requires perseverance, some skill, industry, and a long time, during which the planter must make his living from other sources, to bring such an orchard of semi-tropical fruit to a successful and profitable state. Of all who start, probably less than half will succeed.

Second: The area of land in the whole civilized world suited to the culture of these fruits is very limited. They flourish in California, and they may do, with care, in Florida, and probably nowhere else in the United States. Even in these two States only in parts is the climate suited to them. Southern California, which includes that part of the State south of Stockton and San Francisco, is, in fact, the Italy of this continent; its equal climate, its protection from cold by mountain ranges, its rich soil and healthfulness, give it a place alone among its sister States.

Overproduction, then, of these fruits, which are in universal demand, is not probable, they think, in the next half-century at least. It is believed here by those who have most carefully investigated the matter, that at any probable rate of planting the semi-tropical fruits raised in California for the next thirty years will not increase in quantity in proportion with the demand for them arising from the increased population of the country west of Chicago and St. Louis—all which will be the market for these products.

Third: Not only is the market wide, but these products bear transportation a long distance. They are not perishable, as the strawberry or the cherry. The orange-grower has four months during which his oranges hang on the trees, and may be picked and marketed. Olives and their oil are, of course, marketable at any time; and nuts and almonds may be kept, of course, for months—longer even than apples.

Finally, they say: We have the whole country for our market, from Sitka to Maine; our products bear transportation across the continent, do not need to be put on the market at once, or at any given time, and are in universal demand. We have in our favor a climate which experience has now proved to be peculiarly adapted to these trees; the soil which they require; a region so healthful and pleasant that life in it is a pleasure; and our trees seem, so far, to be secure from any serious disease. We believe ourselves able to compete with Florida, France, Italy, and the Pacific Islands; and thus we have not only our home market, but the whole world; and the present profit is so large that we have a large margin for a fall in prices.

Whether all this is true or not, it is certain that not only small farmers, but capitalists, are turning their attention to this business. Near Santa Barbara, in a most lovely region, Colonel Hollister, well known here and in the East as a successful wool-grower, and one of the ablest men I have met in this State, is preparing to plant four hundred acres in almonds, olives, and walnuts. Near him, Mr. Elwood Cooper, formerly a New York merchant, and resident in Brooklyn, has another beautiful place, where also he is setting out almonds by the thousand; and in Los Angeles County I have found a large number of men of small fortunes, as well as farmers, deliberately giving money and time to the formation of orange, lemon, and nut orchards; while about Visalia and Bakersfield, in the San Joaquin Valley, these fruits begin to attract the attention of the shrewdest farmers. They say, "We will work and wait for eight or ten years, in order that at the end we shall have a small fortune, to make our later years easy;" and if a man may, in ten years, from twenty acres secure himself a regular income of ten or even five thousand dollars per annum, with but trifling labor and care, these persons would seem to be wise.

WINNOWING GOLD NEAR CHINESE CAMP.

CHAPTER XVII.

ANAHEIM—A SUCCESSFUL COLONY—WITH HINTS FOR OTHER COLONISTS.

CALIFORNIA has just now several experiments going on in settlement by colonies. The Southern California Colony is near San Bernardino; the Westminster Colony is near Wilmington, the port of Los Angeles; there is a Methodist Colony on the plain which lies between Los Angeles and the sea; I have heard that another colony is projected on a rancho in Santa Barbara County, called Lompoc, and belonging to Colonel Hollister.

There may be others, for aught I know. I have seen all that have made a beginning, and last I saw also Anaheim, which is the only one which has had time to test fully its plan, and which has achieved a notable success.

Of course, settlement of a new region by colonies, or by the co-operation of families, is nothing new. In all our Western States there were, in the early days, numerous instances of such settlements; and where the Indian disputed the white man's advance, no single family could hold its ground. But the systematic laying out and planting of a tract of country upon a plan decided beforehand and faithfully carried out is, I think, peculiar as yet to Anaheim, though I wonder much that it has not had frequent and numerous imitators in California, which is peculiarly adapted for such experiments.

In 1857—fifteen years ago—several Germans proposed, in San Francisco, to some of their countrymen to purchase, by a general effort, a piece of land, lay it out into small individual farms, plant these with grapes for wine, and to do all this by one general head or manager, and in the cheapest and best manner possible.

After some discussion, fifty men joined to buy a tract of 1165 acres of land south-west of Los Angeles. They paid for this two dollars per acre, and took care to get for this price also a sufficient water-right for irrigation.

The land was selected and bought by the leader in the enterprise, Mr. Hansen, of Los Angeles, a German who had long lived in California, and who is a man of culture and ideas, and desired to see what could be done by co-operation in this direction. He became, subsequently, so much interested in the success of the plan he had formed, that he was the manager of the colony in all its preparatory stages; and as he is an engineer, and a capable, honest, and patient man, he was, I think, a very valuable person.

The Anaheim Company consisted, you must understand, of mechanics, in the main. There were several carpenters, a gunsmith, an engraver, three watch-makers, four blacksmiths, a brewer, a teacher, a shoe-maker, a miller, several merchants, a book-binder, a poet (of course, as they were Germans), four or five musicians, a hatter, some teamsters, a hotel-keeper, and others: not a farmer among them all, pray notice.

Moreover—and this I say with a certain degree of hesitation—there is some reason to believe that the members of this company were not even eminently successful in their callings. They were not getting rich in San Francisco, where most of them lived. Several of them had money ahead, but most of them, I judge from what I hear, were men ready enough to better their fortunes, but to whom it would have been impossible to buy for cash a ready-made farm of even twenty acres.

Well, it was agreed to divide the 1165 acres into fifty twenty-acre lots, and fifty house lots in the village, leaving some lots for school-houses and other public buildings, fourteen in number.

The first contribution or payment toward the common stock bought the land. Thereupon Mr. Hansen was, very wisely, chosen resident manager, and the share-holders quietly went on with their pursuits in San Francisco, taking care only to pay up the calls on their stock as they became due.

It was the manager's duty, meantime, to go on with the improvement of the lots. This he did with hired labor—Indians and Californians.

He dug a main ditch about seven miles long, to lead the irrigating water over the whole area, with four hundred and fifty miles of subsidiary ditches, and twenty-five miles of feeders to these.

He planted on each twenty-acre lot eight acres in vines (8000 vines), and some fruit-trees.

He fenced each lot with willows, making five and a quarter miles of outside, and thirty-five miles of inside fencing.   These willows are now topped for fire-wood, and, as they grow rapidly, they give a very fresh and lovely green to the aspect of Anaheim.   This done, he continued to cultivate, prune, and keep up the whole place.

At the end of three years, in 1860, all the assessments were paid; each stockholder had paid $1200, and a division of the lots was made.   This was done by a kind of lottery.   All the lots were viewed, and assessed at their relative value, from $1400 to $600, according to situation, etc.

When a lot was drawn, if it was valued over $1200, the drawer paid the difference; if less, he received the difference.   Thus he who drew a $1400 lot would pay $200; he who drew a $600 lot would receive $600 additional in cash.

When all were drawn, there was a sale of the effects of the company—tools, horses, etc.; and, on balancing the books, it was found that a sum remained on hand which sufficed for a dividend of over one hundred dollars to each share-holder.   I believe the actual cost of the lots was but $1080.   For this, each had twenty acres and a town lot 150 by 200 feet, with 8000 bearing grape-vines, and some fruit-trees.

Then most of the owners broke up at San Francisco and came down to take possession.   Lumber for building was bought at wholesale; for so many families a school-house was quickly erected; shop-keepers flocked in and bought the town lots; a newspaper was begun; mechanics of different kinds were attracted to the colony; and the colonists themselves had at once about them all the conveniences for which, had they settled singly, they would have had to wait many years.

Now it must be remembered that these colonists were not either farmers or gardeners by trade.   Only one had ever made wine.   They began as green hands; and some of them borrowed money to make their improvements, and had to pay heavy interest.   They had to build their houses, and make their gardens, and support their families.   Here is briefly the results of the experiment:

1. There was a struggle for some years, but in this early time, every body tells me, they all had abundance to eat, a good school for their children, music and pleasant social amusements, and they were their own masters.   There is no winter here for the struggling poor man to dread or provide for.

2. Only one of the original settlers has moved away; and the sheriff has never issued an execution in Anaheim.

3. The property which cost $1080 is now worth from $5000 to $10,000; and I do not believe more than one in ten of the colonists would have been worth to-day, had they remained at their trades in San Francisco, any money at all.

4. There are no poor in Anaheim.

5. It is the general testimony that the making of wine and brandy has not caused drunkenness among the colonists. "When you see a drunken man in our town, it will be an Indian," said several people to me.

6. I have not a doubt that the moral standard of the people has been greatly improved. Their children are well trained; the men are masters of their own lives; they have achieved independence, and what to an average New York mechanic would seem the ideal of a fortunate existence. The average *clear* income from their vineyards, which now contain mostly sixteen acres, is about $1000 per annum. Some few fall below this, but most of them, I was told, go above. They have besides this, of course, their gardens, which here yield vegetables all the year round; their chickens—in short, the greater part of their living. They live well; it is a land of plenty; and to me, who remembered how painful and unpleasant is the life of a mechanic or artisan in New York, it was a delight to see here men and women who had redeemed themselves by their own efforts from this drudgery and slavery.

In repeating such an experiment, naturally, some improvements could be made. I think forty acres would be better than twenty; and this is the opinion of most of the Anaheim settlers. But forty acres are enough in this rich country.

Then, I think, oranges, lemons, almonds, and olives should be planted, not to the exclusion of the vine, but as a considerable part of the planting. The vineyardist has to contend in this State with high freights and very dear casks. The man who can keep his wine till it is three or four years old will make a great deal of money, but he must invest a large sum in casks, which a poor vineyardist can not afford.

Then the raisin grape should be planted, for the raisin crop will be as profitable here, and less expensive, than the wine crop.

Also, for wine, any one would now plant a different grape than the Mission, which is the variety mostly used in this State as yet.

With such changes there is no reason why the Anaheim experiment should not be successfully repeated in a hundred places in this State. In some parts, of course, the land is high in price. But in the great San Joaquin Valley, which is just being opened by the building of the Southern Pacific Railroad, there are three millions of acres open to settlement, and most favorable to such experiments. The vine is already successfully cultivated there, both for wine and raisins; the orange and the olive and lemon will grow, I believe, in every part of the valley where they are watered; the almond will bear in the foot-hills, but will be uncertain, I think, on the plain itself. There Government land can be had in eighty-acre tracts, under the Homestead Act, for nothing, and one hundred and sixty acres at the double minimum rate, two dollars and a half per acre; while the railroad sections can be bought at low prices, and on five years' credit, in whole sections of six hundred and forty acres, or in smaller subdivisions. On this plain there is scarcely any waste land. Usually every acre in a section is good.

If any mechanic or other person in the East, reading of this Anaheim experiment, should ask me what I would advise for a repetition of it, I should say to him:

1st. Look about you for twenty, or, if you can find them, fifty picked men, industrious, saving, and determined. Form yourselves into a society. Select the most trustworthy and experienced one of your number—one in whom you can all confide—to go to California to seek out a place for you. Direct him first to Sacramento. There, in the land-office of the Central Pacific Railroad Company, he can get the best general idea of the vacant land in the State; for in the local United States land-offices he gets, of course, a view only of the lands in the limited jurisdiction of each. Having thus, on the charts, surveyed the ground, he should visit the spot which seems to him most favorable.

2d. There he should inquire what facilities there are for irrigation; what are most suitable for the company's purposes, plain or foot-hill lands—remembering that for the present the foot-hills afford water more handily. And when he finds what he wants, he can buy, of the railroad and Congress together, as yet, in many places a compact body of land sufficient for all purposes. Twenty families, at eighty acres each, would need 1600 acres of land, or two and a half sections.

3d. When the land is bought, it should be fenced as quickly as possible; then the manager should at once bring down water; and he will readily find engineers to manage this cheaply and well. An irrigation canal is not very costly where the soil is twenty feet deep, and without stones.

A nursery should then be begun, in which he should plant orange, lemon, and citron seeds, olive cuttings, and English walnuts, as well as eucalyptus seeds. These, if watered, will grow at once, and a small nursery will cheaply supply the whole colony.

4th. Next come grapes—and here I strongly advise the planting of the white Malaga for raisins. The best authorities assure me that the raisin crop will be very profitable here; first-class raisins are now made in this State, but in limited quantities, as but few vines of the Malaga kind are in bearing. The wine crop is in most places expensive to make; the raisin crop needs no casks, and costs less to send to market.

5th. The manager should lay the land out into eighty-acre tracts, and plant on each one, ten acres in the sub-tropical fruits—orange, lemon, citron, olive, English walnut; ten acres in grapes, an acre or two in common fruit-trees, and put the remainder in barley, to be cut for hay. If the season is favorable, his hay crop will almost pay the expenses of the year. At the same time, he should plant dividing fences of willow or cotton-wood, or both, from which in two years the colonists may cut their fire-wood. He should also plant on each lot at least ten acres in eucalyptus; I should advise even more. It is a graceful evergreen tree, which grows with enormous rapidity, and yields, I am told, a solid and valuable timber. I have known a eucalyptus to grow seventeen feet in a year.

6th. Whatever he plants should be carefully done. Deep ploughing is almost unknown in California; yet many shrewd farmers believe that if you plough thoroughly eighteen inches deep, you need not fear a drought. I do not believe there is to-day a sub-soil plough in the whole San Joaquin Valley; and if a man ploughs five inches deep he thinks himself a hero.

7th. It is easy, in any part of California, to get farm work, such as fencing, planting trees and vines, and building, done by contract. It is not so easy to hire competent farm laborers for the regular operations of the farm. But when the colonists come on it will be easy enough for each to take care of his own tract; and where a community is thus formed, Indians, who make good ploughmen, are always attracted by the prospect of employment.

8th. The manager should continue in sole charge for at least three seasons from the time he begins operations. He should receive a salary, of course; and he should be carefully selected, as upon his faithfulness and capacity the success of the undertaking will greatly, if not entirely depend. It is not absolutely necessary that he should be a farmer; but he should be a competent business man. A shrewd, intelligent mechanic, persevering, and with a proper sense of responsibility to his companions, would do well. He will not need to plough with his own hands; but he must look to the economical use of money in the operations he conducts.

9th. The intending colonists should continue patiently at work in their old homes until the vines come into bearing. They would have assessments to pay for the support of operations in the colony; and they should lay by some money against the time when they will remove to their new homes. If their hearts are in the enterprise, if they have faith and enthusiasm, they will work the harder and save the more, for the incentive before them.

10th. The manager should maintain the nursery of trees; and in the third year, if he can not do it before, he should plough deeply ten acres on each lot, and sow it to alfalfa, which will require watering or irrigating the first year. Alfalfa is the Chilian clover. It is, in fact, a kind of lucern. It yields enormous crops of green grass, or hay, and is relished by cattle, horses, and hogs. An acre of it will maintain ten sheep.

11th. When at last the colonists come on to take possession, a town plot, which ought to be laid out in the beginning, will rapidly fill up with mechanics. Lumber can be bought at wholesale for building, and houses are very cheaply built in California.

12th. Each settler should first make himself a vegetable garden, and plant besides an acre in beets.   Beets grow in Southern California all the year round; and with ten acres in alfalfa and an acre in beets (to be replanted wherever they are pulled up), half a dozen head of good cattle, a span of good horses, and a dozen or twenty sheep or pigs can be kept with no expense except the labor of cutting the feed.

This is the best country to soil cattle in the United States, because you may cut green food all the year round; cows and hogs or sheep give a constant revenue, or supply food; and with a vegetable garden, and chickens, and fruit, the farmer has almost all he needs to eat on his own ground.

At Anaheim, though many of the colonists began with a heavy debt, and had thus to struggle for some years, there was never from the first settlement any question of bread-and-butter.   In fact, the bread-and-butter terror, the struggle for food, the vague fear that some day there may not be enough to eat in the house, which stands behind the chair of many a hard-working man in the East, is not known in this land of plenty.

13th. I trust every such colony would make abundant provision for a church and a good school.

14th. I have allowed eighty acres to each colonist.   Forty acres are enough, but land in the San Joaquin Valley is cheap; and if a party of men can manage to improve eighty acres, they will be the richer in the end, and with but little more expense at first.

15th. Avoid debt, so far as you can; and if you must borrow to build your houses, try to obtain money in the East at seven or eight per cent.   Here you must pay ten or twelve, and even fifteen.   In fact, in Southern California, large amounts are constantly borrowed at two per cent. per month; and—such are the returns for industry there—the borrowers make money, and often get rich, with that enormous rate against them.

16th. Finally, perseverance is the only requirement for success; but perseverance, patient work at one thing, is needed.   Opportunities are still so abundant in California, that excitable men fly off from one pursuit to another in hopes of a speedy fortune—and for the most part fail, because they do nothing thoroughly.   I have yet to see here the first farmer who sat down on a piece of land for five years, and gave it patient and thorough tillage, who was not an independent man at the end.

If any Eastern mechanic, feeling the oppression of his circumstances, desires independence for himself and his children, he has, I verily believe, in this Southern California, and especially in the San Joaquin Valley, the best opportunity in the world to acquire it.   Of Congress land he can get eighty acres for nothing; Southern Pacific Railroad land he can buy at a low price on five years' credit, paying but a tenth down; soil and climate yield many of the costliest products of commerce; the climate is so mild that his children may play out-of-doors almost every day of the year, and his animals need no shelter in the winter, while his house need not be as stout as in the East. With few and local exceptions, the whole of California is singularly healthful. The vegetable garden yields him food in every month of the year, and his fruit-trees begin to bear much earlier than in the East. Let him only keep his Eastern habits of industry, and beware of the curse of California—idleness and unthrift—to which no doubt the mild climate predisposes men.

SOUTH DOME, YOSEMITE VALLEY.

CHAPTER XVIII.

WHEAT FARMING IN THE SAN JOAQUIN VALLEY.

BETWEEN Stockton and Merced lie about six hundred square miles of wheat. The railroad train runs through what appears to be an interminable wheat-field, with small houses and barns at great distances apart, and no fences, except those by which the company has guarded its trains against the cattle, which are turned into the fields after harvest to glean the grain and consume the stubble.

Wheat, wheat, wheat, and nothing but wheat, is what you see on your journey, as far as the eye can reach over the plain in every direction. Fields of two, three, and four thousand acres make but small farms; here is a man who "has in" 20,000 acres; here one with 40,000 acres, and another with some still more preposterous amount—all in wheat.

This is the middle of March, and of course the crop is in and up, and from six inches to a foot high; it is not so fine a sight as it will be two months hence, when the whole plain will be an ocean of waving tassels. Yet, as you look out and see mile after mile without a division fence, fifty or sixty miles apparently in one field, it makes its impression.

The valley of the San Joaquin differs from an Illinois prairie in that it has two magnificent mountain ranges for its boundaries—the Sierra Nevada on the east, and the Coast Range on the west. The mouth of the valley is to the north, as that of the great valley of Virginia, and that of the Nile; the San Joaquin River joins the Sacramento and flows into the sea, and this has been, until this year, the chief avenue for freight transport from the country through which it runs.

Now the railroad is in operation as far as Merced; it will reach Visalia in June, and Bakersfield in September, and Los Angeles or San Bernardino perhaps next spring; and the great rich valley which has so long lain asleep, given up to horses and cattle, is waking up.

It is a singular piece of good-fortune to the farmers and land-owners that they get a remarkably fine season and the railroad in the same year. They have known how to avail themselves of their good luck, for they have put in enormous crops. One of the best informed men in Stockton assured me that the San Joaquin Valley will send to tide-water, in the year 1872, 180,000 tons of wheat. Mr. Friedlander, the great grain buyer of this State, is reported to me to have estimated the probable export of the whole State this year at 700,000 tons.

This means that seven hundred ships of one thousand tons each will be needed to carry California's spare crop to its far-away markets; and it means that 18,000 cars, each carrying ten tons of grain, will be needed to move the surplus wheat of the San Joaquin Valley to San Francisco; or three hundred and sixty trains of fifty cars each; or a single train more than one hundred miles long.

There will be ships needed to market the great crop, and there will be men needed to harvest it; and as the harvest here lasts three months, and as harvesters will this year get at least two dollars a day and food, many a thrifty man will no doubt earn a small farm by his labors in the wheat-fields.

It will surprise you, perhaps, as it did me, to hear that much of this great wheat-field, of which I have spoken, does not bear, even in such a good year as this is, more than from ten to twelve bushels per acre. A large part of the plain between Stockton and Merced is light and sandy. Some of it looks like a mere collection of white sand; and the wind, when it blows strongly, as it often does, blows a man's farm about a great deal.

There is a goodly quantity of heavier soil—a sandy loam, the best of which yields in a good year from twenty to thirty, and even forty bushels per acre;

and on the western side of the San Joaquin there is yet heavier land, adobe, which will bear, when it is not too wet, still larger crops.

A great deal of this land is owned in large tracts of from 20,000 to 40,000, and from that to 100,000 acres. The holders of these great tracts do not usually farm them, but lease or rent them; and this is a vast business in itself, as you shall understand.

But I must first remind you that if it were not for the peculiar climate of this State, wheat raising on such a scale would be impossible. They sow the wheat here from the first of December to the first of March, and they have another three months to harvest it in, with a certainty that no rain will disturb them during their long harvest.

The fields are ploughed with what are called gang-ploughs, which are simply four, six, or eight ploughshares fastened to a stout frame of wood. On the lighter soil eight horses draw a seven-gang plough, and one such team is counted on to put in six hundred and forty acres of wheat in the sowing season, or from eight to ten acres per day. Captain Gray, near Merced, has put in this season 4000 acres with five such teams—his own land and his own teams.

A seed-sower is fastened in front of the plough. It scatters the seed, the ploughs cover it, and the work is done. The plough has no handles, and the ploughman is, in fact, only a driver; he guides the team; the ploughs do their own work. It is easy work, and a smart boy, if his legs are equal to the walk, is as good a ploughman as any body; for the team is trained to turn the corners at the driver's word, and the plough is not handled at all.

It is a striking sight to see, as I saw, ten eight-horse teams following each other over a vast plain cutting "lands" a mile long, and, when all had passed me, leaving a track forty feet wide of ploughed ground.

On the heavier soil the process is somewhat different. An eight-horse team moves a four-gang plough, and gets over about six acres per day. The seed is then sown by a machine which scatters it forty feet, and sows from seventy-five to one hundred acres in a day, and the ground is then harrowed and cross-harrowed.

When the farmer, in this valley, has done his winter sowing, he turns his teams and men into other ground, which he is to summer fallow. This he can do from the first of March to the middle of May; and by it he secures a remunerative crop for the following year even if the season is dry. This discovery is of inestimable importance to the farmers on the drier part of these great plains. Experience has now demonstrated conclusively that if they plough their land in the spring, let it lie until the winter rains come on, then sow their wheat promptly and harrow it in, they are sure of a crop; and the summer will have killed every weed besides.

After the summer fallowing is done, the teams have a rest. The horses and mules are turned out to grass until the fourth of July, when the harvest begins.

It is then the rainless season; and the farmer gets his teams, his headers, his grain wagons, his thresher, and his sacks and men, into the field, and on the light soil cuts, threshes, and puts into sacks the grain at the rate often of one hundred and fifty acres per day.

Three "headers," which cut off only the heads of the wheat stalks, leaving the straw standing, and nine wagons to take the heads from the headers to the thresher, require to work them twenty-three men and eighty-three horses. With this force they get in one hundred and fifty acres per day. The grain, put into sacks, is left on the fields until time and teams can be got to haul it to the railroad; or often until it is sold. It does not sweat nor mold, and there is no fear of rain.

As soon as the crop is harvested, the teams are hitched to a brush—six horses to a twenty-foot brush, which goes over the field at the rate of forty acres per day. This brush scatters the grain which has been dropped in the fields; and sometimes a little more seed is added. When it has been brushed in it is ploughed—two or three inches deep—to cover the seed; and from this comes, without further care, what is called a "volunteer" crop, which is often better than the first, and is as certainly counted on.

Now the horses and men have another interval of rest until the rains begin and ploughing recommences.

Thus, as one farmer pointed out to me, they have work for their teams almost the whole year, and have no horses eating their heads off in idleness.

In the heavier soils, the "volunteer" crop is put in with the harrow instead of the brush; and this is followed by a "chisel cultivator," having from seven to thirteen teeth, four inches deep. If these leave the ground rough, it is again harrowed.

"It would astonish you to see how small a crop pays the farmer on this sandy soil," said an intelligent man with whom I rode over his fields. He told me that from seven hundred acres last year, he got but a bushel and a half per acre, besides the feed of his teams while they were harvesting. They often feed the horses with wheat from the header-wagons, which is a wasteful act, I should say. But, after all, from this small crop he made five hundred dollars.

At five bushels per acre, if wheat brought two dollars and a half a hundred pounds, the farmer on these sandy plains makes three dollars and a half per acre, clear of every expense. This result, which seemed to me incredible, I saw demonstrated by figures of the cost of the crop which were satisfactory to a whole roomful of farmers.

But if you will remember that it is no uncommon thing for a farmer to put in three or four thousand acres, you will see what money they make, even with a small crop, if the price happens to be good, as it often is in a bad year. Two and a half cents is, of course, a high price, and a cent and a quarter is a more usual price in good years. But at that rate a crop of ten bushels per acre pays so well on the sandy plains that farmers down here count confidently on making large fortunes this year.

I was fortunate enough to find myself one afternoon among a dozen farmers, some having sandy soil, and some the heavier loam; and, after discussing the comparative cost of cultivation, which is nearly double on the heavy land, and the product, which is as ten bushels to from twenty to twenty-five, I listened to an earnest argument concerning the relative merits of sand and clay.

I must say that the sand had the best of it, very much to my surprise, for it is not only sand, but it has, I am told, an impenetrable hard-pan from a foot to three feet below the surface. In spite of this, which would seem to make it worthless, it was admitted that the sand did not show as much sign of exhaustion as the clay, and that, taking six or eight years together, it was as profitable as clay.

A very intelligent man, who owned and worked 2000 acres of clay and loam, said, at the close of the discussion, " The sand has many merits; it can be worked very cheaply, and it bears drought surprisingly well; but after all it is only good for wheat; it must always be farmed on a large scale, and circumstances may make it unprofitable some day; whereas, on the clay we can raise any thing we like, and are not dependent on wheat alone." He added, " The clay and loam farms will have to be cut up, and will be before many years. It will pay better on that land to take one hundred and sixty acres and work it in various crops thoroughly, than to exhaust 2000 or 3000 acres by skimming over the surface."

I told you that much of the land is rented. It is customary in such cases for the land-owner to furnish seed, feed for the teams, all the tools and machinery needed for putting in and harvesting the crops, and the land and necessary buildings, and he gets half the crop put in bags on the field, and furnishes the bags for his share. The renter, as the tenant is called, furnishes only the teams and men, the supplies for the men, and his own grain-bags.

This arrangement is not inequitable; and it gives, as you will see, an important advantage to a man without capital. An eight-horse team is worth about six hundred dollars; with five such teams, and five men—who receive in the winter thirty dollars per month and rations—4000 acres can be put into wheat.

When the work is done, the teams can be hired out, or they can be turned into pastures without cost. I was not surprised to hear that many men have become rich as renters. Two or three good crops enable a renter to buy a large tract of his own.

I do not know what is the net profit of the land-owners under this system, but was told that one, who has 40,000 acres, had refused to rent land for one dollar a year per acre. At this rate many of the large land-owners who rent their land for wheat crops must make nearly one hundred per cent. per annum on their original investments; for you must understand that these plains lay for years in the market as Congress land, and could get no buyers; and it was only during the war that men began to think them valuable.

Then thousands of acres were bought for greenbacks, when gold—the currency of this State—was at from 150 to 200; that is to say, these lands cost from sixty to seventy-five cents per acre.

I do not doubt that the whole of the great counties of Fresno, Tulare, and Kern would have been gobbled up by the land monopolists at the same rate, had not the Government given a land grant in these counties to the Southern Pacific Railroad, and withdrawn the whole of the public lands from sale at the same time. From this it results that the " even sections " are now open only to pre-emption or homestead settlement, in tracts of from eighty to one hundred and sixty acres, and thus more than 2,000,000 acres of the most fertile soil in the world were saved for small farmers, who are now coming in in advance of the railroad, and taking up these Congress and railroad lands, most of which are of better quality, and capable of more various production, than the Merced Plains.

The buildings put up for renters are, as you may guess, as slight and poor as can be. There is a shanty for cooking and sleeping—the farm laborer here furnishes his own bedding and does his own washing, and his equipment is usually two shirts and a pair of blankets. There is a well, and a barn roomy enough to hold the hay and barley, and the teams. The renter either has a house of his own elsewhere, or, if he is poor, his family live in this shanty; there is no vegetable garden, there are no trees, there is absolutely nothing to make life endurable or pleasant; and the only care of owner and tenant is to get as much wheat out of the land each year as they can at the least expense.

It is not a pleasant system of agriculture, nor one which can be permanent; but it develops in the farmers who practice it a great deal of enterprise, and very shrewd business habits. They make money by economy in cultivation, and they are very quick in seizing new labor-saving devices. If I may judge from those I met, I should say that these wheat farmers are an unusually intelligent set of men, with great courage. "Last year I fed my teams but once a day the whole season, and worked them hard too," said one to me.

"How could you be so inhuman?" I exclaimed.

"By Jove!" he answered, "I was not inhuman; I was poor; I had very little to eat myself."

A nurseryman wished to have a piece of twenty acres ploughed ten inches deep, but was told it could not be done with the gang ploughs.

"Why not try a single plough?" I ventured to suggest.

"No, sir," a farmer replied; "I don't *sabé* a single plough; you can't get any man to put a hand to his plough here."

One farmer told me, in reply to some questions, that he had lost $15,000 in the last two years. He expected to make at least $10,000 clear of all expenses this year. He had paid for seed and feed, shipped from San Francisco, to put in his crop this past winter, $7000.

Another farmer shrewdly remarked to me that when the wheat crop is large enough to supply the State, and a little over, then wheat was pretty sure to be very low in price—lower than when the crop was very great; "because," said he, "a heavy crop draws ships here to carry it off; with a light crop, the small surplus weighs on the market, because no ships come to take it away."

I reproached some of them for not planting trees, and the answer was, "We don't go a cent on any thing but wheat in this county; we all want to get rich in two years."

But the best men I spoke with saw the evil of this farming, and are prepared to welcome better things. The soil in Merced County is well fitted for many crops. Fruit grows well wherever it has been tried, and the sugar beet culture has been begun on a large scale near Sacramento, where 1200 acres are now sown in beets, and a very complete factory is ready for operation. It has cost $225,000, and the company are satisfied that they will get this year ten barrels of sugar to the acre. They employ three hundred and fifty men in the fields, mostly Chinese, and between seventy and eighty in the works; and they have extensive sheds for storing the beets; have planted willows along the fence lines and irrigating ditches for wind-breaks, and have prepared sheds for fattening five hundred head of cattle with the bagasse or refuse, which last year they found to be very much relished by animals. They mix ten pounds of cut hay with as much bagasse as the beast will eat. The beats are sown in February, and the sugar-making will begin in July.

The beet sugar-works near San Francisco have been, it is said, enormously profitable for the past two seasons.

On the Merced Plains but little attempt has yet been made at irrigation, but some plans have been formed, and experience has shown that if the land is flooded and thoroughly soaked before it is ploughed in December it will bear a profitable crop, no matter how dry the season.

A QUARTZ-MILL.

CHAPTER XIX.

THE CHINESE AS RAILROAD BUILDERS.—A GREAT STOCK-FARMER.

FROM Merced, where the railroad company are building a very large hotel to accommodate the Yosemite travel, which here branches off for the famous valley, I had the curiosity to go down to the San Joaquin River, where the railroad people are at work. I wanted to see how Chinamen do as road-builders.

There are about seven hundred Chinese employed in grading and laying track, and perhaps one hundred white men. The engineer in charge, Mr. Curtis, told me that the Chinese make, on the whole, the best road-builders in the world. The contractor, Mr. Strobridge, told me that they learn all parts of the work very quickly; and I saw them employed on every kind of work. They do not drink, fight, or strike; they do gamble, if it is not prevented; and it is always said of them that they are very cleanly in their habits. It is the custom, among them, after they have had their suppers every evening, to bathe themselves all over; not in the stream here, which is too cold, but with the help of small tubs. I doubt if the white laborers do as much.

These Chinese receive twenty-eight dollars per month of twenty-six working days, and for this they furnish all their own supplies of food, tents, cooking utensils, etc., but the contractor pays the cooks.   They work in gangs of from twelve to twenty men, who form a mess; and the head-man of the gang receives the wages of all, and divides the money among them.

The Chinaman, except when he is in gala dress, is a dingy-looking creature; he is said to be parsimonious; and to an American his quarters always look shabby.   One gets the idea, therefore, that he lives poorly; and I should have said that pork and rice probably made up their bill of fare here on the plains. It will perhaps surprise you, as it did me, to find that they have a greater variety of food than their white neighbors.

They buy their supplies at a store kept in several cars near the end of the track; and this shop was a great curiosity to me.   Here is a list of the food kept and sold there to the Chinese workmen: Dried oysters, dried cuttle-fish, dried fish, sweet rice crackers, dried bamboo sprouts, salted cabbage, Chinese sugar (which tasted to me very much like sorghum sugar), four kinds of dried fruits, five kinds of desiccated vegetables, vermicelli, dried sea-weed, Chinese bacon cut up into salt cutlets, dried meat of the abelona shell, pea-nut oil, dried mushrooms, tea, and rice.   They buy also pork of the butcher, and on holidays they eat poultry.

Compare this bill of fare with the beef, beans, bread-and-butter, and potatoes of the white laborers, and you will see that John has a much greater variety of food.

At this railroad store they sold also pipes, bowls, chop-sticks, large shallow cast-iron bowls for cooking rice, lamps, joss paper, Chinese writing-paper, pencils and India ink, Chinese shoes, and clothing imported ready-made from China.   Also, scales—for the Chinaman is particular, and re-weighs every thing he buys as soon as he gets it to camp.   Finally, there was Chinese tobacco.

The desiccated vegetables were of excellent quality, and dried, evidently, by a process as good as the best in use with us.

The cost of these supplies, imported from China, was surprisingly low, and the contractor told me that the Chinese laborers can save about thirteen dollars per month, and, where they do not gamble, do lay by as much as that.

When you cross Bear Creek near Merced, you come at once into a new and thinly settled country.   Instead of wheat, you see cattle and sheep, and not only these, but herds of antelope feeding contentedly among the cattle.   Three antelopes ran a race with the hand-car on which I made part of my journey to the San Joaquin River, and kept up with us for nearly two miles, at so short a distance that if there had been a rifle at hand we should have dined on antelope steak, which is very good meat.

Below Bear Creek you enter Fresno County, which has, through the bitter and unscrupulous opposition of the cattle-owners, a fence law, and suffers great injury from it.

The question of "fence" or "no fence" is an exciting one in this State; some of the great, and most of the little cattle-owners, meanly use all their influence to maintain a law under which the farmers are obliged to fence their farms. In Merced County, as in many others, this law has been repealed, and the result is an enormous saving to the farmers, who build no fences. In Fresno, a man must pay more for fencing one hundred and sixty acres than the land costs him, or else see his crop eaten up by some other man's cattle. The people in what is called the "Alabama Settlement," near the San Joaquin, have actually to hire vacqueros at their own expense, to keep other people's cattle out of their wheat-fields. They can not afford to fence their farms.

The "no fence" regulation can not be much longer put off, and the more sensible cattle-owners are already setting their houses in order. Before twelve months, I am told, the whole State will have a "no fence" law, and farmers who come here will be relieved from one of the worst and most expensive worries of country life—the care of fences.

At the Alabama Settlement a number of Southern families have bought a large and fine tract of land, much of which they have put into wheat. Their crops look well; and I believe they are well pleased with their location, finding the country healthy, the soil rich, and their prospects this year good. They came here in the midst of the great drought, and lost two crops; but they had means to support themselves, and now will do well. It struck me that they had made the common mistake of getting too much land; and I believe those farmers are correct who assert that in this valley men will make more money on one hundred and sixty or two hundred acres than on 2000 or 3000. But every body must, I suppose, find out such things for himself.

Trees have made a fine growth in the Alabama Settlement; the orange, I was told, grows there—of course, it does not yet bear—and no doubt the olive, walnut, and perhaps the almond, would do well.

From the end of the track the Visalia stage route leads across Firebaugh's Ferry, and at that point I remained, to see something of a life quite different from that on the Merced side of the San Joaquin. On one side of the river are wheat fields; on the other you find only cattle. Miller and Lux own forty miles of land on the western side of the San Joaquin, and other persons own almost equally great tracts. It is said that Mr. Miller is the possessor of half a million of acres in this State; he has nearly 100,000 cattle; and being a shrewd business man, he is fencing in his great estate, to reserve it for his own cattle. He is eager for more land; and is said to have determined that he will not rest until he can drive his cattle over his own land from Los Angeles to the Sacramento.

Two men in San Francisco saw him sitting somewhere, lost in thought, and one asked, "I wonder what Miller is planning now?" The other replied, "He is making a little plan to buy the rest of the State."

Miller and Lux have now about one hundred and twenty-five miles of fence built, and will build one hundred miles more this year. Some other great land-owners have nearly as much. Fencing costs them from five hundred to six hundred and fifty dollars per mile. Of course these are not the men who oppose a "no fence" law.

At Firebaugh's I fell at once from California into Texas. Who drives wild cattle must himself be wild, I suppose. I found myself in the evening, in a large room, used as a store and shop, where eighteen or twenty vacqueros or cattle-herds sat about an open fire, and smoked, and chewed, and swore, and spat, with great gravity and decorum.

Some were Americans, from Missouri or Texas—the persons called "Pikes" in this State; some were Mexicans, who came in with jingling spurs, and with riding-trowsers made of calf-skin with the hair left on, or sometimes of the skin of the California lion, which gave them quite a startling and disgusting satyr-like look.

As I sat among these men after supper, I began to think I should have to take some care not to be spit on; but the accuracy, neatness, and precision of their aim presently re-assured me. One fellow, lounging on the counter behind me, spat over my hat; a vigorous cross-fire was kept up by two others across the toes of my shoes; a scattered but unintermitting rain fell upon the centre of the floor; and occasionally the fire received a douche; but I believe I may safely say that no accident occurred in the whole course of the evening.

It happened that Mr. Miller himself was present that evening. He is a German by birth, short, alert in his movements, neatly dressed, and with a good nose, a low forehead, and a remarkably expressive countenance. He busied himself with instructions to his foremen, smoking meanwhile, and I was amused to see that when once he got up from his chair, a vacquero slipped into it—and as there were more people than chairs, after wandering about the room for a while, exposed to a battery of tobacco-juice, the owner of half a million acres finally squatted down in the wood-box at the side of the fire, and prudently took care not to get up again until he went off to bed.

His men give him a good name for liberality and kindness to them, and to all working-men; and I believe there is no doubt that he is an uncommonly able business man. He began life poor, in this State, less than eighteen years ago, and has made his fortune "in cattle."

The next morning I had opportunity to study a little the manners and customs of these men. They do every thing on horseback; and the lasso—or *riata* as it is more commonly called here, lasso being properly a verb, I find— is a sort of third arm to them. It was desired to single out half a dozen horses from a herd of twenty-five or thirty confined in a stable-yard. So the horses were let out of the yard, cornered by two mounted men in a fence corner, and then one man, fixing his eyes on the horse he wanted, dashed into the herd, flung

his *riata*, and unfailingly secured the prize. In one case the horse, used probably to the operation — for these animals were broken — saw when he was
"wanted," and actually stood still to be caught.

A vacquero came in after a night's watch over cattle, slipped off his horse
at the door, tied the animal, and in a·minute was fast asleep, standing up and
leaning his head on the saddle. His nap lasted half an hour, and was not
broken apparently by the noise about him.

A horse not thoroughly broken had attached to its head-stall a broad leather
band; when the owner wanted to mount, he slipped this band over the horse's
eyes, and removed it as soon as he was securely in the saddle.

The cattle-range is divided into ranchos, each of which has a foreman, responsible to the proprietor for the cattle on the place. These men receive, I
was told, from $1200 to $1800 per annum, and their food and necessary traveling expenses. Under them are vacqueros.

The cattle range as they please over an enormous extent of land; when
market cattle are wanted, or when it is thought expedient to drive a band to
new pastures, a foreman sets out with from twelve to eighteen men on horseback, accompanied by a wagon which bears provisions and the blankets of the
men, as well as a cook. Three horses are taken along for each man, for the
business is not easy. They separate, and hunt up the cattle they want—each
rancho has its distinct brand—and all are driven toward one point. Meeting
there, which may be one hundred or one hundred and fifty miles from their
destination, they combine forces to drive the whole herd slowly to the place
where they are wanted. This demands watchfulness both night and day; and
men are up from twelve o'clock at night until six the next night, one half keeping watch all night; and all, of course, being on horseback all day. The men
receive thirty dollars per month, and own their saddles and accoutrements.

"Do the men marry?" I asked one of the foremen. He seemed a little
puzzled at my question, but presently replied: "No; but they live with
women."

When children are born, if they can't take care of them, some more prosperous friend, who is the man's "padrone," takes charge of them. Very few,
I was told, ever marry. They change about a good deal. There are no schools
for the children, and no churches. The men drink, more or less.

This is the substance of replies to many inquiries I made; and as I rode
over the plain I saw no schools or churches, not even a Catholic priest.

It seems to be a wild, rough, godless, and disreputable sort of life, in which
the rich employer, kind and liberal as he may be, gives no heed to the morals
of his men or to their intelligence.

In the wheat country of Merced, though most of the people were renters,
and the houses were small and mean and far apart, there were school-houses.
I saw the little children riding or driving to school: on Sunday somebody

13

preaches in the little school-house; and there is at least a chance that the children shall grow up into reputable citizens. But what is to become of the children raised in such a cattle district as I have described? Has not the community a right and duty to compel the erection of school-houses, the maintenance of schools, and the attendance of children, as measures of legitimate self-defense?

The land about Firebaugh's and lower down is good, but needs water. The King's River Irrigating Ditch will supply it to a considerable district, and Mr. Miller is reported to have sown 1000 acres of alfalfa this spring, which needs irrigation two years here, but is thereafter a very profitable hay crop. There are also some crops of wheat and barley put in, but most of the land west of the San Joaquin, about Firebaugh's, is given over to cattle and sheep.

As you journey toward Visalia, you will notice that the telegraph poles, which are here of square sawn timber, are rubbed off quite smooth and round for about three feet from the ground. For thirty miles I did not see a single pole which was not thus polished. It is done by the cattle, who rub themselves against the poles until in many places these have had to be re-enforced with heavy posts to prevent their destruction.

NEVADA FALL, YOSEMITE VALLEY.

CHAPTER XX.

THE TULARE LAKE.—CHEAP FARMS FOR THE MILLION.

VISALIA, in these pleasant March days, is in a ferment—a very mild ferment—at the approach of the railroad.

I don't know how the Mohammedans of Mecca would act if a railroad was
within fifty miles of their Holy Place, and approaching at the rate of a mile a
day; but they would regard the engineers, I imagine, with something of the
same horror and aversion with which these emissaries of civilization are regarded by about one-third of Visalia.

For this town has long been the Mecca of the Pike. His cattle wandered
over a million of acres hereabout; his will was law; his vacqueros were the
ministers of his will, and his voice was public opinion. And now comes the
railroad, and—but I must let the Pike speak his own sentence: "Here you're
bringin' in this railroad, and that will bring a crowd of small farmers; the
Germans will rush in here soon; the whole darned country will be fenced in before you know it; and then it will be ruined forever." And having gone thus
far, John Pike opens his mouth a little wider, and lets out a mixture of profan-
ity and tobacco-juice, which presently leaves him in possession of the room.

The railroad is really a great civilizer. It not only quiets the Indians—it drives off the Pikes. They are selling out cheap, and emigrating by scores to Arizona; and if you were here now you might buy town lots and farms at very moderate prices, from men who "don't mean to live near no railroad—not if they know it."

They showed me a man down here who refused, some years ago, to let the telegraph-wires pass over his farm. "He didn't want the whole country to know every time he whipped his children," he said; and when it was explained to him that the wires did not of themselves take cognizance of passing events, he replied, "Well, anyhow, he'd always hearn that it killed corn."

There are Pikes with property, and Pikes without. When he has a farm, you may know it by a house with a room on each side, and a broad, open passage in the middle; carpets there are none; and if you go in, you shall find that they cook by an open fire, and that bacon, and stringy greens, and corn pone are the fare. He may be worth $20,000 or $40,000, but his door-yard is in a litter, and his first offer of hospitality is whisky. He is not a bad creature; profane he is, and rough, till rough seems too mild a word; but he is hospitable after his way; and if you are not a "pre-emptor of one hundred and sixty acres," he will treat you well.

Then there is the Pike who owns no land. Sometimes he is rich, too, for he has cattle, and they feed by hundreds on Congress land, with the rest. But oftenest he is poor; he lives in a wagon. I saw a man who had been living in his wagon for twenty years, and had raised a family in it. After the wagon toils a harmless old cow, with three or four calves following it. "It's wonderful how prolific the cattle of these fellows are, even in a dry season," said a man to me in Visalia; "why, I've seen one of them come into town with an old steer that had at least four calves following it, all born in the same year."

This poor John Pike has the knack of appropriating other people's calves, and turning them, as necessity demands, into sugar, coffee, bacon, and flour.

Well, the Pikes, poor and rich, are panic-struck. They are getting ready to leave the country before the railroad shall utterly ruin it. And they are wise. Their empire is gone. The small farmers are not following the railroad, for they precede it; and all over the great plain south of Visalia, and in the foot-hills, and even down near the shores of the great Tulare Lake, you see little boxes of houses standing far apart, the signs of small farmers who have here chosen each his one hundred and sixty acres, and who will no longer be worried and bullied by the cattle-owners.

You are to understand that the San Joaquin Valley, which contains about 24,000 square miles, or about 15,360,000 acres, and is two hundred and fifty miles long, by from sixty to one hundred and forty miles wide, has been given up, ever since the Americans came into the country, to cattle and horses. The farmers have year after year encroached upon the cattle, so that now few cattle are found north of Merced; and as far south as the San Joaquin River the farmers are disputing the land with cattle and antelopes, and you may see herds of cows and antelopes feeding within half a mile of a thousand-acre field of wheat.

But south of the San Joaquin cattle have been until now supreme, and their owners—who were not and are not always owners of the soil, but often mere squatters—have assumed all the power and airs of lords of the country.

They would have bought up the whole country before now, were it not reserved from the clutches of such land monopolists. When the Southern Pacific Railroad charter was granted by Congress, that corporation received, as has been usual, a land grant of alternate sections for twenty miles on each side of its road. It is entitled to build two lines; one running from Gilroy, or south of that, across the Coast Range, to Visalia, and thence southward, by way of Bakersfield, to the Tehatchapi Pass, and by way of San Bernardino to Fort Yuma; the other south and east of Tulare Lake, through the Bakersfield country again, and, by way of the Tehatchapi Pass, to Fort Mohave. Now, when Congress makes a land grant to a railroad, it reserves, by a custom which is of extreme importance, and which is yet, I think, little understood in the East, all the "even sections" from sale, and holds them exclusively for settlers under the homestead and pre-emption laws.

Thus land monopoly is entirely prevented. You may buy six hundred and forty acres from the railroad company; but you can not buy a single acre from the Government unless you settle on it and improve it for a year; and the country thus withheld from general sale is, in fact, dedicated to the use of small farmers, for no man can acquire a great body of land lying together, and no one man wants two or three alternate sections.

Thus the great fertile San Joaquin Valley is kept open by law for homes for the homeless. It has still, as nearly as I can ascertain, without reckoning the foot-hills, about two millions and a half acres of land owned either by the Government or the railroad company—one half by each; and upon the Congress land any citizen has the right to settle, taking eighty acres as a homestead for nothing, or one hundred and sixty acres by pre-emption and actual settlement, at two dollars and fifty cents per acre. The railroad sections are sold also in eighty, one hundred and sixty, three hundred and twenty, or six hundred and forty acre pieces; and the company gives actual settlers five years in which to make their payments.

Now, over this immense tract of fertile country cattle and horses have been roaming for years, and numbers of men have become rich by grazing, without owning an acre of land. A man may have a farm, but he does not keep his cattle on it. He lets them graze on the great uninclosed common; he gathers them up once a year, in the spring, and brands the calves; he sells them when they are fat; and he resents, as an invasion of his rights, the entrance of farmers upon this soil upon which he has grazed his cattle. He opposes the "no fence" law, because he knows that the pre-emptor can not afford to fence in his one hundred and sixty acres. He drives his cattle upon his poorer neighbor's wheat-field and destroys it in a night. He tells you that the country is not fit for farming; that it is a desert; that his cattle are starving; that it would take fifteen acres to support a sheep; that it has no water—how does his stock live?—that it is too hot, and too cold, and too full of alkali, and too heavy, and too light; and in short, he fibs to you, if he thinks you are a pre-emptor; and if he dared, he would shoot you.

But his empire has departed; he no longer rules supreme; the pre-emptors are in the majority, and defy him. The small farmers have this year given notice to the cattle-owners that if the cattle trespass they will be killed; and the courts and the juries have their sympathies with the small farmers. Many cattle-owners are already herding their stock; others are selling out; and yet others are driving their stock away into the mountains and far off districts.

The country about Visalia, for six or eight miles in every direction, looks like an old park, because of its magnificent oaks. These trees, like the oak generally in California, are low-branched, wide-spreading, gnarled; they are magnificent in size; many of them must be hundreds of years old; and they are disposed on the plain in most lovely groups, masses, and single specimens. You drive for miles among them; and you meet, very frequently, single trees so large, so stately and perfect, that a painter of trees would be enchanted with them. The mistletoe, which is the enemy of the oak in California, does not seem to trouble these trees about Visalia; I do not remember seeing any of this parasite, except on some oaks and cotton-woods near Tulare Lake.

I suspect that the oak groves make Visalia hotter in summer than the more open plain surrounding it. It has the reputation of being a hot place. Some years ago it was affected with malarious fevers; but the drainage caused by irrigation has, I suppose, removed the cause of these fevers, for it is now said to be healthful.

The whole San Joaquin Valley is hot; but the heat being dry, people do not suffer from it—such is the universal testimony—nearly as much as they do in the more eastern States. A farmer from Northern Illinois, who has lived near here two years, told me that he had seen the mercury at 100° in the shade. I asked him if he was not prostrated, and he said he did not feel it as much as 90° in Illinois; he could ride over the plains in the heat of the day, and did actually pursue his usual and necessary occupations.

"Then," said he, "the nights are always cool. Let it be ever so hot in the day, as soon as the sun sets the air is cool, and at night, after one of our hot days, we always sleep under blankets. Thus there is no such exhaustion from restless nights as in the East."

In fact, the climate is most kindly to little children, which is perhaps one of its best tests. One can not travel anywhere in California without noticing that the forms of the women who have lived some years here are more full and robust than with us; while the children are universally chubby, fat, and red-cheeked. I do not remember seeing anywhere in the State a single weakly, or what the Yankees call "peaked" looking child.

The Spanish California women begin to take on fat at an early age, and "lose their figure" often before they are twenty-five. All animals also fatten easily here, and horses are very commonly so fleshy that they would be thought unfit to drive or ride in the East.*

I found, to my surprise, that a good deal of wine is made around Visalia. The grape does admirably on the plains; it will do still better in the foot-hills, which are as yet but little occupied. A German, some miles from the town, makes a good wine; but none of the vineyardists have yet discovered how to make a mild table wine.

---

* As I was sending this page to the printer, my eye fell upon some sentences upon the climate of California in a work upon that State, "Californien, Land und Leute"—"California, its Land and People," by the eminent German traveler and savant Robert von Schlagintweit, just published in Leipzig. He writes: "The climate of California, with all the varieties which it manifests in different parts of the State, is yet, undoubtedly, in a high degree healthful. He who comes to this State from the Eastern States of America wonders at the fresh complexion of the people; he is pleasantly surprised at their healthful color, and the red blood in their cheeks, which he by no means commonly meets in his home. It is not an overstatement that all California is exempt from a number of diseases which are burdensome and dangerous in other regions; so that one may here expose himself, without danger, in many ways which in other regions would entail serious consequences to the health. Only in low-lying lands, which, as some parts of the Sacramento and San Joaquin valleys, are subject to overflow, and of which the quantity is less now than formerly, is miasma found; but the spread of this is narrowly limited by the universal dryness of the atmosphere. A thoroughly or constantly sickly region is not to be found in all California. * * * Where else except in California would men venture to settle permanently on land where, for miles around, the beds of rivers and brooks are emptied by turning the streams, and the bottom, consisting of alluvial deposit, is turned over by the gold-seekers, or where they dig away the river banks, and so soak the earth with water that it steams during the warm days?"

"The climate of California," continues Mr. Von Schlagintweit, "on the whole, resembles that of Italy, but without the unpleasant peculiarities of the Italian climate, whose chief injurious effect is to indispose the people to labor of hand or brain. The *dolce far niente* of the Southern Italian is unknown in California. The peculiarities of the Californian climate, which distinguish it from that of the States east of the Rocky Mountains, are that the summers are cooler and the winters warmer, and that there is neither a frequent nor a sharp change from heat to cold, or the reverse. The air, too, is drier; there are fewer cloudy days, less thunder, and fewer storms than in the Eastern United States. To this must be added a circumstance most important and delightful to the inhabitants of California, that the nights are always cool and refreshing, even where, as in the low-lying valleys of the southern part of the State, the days are sometimes very hot. In some parts of the Sacramento and San Joaquin valleys the mercury rises at times to ninety-one degrees, and even, exceptionally, to one hundred degrees in the shade; but the dryness of the atmosphere, which favors a quick dispersion of the perspiration, makes even this heat by far easier to bear than the same temperature in a damper climate."

Several farmers make raisins, and at one farm I found them of excellent quality. I was told that a small crop had been sold at twenty-five cents per pound. The process of curing the grapes is very simple and easily carried on. They are dried partly in the sun, and afterward under cover—as in the loft of a barn. The Mission Grape does not make good raisins, but in several parts of the State men have planted the true raisin grape of Malaga, and it does well. The manufacture of raisins ought to be as profitable as that of wine, and far more beneficial to the State. Dried grapes are very commonly sold in the shops, and for cooking do nearly as well as raisins; but they are not very good to eat, and would not, I imagine, bear transportation.

When one compares the possibilities of this region with what he finds actually accomplished, he is always disappointed. The orange grows near and in Visalia; the olive would flourish there; of the English walnut there are some good trees, and in the foot-hills all these and the almond also would do well, even better, I think, than about Los Angeles; for in the foot-hills they have scarcely a touch of frost. But there are not more than six bearing orange-trees, nor a dozen olives within twenty miles of Visalia, and the culture of these profitable fruits is scarcely known.

The old settlers have but little energy for such new pursuits; and in general, where they do not keep cattle, they content themselves with wheat, barley, and other field crops, and do not plant trees. Yet the planting of trees for timber and fire-wood alone would be very profitable all over this valley; and no one who owns one hundred and sixty acres ought to lose a year without putting twenty acres into such trees as the locust and the eucalyptus.

It is not that the farmers are unintelligent. As a class, the people about here who raise grain are an admirable set of men, hardy, enterprising, not easily discouraged, and with a remarkable faculty for acting together for the general good. But they have lived a long time away from the rest of the State. Until this year, one could reach Visalia only by a tedious stage ride of thirty-six hours, and the people were not sufficiently in contact with the rest of the State. Moreover, most of them are poor.

There is a great deal of wealth in the immediate vicinity of Visalia, but it is chiefly in the hands of the cattle-owners, who are, every body tells me, the least civilized part of the community, and whose manner of living is poor and common. Men worth from $40,000 to $60,000 sometimes live in shanties, and, aside from a peach-orchard, have no sign of thrift or forethought about their places.

The truth is, that much of this great valley is so fit for a garden that it is wasteful to use it for a cattle or sheep range, or for field crops. Wherever the farmer can have water for irrigation, the careful culture of small tracts will pay, for many years to come, extraordinary profits. The hop will grow well anywhere about here, and as there is no rain to interfere with its maturing and gathering, it will, I suspect, some day be one of the staples of this region.

The vine, grown for raisins, will be found to yield here five times the profit per acre of wheat, and it is as cheaply cultivated.

The true way to keep cattle here is to soil them—for the beet and alfalfa grow all the year round. An intelligent sheep farmer remarked to me that he thought the whole present system of farming in this valley—which yet he follows—was a mistake. "The small farmers will make more money by soiling cattle by-and-by than the great stock-owners ever made, and will drive them out of the market," he said.

When I asked him why he did not change his system, he replied, "It is too late; I have grown old here, and can not change. But the new people will drive us all out. In the aggregate, the small farmers will raise many more cattle and sheep than we do, and they will sell them for a higher price, because they will be uniformly in better condition."

This I judge to be true; in fact, I do not know a country which is better adapted to farming, as we understand the word in the East. The seasons are such as to play into the farmer's hands; the soil is rich, and easily worked; one may plough during all those three months which are, in the East, the frozen winter months; and with irrigation every crop is sure, and every thing grows marvelously.

Without water, even in such years as this, full and very remunerative crops are obtained; but the farmer is exposed to the risk of droughts, and I advise every one who comes to California to farm to take care that the place he selects shall have sufficient water. In this valley there are as yet no artesian wells; but, lying as it does between two great mountain ranges, there is no reason to doubt that flowing wells can be got. There has not been enterprise enough in the whole valley to give artesian boring a trial, and in this particular it is far behind San Bernardino, which has an abundance of flowing wells. The stock and sheep owners who graze on these plains content themselves, when they have no natural water at hand, with digging wells, and pumping water for their stock. As they do not own the land, they are of course careless as to its permanent improvement. Irrigation is largely practiced about Visalia, and of one of the ditches I give some account in the next chapter.

FLUTTER-WHEEL ON THE TUOLUMNE.

CHAPTER XXI.

CO-OPERATIVE FARMING.—HOW IRRIGATING DITCHES ARE MADE.

SIX or seven miles north-east of Visalia lies a little hamlet called Farmersville. As you approach it, you find the land well fenced, the houses so near each other as to betoken what here are called small farms—one hundred and sixty-acre tracts; and orchards, and vineyards, and grain-fields in such numbers as to show a thrifty community.

This continues for some miles beyond Farmersville Post-office—up to the foot-hills indeed, and the farther you drive onward, the more water you see—running water, in ditches, large and small, until at last you come to a mill, which stands near the lower end of what is called the "People's Ditch," and has its water-power from that.

The aspect of the whole country-side which is included in this drive is that of a prosperous, well-established community, and, except that the farm-houses are insignificant and poor, as they are almost everywhere in this State, you might think yourself, in these March days, in a thrifty farming country in New York in the month of June; for the wheat and barley fields look green and rich, the peach-trees are just past their bloom, the roads are good, and little brooks run through pastures of what at a distance you might mistake for clover, but which is really alfalfa.

Now all this prosperity, which is not only apparent but real—for the drought of last year did not rob these farmers of a crop—comes of the "People's Ditch," and that, as its name denotes, came from the people themselves. Here is the story of this People's Ditch:

Four years ago several farmers about here saw the necessity of irrigation for their lands. They talked the matter over, and finally called a meeting of their neighbors. At this meeting it was resolved:

To dig a ditch;

To do it by a general effort of those who should subscribe to the stock;

To have one hundred shares, each share to be entitled to water enough for one hundred and sixty acres;

To elect a president, who should call out the stockholders to labor, which call should be promptly obeyed;

To engage an engineer to lay out the work, and to obey his instructions;

And, finally, to begin the work "next Monday."

The engineer was himself one of the stockholders, Mr. William S. Powell, of Visalia, an energetic and competent man, and the leader in the enterprise. Work was begun on the following Monday, and in six weeks the People's Ditch—eight miles long, twenty-four feet wide, and three feet deep—was completed. The sum of six hundred dollars was expended upon it, in money, for lumber for flumes and gates, etc.; all the rest of the work was done without the expenditure of a cent of money.

It was afterward found that this ditch did not give water enough, and the stockholders enlarged it and took in another stream, so that it is now fourteen miles long and four feet deep, with a pitch of eight feet to the mile.

It supplies more than enough water in the driest season to irrigate 16,000 acres of land—namely, one hundred 160-acre lots. Near the lower end of the ditch stands a grist-mill, which is a very great convenience to the neighborhood, and, I believe, a source of income to the Ditch Association. Out of the main ditch proceed three arms, and out of these, again, numerous smaller arms —as many, of course, as there are fields to irrigate. The water is divided by self-acting gates, and the arms or branches are dug, not by the company, but by those members interested.

The labor is far less difficult or tedious than any one who had not seen it done would suppose, and the success is complete. Last year the irrigated crops were almost, not quite, as great as those of a rainy year; and as prices were high, the farmers made more money. The man who can raise a crop in a year of severe drought is sure of a good price.

There is a water-master, who is paid to go over the ditch and see that all goes right with it; and a president who is not salaried, but has authority to call on the stockholders for repairs; and once a year, in March, when the farmer's work here is done, and he and his teams are idle, all hands meet to clean out the ditch, which is a labor of a few days. This annual ditch-meeting was held while I was in Visalia.

Now the work of six weeks of these farmers doubled the value of their land at once. It was about the cheapest way to make money that they could have devised. It made them sure of a crop, no matter how dry the year. It gave them a perpetual fund of manure; for the testimony of every man I have seen in the State who has practiced irrigation for a long term of years is positive that with this the fertility of the land does not deteriorate.

I was surprised and delighted to hear of one hundred farmers joining hands for such a work as this, and energetically carrying it through; but I have found since that this is not uncommon here. I have been present at several " ditch meetings;" they are usually held in the open field, and what they determine on they do.

I suspect that the frequent ploughing which irrigation in orchards and gardens necessitates has something to do with its efficacy. The soil bakes after it has been flooded, and must be ploughed to keep it mellow, else irrigation is a hinderance rather than a help. Orange orchards are irrigated about Los Angeles once in six weeks, and the plough is run through the ground two or three days after every irrigation. Grain fields in this part of the country are irrigated thoroughly before they are sowed.

" When you soak your field before the rains come on, and plough and sow so that the first rain shall catch the seed sprouting, that is high farming," said an intelligent farmer to me near Visalia.

They get, on the lighter soil, an average of twenty-three bushels of wheat and forty of barley to the acre about Visalia. On the best soil, forty bushels of wheat to the acre, I was assured, is not extraordinary. It is not a good corn country.

Unimproved land, within from two to five miles of the town, can be bought for from two dollars and fifty cents to four dollars per acre, in tracts of one hundred and sixty acres. Such land can be irrigated, but has no ditches dug; in common years it will bear a crop without water.

For improved farms, fenced, with wells, houses, out-buildings, and orchards, and with ditches dug for irrigating, thirty dollars per acre is thought a fair price. In the orchards I found plums, peaches, pears, apricots, apples, and small fruits. The apple does well, but the fruit does not keep well here. The subtropical fruits are not yet grown here, though they would do well. All the finer varieties of the vine flourish.

Gang-ploughs are used in the grain-fields; usually a sulky-plough, with two shares, drawn by two or three horses, the driver riding on the plough. Five acres can be got over in a day with this force. Summer fallowing, which,

TURNING A RIVER.

as practiced in this State, I have described in a previous chapter, is used here with eminent success, and is said to add a third to the crop, besides insuring a crop without irrigation, even in a dry year.

Alfalfa gives, with irrigation, four or five crops in the year, or from ten to twelve tons, and affords some pasture besides.

Horses cost from twenty to eighty dollars, the higher price bringing a good stout creature. Milch-cows cost fifty dollars. The whole country is full of chickens and turkeys. Farm hands receive thirty dollars a month and their food. It is the custom here for farm laborers to furnish their own bedding and wash their own clothes. Harvest hands get two dollars a day and food, and they will get more this year.

There are as yet only about seventy acres of vineyard in the whole of Tulare County. The vine does admirably, and vineyards will be even more profitable than before, now that the railroad makes cheap shipment possible.

To prepare the ground and plant a vineyard costs, exclusive of the cuttings, about ten dollars per acre. At five years of age the product is reckoned at 1000 gallons to the acre, of must or grape juice. This is sold on the ground at twenty cents per gallon, or two hundred dollars, and the cost of cultivation is about fifty dollars per acre. The vine bears in the second year from the cutting. It is usual to irrigate it for a year after planting; after that it makes its own way, and there is no doubt that vineyards not irrigated produce the best wine.

Of course you will remember that the varieties grown here are those which we can grow only in hot-houses in the East. They bear prodigiously here, and I believe are entirely free from disease. The Rose of Peru, one vineyardist told me, gave him, the past dry season, forty pounds to the vine. The White Muscat does not bear so well here as most other varieties, but the Malaga grape does excellently, and it is from this that raisins are made.

The farmers about Visalia are, in the main, an intelligent and hospitable class, ready to welcome new-comers, and helpful in every way. Many of them are quite poor, but poverty is not so oppressive in this mild climate as with us, and the railroad, which will cheapen their supplies and widen their market, will add very much to their prosperity.

Lumber has been very dear here—fifty dollars per 1000 for fencing boards—and this has really retarded the advancement of the country. But the railroad will give them cheap lumber, and the no-fence law, which Tulare, Kern, and Fresno counties are sure to have from the next Legislature, will make the farmers independent of the stock-owners.

Visalia will, I think, be the largest city in the valley; it has a number of intelligent and enterprising merchants, who will not let slip their opportunity. Both Visalia and Bakersfield will make a rapid growth, now that they are to have railroad communications with the rest of the world.

From Visalia I drove, in company with Mr. Powell, the engineer I spoke of above, down to Tulare Lake, along the lake shore for some miles, and then across the broad plain to the foot-hills. We drove, in fact, over a vast flower-garden. The plain, in this month of March, is in a blaze of color. Yellow, orange, purple, blue, and white are the predominant hues; and they lie in broad sheets of separate and distinct colors, massed as the landscape-gardeners say, so that you see now a thousand acres glowing like a fierce fire with the orange eschscholtzia; and again a square mile or two, or a broad stripe, of the delicate purple and white of the lupine, with which, where it lies thus in masses, the sunlight plays the most fantastic tricks, now to your eyes obliterating the white, and again, as the light strikes in some different direction, bringing it out so that at a distance your field of purple lupines shines white almost, as though the snow covered the ground. The phlox and a delicate little yellow flower fill the air with a delicious fragrance, through which we drove for miles, the horses wading knee-high, and in many places breast-high through vast flower-beds.

We camped near the lake, and in the morning I was awakened by a noise like the rush of a distant railroad train. I saw a long line of fluttering white in the far distance toward the lake, which represented, I found, an immense body of wild geese, whose wings and cries, as they moved from place to place, caused this kind of roaring noise. When, later in the day, we drove along the flat shore of the lake, clouds of geese rose on all sides of us, and at one point a long white line, shining like the surf on a sea-beach, showed us a great flock, extending more than two miles along the shore, which presently began to shiver and flare in the bright sunlight, as the whole mass rose with a great rush, flew off a mile or two into the lake, and once more settled down.

A great part of the bottom of Tulare Lake is so shallow that a fall of two or three feet in the waters would leave thousands of acres of rich land dry and fit for cultivation. In fact, probably 15,000 acres on the eastern side of the lake alone have become dry land within eighteen months, and are now covered with cattle, grazing on nutritious grasses.

An English company has bought, I hear, 30,000 or 40,000 acres of land on the shore of the lake, and proposes to permanently redeem this tract and a large body besides, by surrounding the lake with a levee to confine its waters. This seemed to me at a distance a difficult undertaking, but it is very easy and cheaply done, for the plough will do most of the work, and the water is so shallow—hogs wade out in the summer season half a mile into the lake to root up shell-fish—that the embankment may lie far out and yet need not be very high.

A double end will be gained by this embankment, for the land for miles around the lake is so level that it may be easily and cheaply irrigated if the levee raises the surface of the lake only a few feet; and thus an extensive and valuable tract of agricultural land will be redeemed and brought under cultivation.

It is amazing to see so large and fine a country as this lying unoccupied. The land is clear and ready for the plough, and almost the whole of it is fertile. There are here and there patches of alkali land, but they are of inconsiderable extent, and the farmer, now that the Southern Pacific Road is opening this country by giving it quick and cheap connection with markets, may pay for his land twice over with a single crop. There is no danger from land monopoly, for no man can obtain more than six hundred and forty acres in a single tract; and at the Visalia land-office they told me that a great many pre-emptors and homestead settlers are coming in already.

I found that it is one of the advantages of the farmers here that they can pasture horses and cattle on the public and railroad lands near them which are unoccupied. A farmer stakes out his few cattle or horses during the winter, spring, and summer, and they get abundant food from the pastures.

Even working cattle are fed here without grain. I drove a hundred miles with a pair of horses which did not in the whole distance receive an ounce of barley; when we camped at night the horses were staked out in the open plain; they ate themselves full during the night, and kept fat.

Even hogs are turned adrift on the plain. They make their way to the shore of Tulare Lake, where they spend the summer hunting roots and shellfish among the tule reeds; when the acorns ripen they return to the oak groves about Visalia to feed on the mast, and they keep fat all the time. Each farmer marks his own, and toward winter hunts them. Black hogs seem to do better here than the white, and Chester Whites, which have been tried, have given place to the Essex, of which I saw numbers of fine specimens.

Among the younger cattle on the plains there is evidence of improved blood, and some fine Devon bulls are kept in the country, I was told; but the immense horns and savage front which make the Texas cattle disagreeable objects are still common here. All the cattle are fat, and everywhere we saw them contentedly lying down in the middle of the day, which is a sign that food is abundant.

14

A FLUME.

CHAPTER XXII.

BEET SUGAR, SILK, ETC.

THE beet grows so well in Southern California that I do not doubt the
State will make, in a few years, a very large quantity of beet sugar.   I
have seen beets that had grown for eighteen months; and wherever in the
State I found a thrifty farmer, there I found that he "soiled" his cows on
beets, with great ease and profit.

A region in which green crops grow all the year round is, of course, the
best for this manner of keeping stock.   In an Eastern State, farmers who
soil their cattle can cut green food for them only during six, or at most
eight months in the year; but here you may cut in every month the most suc-
culent vegetables and grasses for the beasts.   You need only plant beets and
alfalfa.

But it was of beet sugar that I began to speak.   There are, so far as I
know, but two beet-sugar manufactories now in California.   One of these lies
four miles east of Sacramento.   It is very completely furnished, and its manager is a German engineer of approved experience and skill in the business, who
has been brought out by the company.   I walked with him over the factory,

and later rode over the beet-fields. The machinery used is of the latest and best kind; much of it was imported from Germany; some parts have been made in this State, from the manager's drawings.

I shall not attempt to describe the machinery itself. Some parts of it, as Lord Dundreary would say, no fellow could be expected to understand. What struck me here, as it has in other California manufactories, is the great advantage they have in not being obliged to use any precautions against frost, cold, and snow. Machinery must, of course, be well bedded and braced; but otherwise a manufacturing building in this State may be as slight and airy as you please, and thus a large expense is saved.

Here, for instance, the water used in the different processes is pumped into the upper story from an artesian well one hundred and fifty feet deep. The pump stands in a shed; and the water-pipes run up on the outside of the building. The storage-house for beets is by no means such a frost-proof structure as it would have to be with us.

It seems to me that these advantages, arising out of a mild climate, will do somewhat—how much I can not tell—to counterbalance the higher price of labor in this country.

In other respects the climate, too, appears to be singularly favorable to the successful culture of the beet, and the development in it of the greatest quantity of saccharine matter. In the first place, the seasons in this State are certain and sharply marked. The rains begin in November. Beets, which in France are sown between April 24 and May 10, are here sown in January and February. Voelcker, a writer of authority on this subject, states that the more rain falls on the land during the first two months of the growth of the beet, the better the crop is likely to be—if a dry season follows. Now, in California, all the rain-fall of the year occurs from November to April, and after April—that is to say, when the beet begins to require a dry season, to develop its saccharine quality—comes here the dry season, when rain is so absolutely unknown that, during the summer, the farmers leave their grain piled up in bags along the railroads, often for two months. The rain-fall and the absence of rain come with precision and certainty, at the proper times for the beet.

The Sacramento Beet Sugar Company have expended, in buildings, machinery, and five hundred and forty acres of choice land, $225,000. They have rented other land, so that they have sown to beets, this season, 1100 acres, from which they hope to get an average of ten tons of beets to the acre. In France they get from twelve to fifteen tons to the acre; in England, it is reported, they have got eighteen tons to the acre. At Chatsworth, in Illinois, and also in Wisconsin, I believe they got but ten tons to the acre.

I am satisfied that the methods of culture can be improved in California. Deep ploughing is hardly understood, as yet, in this State; and thus the real wealth and producing power of the soil are not utilized.   But the beet here yields a much larger percentage of sugar than in Europe; and with the favorable climate, and rich virgin soil, this does not surprise me.   The polariscope test gives from twelve to sixteen and a half per cent. of saccharine, which is from one to three per cent. more than in Europe.

The field culture and general work of the farm are done by Chinese laborers.   The manager has perfected a seed-sower, which sows twelve rows at once, and is believed to be an improvement over all machines used for this purpose hitherto.   The seed this year came up very evenly and regularly.

The beets are thinned in the rows, weeded, and dug, by hand.   In Europe a digger is used; but this has not yet been introduced here.   The Chinese, who work in gangs, each gang under a leader chosen by themselves, receive five dollars per week.   For this they feed themselves, the company paying a cook for every thirty men.   They furnish, also, their own bedding and cooking utensils, and are lodged in very cheap shanties, the climate making substantial houses for them needless.

The 1100 acres planted this year will employ the factory about eight months, and the manager hopes to turn out at least 10,000 barrels of sugar.   Only the whitest sugar is made.   A ton of beets ought to yield, I am told, a barrel of sugar.   The refuse of the beets is fed to stock, and I saw cows leaving green grass and grain to eat this bagasse.   A milkman told me that cows fed on this refuse made good butter and milk; but I should think it would be found especially valuable for fattening cattle.   For this it is much used in France, a little grain being fed only for a few days before the beasts are sent to the shambles.

France, the German Empire, and Austria now produce nearly as much sugar as all the tropical world exports, yet the industry dates in Europe only from the beginning of this century.   As population increases in California, I see no reason to doubt that beet-sugar making will become one of the most profitable and one of the most important industries in the State.   That it has had an important beneficial effect upon the preservation of the land, and largely increased the wealth of the farmers who have engaged in it in France and Germany, is well known; and in California, where so much of the land is year after year sown to wheat, it will be a very great advantage to farmers, and encourage a more solid and thrifty style of farming, to introduce this culture.

At present it is necessary for a manufacturer to grow his own beets, just as the vineyardist makes his own wine; but a sounder system will come in, as factories increase, under which the manufacturer will contract for beets grown by farmers.   In some parts of Europe this is done to a great extent, and the farmer is guaranteed a certain price per ton for his beets, on the condition that he conforms in his field-work to certain specified rules of the manufacturer.

At the Sacramento works the beet seed cost this year $10,000—an important item, which will be saved next year, for the company will raise their own seed. The two manufactories—that at Sacramento and that at Alvarado—have been at work for a season only previous to this. Of course this first season was experimental; but I have heard in San Francisco, not from the manufacturers, that the profit from the investment was so large as to satisfy even the high rates of interest which prevail here, and to promise returns so handsome that, if they are realized, there will soon be dozens of beet-sugar factories where now there are but two.

In the San Joaquin Valley alone there are hundreds of thousands of acres admirably suited to beet culture. The soil is light and yet rich, easily pene- trated by the plough, and needing only deep culture to produce a sure crop even in dry years. The Chinese, who are so excellent in every thing which re- quires minute care and patient toil, will make the very best field-hands for beet farming; and their manner of life—they furnish always their own supplies of every kind—will make their employment much less burdensome than is that of white laborers, who have to be fed and lodged.

California is also capable of producing silk of good quality; climate and soil both favor the mulberry-tree and the silk-worm; yet a great deal of money has been lost or wasted in silk-culture.

One need not remain long in California to discover that prudence rarely be- comes a vice among its people. They are quick-witted, enterprising, and very ready to turn to new employments. They have done many new things so well, that they do not lack faith in themselves. And they have a singular way of using the multiplication-table. For instance: some ingenious, laborious, and careful person tried the culture of silk-worms on a small scale. He planted an acre or two with trees; and he was able to demonstrate that, when the trees were sufficiently grown, he had cleared in a year some prodigious sum—say two thousand dollars per acre—and he had achieved this without severe labor.

Now if one can clear two thousand dollars from an acre of mulberry-trees, any school-boy who has got his multiplication-table by heart can tell you that you should, at the same rate, clear two hundred thousand dollars from a hun- dred acres. Land is cheap; mulberry-trees cost but a trifle in the nurseries; the price of labor, of silk-worm eggs, etc., is known beforehand; knock off fifty per cent. for bad seasons and inexperience, and there remains still a handsome fortune per year from a hundred acres of land.

Can any thing be plainer—or safer? Not to a rapidly-calculating Califor- nian, certainly; and accordingly, as a matter of fact, some investments were made on this scale; and to the amazement and disgust of the investors, they failed. What was true of an acre was not true of a hundred acres. "Figures don't lie," is an old and very foolish proverb. In fact, nothing lies so fright- fully as the multiplication-table.

Silk culture will succeed in California wherever it is pursued cautiously and intelligently, upon a moderate scale. In the haste and fury to work what was thought to be an enormously profitable field, men planted in hundreds of cases the wrong kind of tree—the *Morus multicaulis* instead of the *Morus alba* and *moretti*. One farmer planted a million of such trees, and, I have heard, never raised an ounce of worms or a pound of silk.

Moreover, they planted the trees in swampy and low places, because there they made the rankest growth; forgetting that the worm must have for its food wholesome, well-matured leaves. They would not wait for the trees to mature, but began to feed from young, immature trees. They planted the trees too close together; I have myself seen plantations where they stood almost as thickly as corn; this was to get the State's premium of three hundred dollars for a thousand trees of a certain age.

In short, the business was not rightly conducted in most cases; wherever it has been well managed it has succeeded. But my own conviction, as that of many Californians, is, that silk-worms will do best in the hands of the farmer's family; and that silk will become an important product of the State only when small farmers commonly plant a dozen or a hundred trees near their houses, and let their wives and children manage a few worms.

This can be easily done; the care is not great, the labor is very light, and in such cases no extra buildings are needed; and thus, with American ingenuity, will be produced some day, a large quantity of silk in California.

CATHEDRAL ROCKS, YOSEMITE VALLEY.

CHAPTER XXIII.

WINE-GROWING IN CALIFORNIA.—SOME ESTIMATES OF COST.—RAISINS.

ON our way through Tuolomne County, at Columbia, a hamlet among the mountains, our stage-coach was stopped to water the horses. As the day was warm some of us asked for water for ourselves, whereupon a man standing at the gate of the farm-house remarked, "If you prefer wine, there is a wine-cellar at the house."

Accordingly we walked up to the house and found a cellar well stocked with wine—a red wine which they call claret here, but which is thin, and to my taste too strong for claret, and a very sweet angelica, almost like sirup. Both kinds were drawn for four or five of us, freely, and the charge for all, modestly asked, was "six bits"—seventy-five cents. For a bottle of "claret" to be taken away, seventy-five cents was also demanded. The man had an excellent vineyard; and you see the vine on all the hill-tops in this and the adjoining counties.

Dining with a friend in San Francisco, we found on the table California claret, two kinds of white wine—one made from the German Riesling grape, and very good indeed—angelica, port, sherry, and a native sparkling wine. At

San José and elsewhere in country hotels you find a considerable list of native wines, but they bring you French wines unless you insist upon the native product.

The native wine is cheap; but it is "the thing" to put French wines on the table; and, though Landsberger's dry Champagne, or his sweeter sparkling muscatel, is both cheap and pure and good, your friend will not present it without an apology, and takes care, in his eager hospitality, to press upon you French Champagne.

The business of raising grapes and making them into wine is already a very great one in California, and will increase rapidly for years to come. As I have traveled through the State, and have seen the vineyards, I have again and again wondered what becomes of all the wine that is already made here.

Yet it is all consumed; there is very little three-year-old wine in any of the vineyards or cellars; and no matter how remote or how far from the great markets he may be, the wine-maker sells his wine oftenest at what is really a high price, as fast as he can make it.

There are, for instance, seventy acres of vineyard about Visalia, in the San Joaquin Valley. Of course this is not much; but Visalia has, until this year, lain almost as much out of the world as though it were in the Sandwich Islands. It had no railroad—the Southern Pacific Railroad has but just reached it, and will, before October, extend through the whole great valley to Bakersfield—and wine does not bear transportation by wagon by reason of its bulkiness; yet there is no old wine about Visalia.

At San Bernardino, too, the wine-makers could hardly supply the demand, they told me; and Dr. Edgar's vineyard, which lies twenty-five miles east of San Bernardino, in the San Gorgonio Pass, sells all its wine, an excellent mild wine like a good Sauterne, before it is two years old.

As for the Sonoma and Napa vineyards near San Francisco, a few of their owners, men of capital, purposely keep their wine, as do Dr. Bugby and some other vineyardists in other counties; but most of them sell it, as fast as it is made, to the wine houses in San Francisco or in the East. It will perhaps show you how great is the consumption of California wines, if I tell you that the house of Landsberger and Company in San Francisco, which successfully manufactures Champagne, and is, I believe, the only house which has succeeded in this business in San Francisco, finds it difficult to supply the demand for its sparkling wines west of St. Louis.

All this means that wine-growing in California, so far from being overdone, as I imagined it might be, is still in its infancy, with the demand increasing every year faster than the production. The planting of vineyards goes on steadily, and every year men learn better where and what to plant, and how to manage the wine.

There is one fact about California wine which entitles it to the preference of wine-drinkers—it is pure grape-juice. The grape grows so freely, bears so abundantly, and ripens so well, in this State, that it does not pay to adulterate the grape-juice. The wine producer can better afford to sell the juice of his grapes than he could to manufacture any artificial compound. What may be done with the wine when it gets to the East I do not know, but here the wine-maker tells you openly this (white or red wine) is the pure juice of the grape; this (port-wine) has such a quantity of brandy added to it, to make it keep, and to make it port-wine; this (angelica) has also brandy. The brandy is made in the vineyard, from the same grapes which yield the wine, and is added by the vineyardist. It is no secret at all; and I am persuaded that he who wants pure grape-juice can buy it in California without the least danger of being cheated by adulterations.

The famous Sonoma and Napa vineyards are, in May, a most lovely sight. The heavy frost which came late in April this year did not hurt them seriously, and the vines are crowded with young bunches of grapes. The crop promises well.

I was surprised to find the Sonoma Valley to consist in large part of a gravelly, red, arid soil, which would scarcely pay to plant with grain; I think it would make even poor pasture. But it is precisely the soil required by the vine; and it was a valuable discovery of the Hungarian Haraszthy, the father of wine-culture in this State, that the barren Sonoma hills would grow wine. He did not live to see how great a business his zeal and knowledge was to found, but his sons are yet engaged in the culture of the vine in the valley, so large a part of which he was instrumental in planting.

As the grape can be successfully grown in almost every part of Southern California, I shall be doing some of my readers a service, perhaps, by giving some account of the cost of making a vineyard. The following details apply to Sonoma and Napa; but they will, I am told, vary little, if at all, in other parts of the State, except as to the price of land, vine land being cheaper in the San Joaquin Valley than in Sonoma, and dearer in some other parts of the State.

Good grape land can be bought from four to seven miles of Sonoma for from twenty to twenty-five dollars per acre. If it lies high up on the hill-sides it may be a little cheaper, but it will cost more to clear it. Such land, on which the best grapes grow well, is often so poor that it would hardly support goats.

The average size of vineyards is, I find, from twenty-five to thirty-five acres. Of course there are some larger. One man with one horse can cultivate and keep in order twenty-five acres, but he will need help at the time of picking.

Fencing costs, in the Sonoma Valley, four hundred and fifty dollars per mile, for a four-board fence. In some parts of the State it would cost more; but there I should advise the planting of willows and sycamores for fences.

Ploughing to break the ground costs three dollars per acre. On the steeper hill-sides it would cost five dollars, and from ten to fifteen dollars for grub-bing and taking out the stones, where that is necessary; harrowing, one dollar and fifty cents per acre; laying off, two dollars; digging holes, three dollars. The holes are usually fifteen inches in diameter, and a spade and a half deep.

Cuttings of the vine cost seven dollars per thousand, and of the foreign va-rieties they now plant one thousand to the acre.

Planting, three to five dollars per acre.

Cultivation in the year of planting—Suckering, one dollar; cultivating and harrowing, three dollars; total, four dollars. Second year—pruning, one dol-lar and fifty cents, and fifty cents to take away the brush; ploughing and cul-tivating, seven dollars; suckering, two dollars; total, eleven dollars. Third year—pruning, five dollars; taking away brush, one dollar; ploughing and cul-tivation, one dollar; suckering, two dollars; total, eighteen dollars. In this year the vines will produce a little, say ten dollars per acre.

In the fourth year the vineyard pays, or should pay, if it has been carefully attended, a profit. It should yield an average of three thousand pounds of grapes to the acre. The cost of picking and hauling is about one dollar and fifty cents per acre; and there should be a net or clear profit in this year of eleven dollars and fifty cents per acre.

In the fifth year the vines will yield (one thousand vines to the acre) six thousand pounds; in the sixth year, eight thousand pounds; and this is a fair product. There are vineyards which produce twice as much as this, but they are exceptional.

According to this account, which I received in the Sonoma Valley, and in which a number of experienced vineyardists concurred, a vineyard should cost, at the close of the third year, fifty dollars and fifty cents per acre, less ten dol-lars received that year, or net, forty dollars and fifty cents.

As the business is now conducted, every vineyardist makes his own wine, and this, which seems to me a thoroughly bad and unbusiness-like system, nec-essarily involves the grape-grower in new and continually increasing expenses. For he must add to his vineyard a wine-cellar, which is as though a wheat-grower should also have to build a flour-mill.

For a vineyard of thirty acres there are required: a cellar thirty feet square, with a press-house over it, which will cost, in Sonoma, one thousand dollars; and casks, which will cost—fourteen thousand gallons at eleven cents —one thousand five hundred and forty dollars. He must also have a crusher and presses, one hundred and fifty dollars; two vats, one hundred and fifty dol-lars; hose, pumps, etc., one hundred dollars; so that he needs at once nearly three thousand dollars of capital. If he has it, well enough; but if he must borrow it, at from one to one and a half per cent. per month, it will keep him poor for some years.

A better way, to my mind, would be to let the grape-grower sell his grapes to the wine-maker, and thus save himself an investment for which his capital is oftenest inadequate. This is now done to some extent; and as the business is more systematized, I imagine it will be the usual way.

At present, I am told, when the grape-grower also makes wine, the vineyard in the fifth year will yield ten thousand gallons of wine, worth, in the cellar, three thousand dollars if from native, or four thousand five hundred dollars if from foreign grapes, for a crop of thirty acres. Cultivation will have cost eighteen dollars per acre; picking the grapes, three dollars per acre; making the wine, thirteen dollars and twenty cents per acre; or a total of expenses of thirty-four dollars and twenty cents per acre; which would leave a net profit from native grapes of sixty-five dollars and eighty cents per acre, in the fifth year of the vineyard, from which must still be deducted interest on the investment.

It is a part of the profit of the vineyardist to make brandy from the refuse of the wine-press. But here, again, he must invest more money in a still, in casks and barrels, and in stamps and taxes; so that in the majority of the smaller vineyards the refuse is thrown away.

Many of the foreign varieties of grapes which were brought to this State by the late Mr. Haraszthy thrive here; and the new vineyards are planted almost entirely with these. The native or mission grape will continue to do the best on the foot-hills of the Sierra, where it is hot in the summer. Elsewhere —and probably there too, the Muscat of Frontignan, Black Pineau, Zinfandel, Riesling, Black Malvoisia, Chasselas, Berger, Traminer, White Malaga, and some others, do well. There are probably others; and the experience from which men judge is not yet very wide. But those I have mentioned, it is certain now, will if properly planted yield good wine.

I notice that many of the new vineyards are planted more closely than the old. Formerly they put six hundred and eighty vines to the acre; now one thousand is thought better, and I saw in some places even one thousand six hundred to the acre.

I was surprised to find that it is not thought useful to break vine-ground with a subsoil plough. They plough about seven or eight inches deep, and I was told that in Sonoma there is a "hard-pan" in many of the best vineyards within a spade's depth of the surface. They do not irrigate the vineyards there, and I believe that if the ground is properly prepared it will not be found necessary to irrigate vineyards anywhere where vines should be planted.

In Sonoma and Napa a large proportion of the vineyardists are Germans. There are some Frenchmen, and many Americans. I was told that the Americans, where they attend to the business, become the most skillful and successful of all, and that the French do the least well.

Chinese laborers are employed in all parts of the business. They quickly learn to prune and take care of the vines, and their labor is indispensable. In the San Joaquin Valley, and in Southern California generally, the Indians, who are there a laboring force as valuable as the Chinese here, are equally useful in the vineyard. I have seen them pruning the vines, and they are used in all the operations of the vine producer.

The area in California on which the grape can be successfully grown for wine is so great that this State will some day—and that before many years— produce wine and brandy for the whole world.

In thirty-five out of the forty-four counties of the State, the grape for wine has been and is now successfully grown, though the larger part of the wine is produced in Sonoma, Napa, Los Angeles, El Dorado, Yuba, Solana, Santa Cruz, Santa Clara, Sacramento, and Tulare counties.

The climate is perfect—the grape ripens fully every year. There are no early frosts, as in Germany and France, to hasten the picking. An experienced wine-maker said to me, "With us, here, every year is a comet year. We have as good a season every year as they have only once in a dozen years in France and Germany." And every year they are learning here how to make better and lighter wine.

Not only, as I was assured by German wine-growers, do the California vineyardists manage their part of the business—the picking and pressing of the grapes and the earlier fermentation of the wine—more cleanly, intelligently, and skillfully than in Europe, but the whole after-process of manufacture is a great improvement over European processes; better casks are used; the cellars, which are here almost always above ground, owing to the evenness of the temperature, are cleaner, and the whole treatment is better. And finally, the great aim and chief difficulty of the California wine-maker being to produce a light wine—or what he imagines to be such—he is not tempted to give "body" to his product by adulterating it with spirits.

The wine merchants and exporters buy the grape-juice of the vineyardists. They watch the crop with some care as it is growing. They advise the farmers of whom they propose to buy concerning the treatment of their vineyards; but they do not buy the grapes, but only the juice, and of that only such as on trial they are satisfied with; of what is left unsold the farmers make brandy.

Every large vineyard, I am told, presently acquires a character of its own, either by reason of its soil or for the method and carefulness of culture.

I think an Eastern man has little idea, until he visits one of the large winehouses in San Francisco, what an immense business this has become. Mr. Haraszthy, of the house of Landsberger and Co., showed us through his large establishment, and we were permitted to see the whole process of making sparkling wines, which can be conducted in the cool and equal climate of San Francisco entirely above ground. It is much simpler than I supposed, and takes much less time than in France. The white wine from various vineyards is so mixed that fifty or even a hundred and fifty thousand gallons are obtained of precisely the same quality. This wine is then run into vats, from which—being first carefully tested with the saccharometer, it is decanted into bottles. These are placed on racks, in a warm room, where the process of change in the wines begins which makes them sparkling and effervescing. Both the filling and corking are done by machinery. When the wine has begun to clear itself, the bottles are placed cork downward, and the sediment is gradually deposited near the cork.

In the next process, a man takes each bottle gently in his hand and cuts the string which confines the cork, holding the bottle in a little closet. Out goes the cork, and with it the whole sediment, and a very little wine. Now it is passed to another hand, who pours in a small, fixed quantity of sirup made from rock-candy; the next man puts the bottle under an engine which rapidly corks it; the next wires it; and then it is carried to a lower apartment, where we saw 60,000 bottles on racks, with their noses slanted toward the ground. Here each bottle is slightly shaken in the rack, once a day for six weeks, by men who wear wire masks to save their eyes when a bottle explodes. They lose about four per cent. by breakage in this process; and when this is done the wine is clear; and, after "seasoning" for three or four months, is "complete," or fit for consumption.

The demand, however, is so great for this sparkling wine that it has seldom time to season. It is sold and consumed for the most part in the territories and the States west of the Mississippi, though the manufacturers have some regular customers as far east as Boston. As it is both cheap and pure, I imagine that those who use it do better than those who drink French Champagne at a higher price, and certainly far better than those who buy the cheap, gas-impregnated sparkling wines which are "made" in New York, and sold with French labels. Three kinds of sparkling wine are made by this house—one, a dry wine, from what is called the Mission grape, which was introduced here by the Spanish priests; another, made from a selection of foreign varieties of grapes; and a third, the sparkling Muscatel, which seems to be the favorite in California, which comes from the White Muscat of Frontignan.

There are, of course, other manufacturers of sparkling wines; and some idea of the magnitude of the business may be got from the fact that of the bottles—which are still imported from France—150,000 are kept on hand, empty, at all times by this one house, besides those filled and in the manufactory, which number 80,000 or 90,000.

Though the cork-tree would grow well in California, there are no plantations, and corks also are imported. The first corks cost two cents, and the last six cents, apiece, and about one third are rejected as unsound.

A company of capitalists are now planning an enterprise which will considerably facilitate the work of the vineyardist in the neighborhood of San Francisco Bay. It is proposed to erect at Vallejo a building roomy enough to store half a million gallons of wine; and intended to receive wine on storage, the company selling it on commission, and making advances on it to the wine-growers.   It is proposed to rent casks to the wine-growers, and thus to save these the expense of constantly increasing cellars of their own.   The railroads centering at Vallejo now connect, I was told, with vineyards containing not less than twenty millions of vines, which will yield, when they come into full bearing, probably ten million gallons of wine.   The wine product of the whole State was but six and a half million gallons last year; it can be easily seen, therefore, with what rapidity the wine crop is likely to increase in the next half-dozen years.

There is no reason to doubt that raisins will also, before many years, form an important crop in California.   Raisins are already made in the State—a few of excellent quality; but the business is not well understood, and the vineyards planted with the White Malaga grape have not come into full bearing.

The White Malaga is the true raisin grape.   It has a thin skin and small seeds.   Raisins made of the Mission grape are tough and have large seeds, and are thus of poor quality.   The White Malaga needs, I am told, a rich soil and a hot summer, and it is supposed that it will do best in the foot-hills, though I have seen it flourish also on the plains.   It should yield in this State, if well planted, I am assured, about ten thousand pounds of grapes to the acre; and raisin-makers here reckon four pounds of grapes to one of raisins.

The long dry summer and fall of California offer peculiar advantages for drying all fruits; what is needed here for raisins is experience in making them. The grapes must be picked before they are too ripe; the unsound ones must be cut from the bunches; they must be dried in places sheltered from the winds; and the whole process requires a certain amount of care, without which success is not to be achieved.

HYDRAULIC MINING, AT FRENCH CORRAL.

CHAPTER XXIV.

A GOLDEN VALLEY.

BAKERSFIELD lies on what is called Kern Island, a large tract of extraordinarily rich alluvial land, abundantly watered by the Kern River, which flows about and past it into Kern Lake after emerging from the mountains through a romantic pass within sight of the town.

This pass, as well as Kern Lake, I hear, Bierstadt is soon to visit at the instance of General Beale, the owner of the Tejon Rancho near here. It is too early in April to go into the mountains, or I should be tempted to precede Mr. Bierstadt; for the head-waters of the Kern are said to contain some scenery equal to the Yosemite in grandeur and stupendous proportions, and the region is very little known except to a few hunters and frontiersmen.

The distance from Bakersville is not great; and as the railroad is to be here on the first of September, no doubt by next year a road will be made over which tourists can conveniently visit what I believe, from descriptions I have heard down here, a very remarkable piece of country.

Moreover, along the Sierra foot-hills, for the whole distance from abreast of Visalia to opposite Bakersfield, there extends a forest of the great sequoia—

the Big Tree of California—a belt of this timber nearly one hundred and fifty miles long by about ten wide, which contains trees said to be larger even than the largest in the Mariposa and Calaveras groves.   One tree was measured and found to be forty-three feet in diameter—so I was assured by the person who measured it, the owner of a saw-mill in this timber region.   I told this man my hope that the saw-mill owners would spare these great trees.   He replied, "We have to spare them, for they are too big for us to handle.   We can use the smaller specimens, but one of these big fellows can not be cut down or sawed with any tools which we can use."

The slope of the Sierra from Visalia down to Bakersfield will, now that the region is easily accessible to tourists, become for the first time generally known, and I do not doubt it will next year be one of the great haunts of travelers to this State; for, aside from the mountain scenery, to persons fond of hunting and fishing, Kern River, and Kern and Buena Vista lakes offer greater attractions than perhaps any part of the United States.   The river abounds in large trout; the lakes and the slough or strait which unites them are also filled with fish, and abound with wild life of almost every kind.   Ducks, geese, cranes, swans, and snipe swarm on and near the shores.   In the tule reeds, far out in the lake, you find the raccoon perched on high, watching for fish and ducks; otter and beaver, the first in large numbers, are shot by neighboring sportsmen; and in the mountains which surround these lakes, at a little distance, the California lion, the grizzly and cinnamon bears, the wild-cat (a formidable little beast), antelope, deer, and fox are to be found by those who care to look for them.

On the Mohave Desert—which is so far from being a desert that it is covered with luxuriant vegetation, and is only called a desert because it is without running streams of water—great herds of antelope are grazing at this time, and the young are frequently caught with the lasso by Mexicans.

All this, with the grand and novel scenery of the Kern River and the country adjoining, will form no slight inducement to travelers; indeed, I advise every man who comes over here for four or six weeks to give at least two weeks to this Southern country; and he will regret that he has not three times the time to give it.

You will hear in San Francisco, no doubt, as I did, that it is a wild country in which every one goes armed, and where you may with very little trouble lose your life or your purse.   But it is not true.   Contrary to the advice of friends, I brought no arms with me; I found every body civil, and my precious person and property perfectly secure.

Bakersfield has as yet no hotel; but this I hear is to be remedied this summer.   Until it is, no one should take ladies down there, for the accommodations are of the rudest.   A traveler in this part of Southern California will do well to provide himself with a pair of good blankets in San Francisco, Stockton, or Visalia; then he is independent; for with these and an overcoat he can, if it is necessary, sleep on the verandah of a store or on the ground, and he need not fear catching cold.

Bakersfield is a new town; it has decidedly a frontier look. It is already, however, the centre of an important commerce with the mining country of Havilah and Owen's River, which makes a market for all the products of the country about Bakersfield. The railroad will very largely increase its trade, and make it, I do not doubt, one of the larger cities of the State within three or four years. It has magnificent natural advantages in the large area of deep and fertile soil which surrounds it, and in its abundant water for irrigation. Its climate is hot in summer; frosts are very slight in winter; all the semi-tropical fruits, as the almond, orange, and olive, will flourish here; cotton, tobacco, and hops have been successfully cultivated; and the soil bears, with irrigation, two grain-crops per year; for they sow wheat in December, which ripens in May, and follow this with corn, which grows eighteen feet high, and matures before the season closes.

Immense tracts of fertile land, with abundant water for irrigation, lie here awaiting settlement and occupation, as public or railroad lands. A number of San Francisco capitalists have bought up 10,000 acres of "swamp land," including part of the town of Bakersfield and Kern Island, and I found there an agent of this company — the California Cotton Growers' and Manufacturers' Association—preparing to plant 1200 acres of cotton this spring, on ground made ready last fall for that use. He intends also to plant sesame for oil, and to try the opium poppy and madder. The latter, East Indians believe, can be profitably grown here.

One hundred and twenty acres of cotton have yielded here five hundred and eighty pounds of clean cotton to the acre.

Though the town appears to the eye to lie in a vast plain, the river runs almost as rapidly as a mill-race; and Bakersfield has important water-power, which will help it some day to become a manufacturing place. It has already a large grist-mill.

The dearness of lumber has been a serious disadvantage; fifty dollars per thousand is the usual price, and even at this rate, just now, none can be bought. The only saw-mill lies some thirty miles away in the mountains, and transportation is difficult and dear. But the railroad will, in part, remedy this difficulty; and a canal is projected, by which logs are to be floated down to the town and sawed there. The machinery of a saw-mill for this purpose is now on the way, I hear.

It is a mistake, I think, to grow so exclusively wheat, barley, or corn, on the land about Bakersfield. The farmers plead that they get high prices for all the grain they raise, which is true enough; but they could make more money by raising cotton and the sub-tropical fruits. However, most of the present set-

15

tlers are poor, and their first aim is to "raise enough to feed their families and stock." Moreover, fencing stuff has been too dear, and without fences it is too great a risk to plant valuable trees, so long as there is no trespass law.

Bakersfield and the surrounding country offer considerable advantages to persons familiar with cotton-planting. Good cotton lands within reach of water may be obtained for two dollars and fifty cents per acre, and I have no doubt a considerable immigration from the cotton-planting States will come here within two or three years. At present there is but a small population, and this consists partly of Mexicans, Indians, and Chinese. The latter seemed to me the most steadily industrious people in the neighborhood; they have made excellent vegetable gardens. The Spanish-speaking population, though they live wretchedly, and are not of as high character as those I have met elsewhere in the State, have some fine fields of grain, and, of course, numerous horses.

Bakersfield and its immediate vicinity suffer in the summer months from fever and ague, and new settlers should be careful about their food, and living generally. I asked the principal physician of the place, who lived formerly in Illinois, how severe the malaria is here, and he replied, "Not so bad as in Illinois ten years ago; and as drainage is carried on here on a large scale for irrigating purposes, I think we shall have a healthy place, as soon as all the alluvial bottom has been ploughed up and turned to the sun for a couple of seasons."

I think he was not too sanguine; for the stream has a rapid current, and all irrigating ditches in the country also flow rapidly.

Twenty miles south of Bakersfield the San Joaquin Valley ends, the mountains close around it, and the Sierra meets the Coast Range at the gorge known as the Tejon Pass.

I have in several chapters described, as I saw it, the whole of this great Valley, which is the least known part of California. It is a very remarkable body of fertile land. While it lay between the Sierra and the Coast Range without railroad communication, it was necessarily given up to cattle and sheep; for the farmer in these days needs cheap transportation above every thing else except a good soil. But nature has given it every thing else except a railroad; a soil of remarkable fertility; a climate, according to the opinion of Eastern men with whom I spoke, who have lived here for some years, far more pleasant in the hottest summer heats than New York or Illinois, and in winter charmingly mild; healthful breezes, and freedom from malarious diseases except in the vicinity of Bakersfield; lovely mountain scenery; the capacity for a great variety of products; and water enough, flowing from the mountains on each side, if it is properly saved, to irrigate every acre of soil which needs it.

An English engineer, Mr. Brereton, long experienced in irrigation works in

India, last year made at the cost of San Francisco capitalists a careful reconnaissance of the valley, foot-hills, and mountains; he ascertained the levels of Tulare, Kern, and Buena Vista lakes, and his report (which I have seen) asserts that the water which comes from the mountains and lakes is more than sufficient for irrigation; and he has proposed a general system of canals, to be carried out this summer in small part only, but to be completed as population comes in, which will supply the entire valley with water.

The moneyed men of California begin to comprehend what, if they were not short-sighted, they would have perceived long ago, that it is far more profitable to build a canal for irrigation than for mining purposes. Yet, to bring and sell water to miners, hundreds of miles of canals and expensive flumes have been dug and built, and at far greater cost than is necessary for irrigation. But a mine is always uncertain, and is sure, some day, to " peter out ;" while irrigated land never ceases to be productive.

But the truth is that agriculture is yet in its infancy in California. Mining and trading have long been the chief occupations for capital and enterprise. Deep, thorough ploughing is almost unknown in the State. I saw a dozen alfalfa fields prepared last winter—alfalfa is the Chilian clover, which sends its roots down to water, gives enormous crops, and will last twenty years. It is a most important crop. I have no reason to doubt that a good alfalfa field will keep ten sheep to the acre the year round. Yet I have not seen one such field subsoiled, and scarcely one ploughed five inches deep. Alfilieria, the most important native grass here, is probably the richest food for cattle in the world. The pastures have been tramped down for years, until the soil is as hard as a brick, and you wonder that it bears any thing. It is well known that to run a plough only five inches deep through a field will cause the alfilleria to come up knee-high the next season; I have seen this myself. Yet I doubt if a dozen men in the whole State have ever taken the trouble to turn their sheep or cattle pastures over with a plough. I did not see a subsoil plough in the whole San Joaquin Valley, and I do not believe there is one.

Repeated experiment on a small scale has proved that land ploughed ten inches deep will give more than half a crop, without irrigation, even in the driest season; and it is now well known that summer fallowing insures a crop, no matter how severe the drought. But summer fallowing is practiced to only a limited extent, and as for deep ploughing, a farmer is so sure of a good crop with only a tolerable season, that he will risk failure rather than be at the trouble of sending his plough down eight or ten inches.

There is magnificent opportunity in this great Valley for industrious and thrifty farmers. Millions of acres of fertile land lie open to settlement, and are reserved by Government, at a low price, for actual settlers. Horses, cattle, and sheep are cheap, and cheaply kept, needing no costly barns nor any expensive storage of food.

The climate is so mild that the farmer is saved the tedious trouble of laying in stores of winter fire-wood, and his family's clothing need not cost half what it must cost in the East.

The most valuable fruits and other products known to commerce grow here safely and easily; life and property are secure; there is nothing here, except idleness, ignorance, and unthrift, to prevent farmers, in a few years, becoming rich. Every thing that is planted bears with a rapidity surprising to an Eastern man. A peach orchard begins to bear the second year after planting the pits; I have seen vines—such as grow only in hot-houses with us at home—which bore and matured clusters of grapes the same year in which the cuttings were planted; the apple bears handsomely at three years from the nursery; the dwarf pear, which has so generally failed with us, every body tells me bears here constantly; in the vegetable-garden the tomato ripens in almost every month of the year; the strawberry blossoms in February, and there is no month in which, with but little care, the family can not get an abundant and varied supply of vegetables from the garden.

But the farming is, for the most part, slipshod and disgraceful. In the whole San Joaquin Valley, from Stockton to the Tejon Pass, I have not seen even a dozen well-kept farms, and yet I have traveled slowly and kept my eyes open. In some other parts of the State I have seen thorough and intelligent farming; and I have always found the men who practiced it not merely comfortable, but rich, or rapidly becoming rich.

It should be said that the Valley has hitherto attracted but little attention from farmers with capital. Without railroad communications, it did not tempt them; and it must be added that a great many people have quietly got rich in it by the most slip-shod farming. You would be surprised to see how much wealth is in the hands of farmers and graziers about a place like Visalia—and what poor use they make of it.

THE GEYSERS.

CHAPTER XXV.

SHEEP FARMING—WITH A NIGHT AROUND A CAMP-FIRE.

"THAT a new place like Bakersfield should not have a church is not surprising," said I to the judge; "but you Havilah people ought to be ashamed that your town has neither church nor Sunday-school."

We were lying about the fire after supper, smoking our cigars, with that lazy contentment which follows a long day in the saddle.   There were half a dozen of us—a Californian, who had lived in Arizona; an Englishman, who had lived in California; a Boston physician, whose name is not unknown to fame, and who has for some years played hermit in these mountains; our host, a sparkling combination of scholar, gentleman, and Indian fighter, the companion and friend of Kit Carson in other days, the surveyor of trans-continental wagon-roads, and the owner to-day of what seems to me the most magnificent estate, in a single hand, in America; and, lastly, the judge and myself.

"Californians may be a wicked set, as you Eastern people pretend," said the general, "but you must admit that they lose no time usually in building schools and churches."

He spoke the truth. Nothing has more constantly surprised me, in this thinly-populated Southern California, than to find everywhere churches and excellent school-houses. Even Bakersfield, which is but a town of yesterday, where the inhabitants have hardly a decent shelter over their heads, has a neat and roomy school-house, one of the most substantial buildings in the place.

"Therefore," said I, "it is the more abominable that you have no church at Havilah."

"Well," replied the judge, who is one of the leading citizens of that mining town, "I agree with you, and we did make an effort to get up a church, but somehow it did not succeed. My wife and I talked it over; she said she preferred an Episcopal Church, and I called a meeting of the most respectable men of the place to choose a vestry. They voted me into the chair, and I nominated Mr. Johnson for a vestryman. Mr. Johnson, who is a prominent citizen, declined to serve; he modestly said he thought himself not fit for the office; he liked an occasional game of draw-poker, he said; he was given to some other worldly amusements, like dancing, when there was a fiddler anywhere around; he couldn't resist a horse-race, and, unfortunately, all the horse-racing in Havilah took place on Sunday, which was sure to interfere with his duties as vestryman; and so he would rather not serve.

"I told him," continued the judge, "that men were not expected to be absolutely perfect in these days; that the chair itself was fond of an occasional little game of poker; and that the office of vestryman was, in the judgment of the chair, purely ministerial. But somehow he did not see it in that light; he is a modest man, and he wouldn't consent to serve. When he backed out every body else did too, and so this effort of ours to get up a church fell through.

"I've always been sorry for it," added the judge, frankly, "for I think a church an excellent thing to have in a place."

Now, though we listeners may have smiled at the judge's story, he, I beg you to believe, was perfectly sincere in his regrets, and we could do no less than admit that he had "done his level best" in the matter.

"The fact is," said the Arizonian, "that Havilah is, like many mining towns, a rude place. I was going down the main street there one evening some years ago, when I got among a crowd of rough fellows, and I happened to say to Jack Thompson, whom I knew, that it seemed to be very quiet nowadays; I had not seen a man killed for a long time."

" ' Haven't you? By the powers! come along with me,' said he, reaching around to the back of his trowsers for his revolver, and grasping my arm. ' I'll show you how it's done; there's a whole billiard-room full of them up there!' and he waved his six-shooter over his head, and I believe if I hadn't quieted him down, he'd have gone up and shot into the crowd. But that's some years ago, and they hung that scoundrel to a tree afterward, and that scared most of his kind away."

" The same fellow told me once," said the general, " of a little disappointment of his. He had a difficulty with a man, and no arms at hand except a shot-gun; so he ' went for him with the scatter-gun,' he said, ' and the contemptible weapon missed, and he just grazed him.' "

" Your courts did not execute justice very vigorously in those days," I suggested.

" Well, no," replied the judge, " they were too often like a judge they had in early days up in Toulumne County. This judge had a quarrel with a lawyer, and the result was what he used regularly to charge the jury against any party whom this lawyer represented. At last Tom said one day in court, with some vexation, when he heard the judge begin to charge against him again, that he did not expect ever to get justice in that court. To which his honor replied promptly, and with contempt, that he would take d—d good care Tom should get no justice in that court."

" That fellow ought to have been a Tammany judge in New York," said some one, and turned the laugh handsomely against the East.

" It's astonishing," said the Englishman, " how rough and how ignorant men are who go about these mountains prospecting for gold. Some years ago, when the Temiscal tin mine was opened, and found to contain some valuable ores, there was great excitement around San Bernardino about tin. Dozens of people who knew nothing about indications of tin went out to prospect, and up in the Bainbridge District a fellow actually set up an assay shop, and made money for a month or two by pretended assays of the rock which credulous prospectors brought him. Of course he found tin in every kind of rock. It was discovered afterward that the scoundrel had stolen a pewter faucet, and made his assay buttons out of that. When that was used up, he melted the solder from old tin cans for the same use."

" He ought to have been the man who told an English tourist near San Bernardino that up in the mountain there they had recently discovered a brass mine—' very rich ore too,' he added, when he saw the Englishman open his eyes with amazement."

" We had such a fellow down in our country," said the Arizonian, " but he went off in disgust. He came into the hotel at Prescott one night, and at supper the landlord asked him if he'd have some teal.

" ' What's teal?' says the fellow.

" ' Why, a kind of duck,' says the landlord.

" ' Had it wings ?' says the fellow.

" ' Certainly,' says the landlord.

" 'And could it fly ?' says the fellow.

" ' Yes,' says the landlord.

" ' Well,' says he, ' I don't want any, then; any thing that had wings, and could fly, and didn't fly out of this accursed country, I don't want to have any thing to do with.' "

" You've got some droll Pikes down there," said the general; "one of them met me once, and said he had traveled on the Gila with a certain person, a friend of mine.

" ' You like that John Nugent ?' he remarked; ' but he's a nasty little beast.'

" Now Nugent is remarkable for his scrupulous neatness, and I said, ' I guess you must be mistaken; he always passed for a very clean man.'

" ' *I* know him,' said the Pike, with a sneer of disgust; ' didn't I travel with him for three weeks down along the Gila River?   And didn't I use to see him go down to the river every morning, with a dirty little tin cup, and a confounded nasty little brush he used to carry in his pocket, and scrub, and hawk, and spit, till it almost made me puke to see him?   I tell you he's a nasty little beast.'

" I believe there's not a hard story in this country that is not fathered either on Arizona or on the Pikes," said the Arizonian. " Yet our territory is one of the richest in the Union, as you would soon know if Uncle Sam would protect us against the Apaches; and as for the Pike, who is the hero of almost every Californian drollery, you all know that the Pike has many excellent qualities; he is hospitable, true to his friends, and though his ways may not be ours, and he is apt to think more of cattle than other men, he is not, on the whole, a bad creature."

The Arizonian spoke truly; and as I have in other parts of this book related the odd stories which are put upon the Pike, it is only right for me here to note this. The " Pike " is the " backwoodsman " of California; the name comes to him from the fact that among the early settlers of the State were many people from Pike County, in Missouri. " The Pike," said the Californian to me, " is only the south-western frontiersman; we got him because he was, as you know, always ' moving West;' and we keep him because here, no doubt to his own amazement and disgust, he butted up against the Pacific Ocean. He owns hundreds of cows, yet scarcely ever tastes milk; his wife still spins and weaves at home; and he and his family live here a thoroughly shiftless and happy life, and manfully resist civilization and its comforts.

" There is a fellow up in Colusa, whom they call Nick, a bar-keeper, who never tires of stories of the Pikes," remarked the judge; " he told me once that he had determined to keep the next fourth of July, having suffered one to pass over without any demonstrations. ' So this year,' said Nick, ' two or three of us took an old anvil down to the river, loaded it up, and began to blaze away. By-and-by I saw a lot of black objects bobbing up and down in the river away up stream. I thought they were ducks at first, but presently discovered them to be a lot of Pikes swimming the river, with their rifles held up out of the water. Soon they came along to us, and the head-man, a gaunt six-footer in butternut, sung out to me, 'Stranger, whar's the war?'

"I couldn't get their whisky strong enough for them," said Nick; "so after trying every way, I at last made a mixture of poison-oak and butternut. That fetched 'em. I called it the sheep-herders' delight; and it was a popular drink. The first Pike I tried it on yelled with delight; the next one took two drinks, and turned a double summerset in the road before the house. A peddler came along, and after taking several drinks of my sheep-herders' delight, he went off and stole his own pack, and hid it in the woods. When he came to himself he made a complaint of the theft; but I guessed how it was, and helped him to find the goods.

"The poor old judge!" said the same fellow, "he complained, on election evening, that he was quite worn out with signing checks all day." I sincerely hope this was a libel on the court.

"Do you know how they carry on agriculture down in Arizona?" asked the judge, looking quizzically at the Arizonian. "There was a fellow who hired himself out as a farm hand in Arizona, and the first day his master told him to cut some wood. So he asked for an axe, but the farmer said, 'No, we don't cut wood with an axe here;' and gave him a sledge-hammer to knock and break off the mesquit which they burn down there.

"The next day John was ordered to cut some hay, and was looking about for a scythe, when his master said, 'We don't cut hay with a scythe down here,' and gave him a hoe to chop down the woody stalks with which they swindle the horses there for hay.

"The third morning the farmer called his man to come out and plant corn. John looked for a hoe, but his master said, 'We don't plant corn with a hoe out here,' and gave him a crowbar with which to punch holes in the ground, wherein to drop corn. They say John left the country in disgust.

"This country is quiet now," said the general; "but when I first came into it it contained some rough people. The head of the famous robber Joaquin Murieta, and the hand of his lieutenant, Three-fingered Jack, were brought into my camp but a few hours after those two scoundrels were shot; Jack Powers and his gang used to herd their bands of stolen horses on my own rancho as they drove them through the country; and Jack once kindly came to tell me that he would kill the first man of his gang that took any thing from me. Mason and Henry, the worst of all the road agents in this State, used to go through Kern County waylaying and robbing; and in those days a man had need to be careful, not only of his money, but of his life."

"They have a story here," said the doctor, "of a courageous woman in this county, who was alone in a stage which Mason and one of his gang stopped. The driver threw down the treasure-box when the two robbers stopped his horses, and Mason thereupon opened the stage door, and, leaning into the stage, ordered the woman to give up her money and rings, pointing a cocked pistol at her at the same time.

"The woman looked at him coolly, and said: 'Look here, don't you see that you're pointing that pistol directly at me, and that it's cocked? You seem to be a little nervous, for your hand trembles; I wish you'd point it away from me; it might go off and hurt me.'

"Mason was so much struck by the woman's coolness, that with an oath he slammed the stage door, and told her to keep her valuables."

"She was lucky," said the Californian; "with these road agents you can't sometimes most generally tell how good-tempered they're going to be, or in how much of a hurry; and they are not always as polite as a fellow who recently, at San Luis Rey, in a written notice, 'begged to intimate to the public' that he was about to open a telegraph office."

Thus the stories went around until, one after another, we dropped to sleep under the clear sky of the mountain, with our feet to the fire and abundance of blankets over us.

To one who likes a free outdoor life, I think nothing can be more delightful than the life of a farmer of sheep or cattle in Southern California. The weather is almost always fine; neither heat nor cold ever goes to extremes; you ride everywhere across country, for there are no fences; game is abundant in the season; and to one who has been accustomed to the busy life of a great city like New York, the work of a sheep or cattle rancho seems to be mere play.

The rancho from which I write this—the Tejon it is called—seems to me, as I said above, the finest property in the United States in a single hand. It contains nearly 200,000 acres, and lies at the junction of the Sierra Nevada with the Coast Range. These two mountain ranges bend around toward each other here in a vast sweep, and form the bottom of the San Joaquin Valley. They do not quite meet. The Tejon Pass, a narrow defile, separates them, and gives egress from the Valley into the Los Angeles country.

You may ride for eighty miles on the county road upon this great estate. It supports this year over 100,000 sheep; and it has a peasantry of its own, about whom I shall tell you something presently.

The Tejon is devoted to sheep, and here I saw the operation of shearing—eight or nine weeks are required to shear the whole flock—as well as the various details of the management of a California sheep farm.

What we call at home a flock is in California called a band of sheep. These bands consist usually of from 1300 to 2000 sheep, and each band is in the charge of a shepherd.

Of course the sheep are scattered over many miles of territory, but each band has a limited range, defined somewhat by the vicinity of water, and it is customary in California to drive the animals every night into a corral, or inclosure, usually fenced with brush, and with a narrow entrance. This corral is near water, and the sheep drink at morning and evening. The shepherd sleeps near by in a hut, or, in the mountain part of the Tejon Rancho, on a *tepestra*.

The corral is to keep the sheep together at night, and protect them in a measure from the attacks of wild beasts, which, curiously enough, are too cowardly to venture after dark over even a low fence.

The *tepestra* is to protect the shepherd himself against the attacks of grizzly bears, which are still abundant in the mountains, especially in the Coast Range. The *tepestra* is a platform about twelve feet high, built upon stout poles solidly set into the ground. Upon this platform the shepherd sleeps, in the mountains, at the entrance of the corral. The grizzly bear can not climb a pole, though he can get up a tree large enough to give his claws a hold. It is, I believe, not infrequent for a grizzly to stand up at the side of a *tepestra* at night, and try to rouse out the shepherd. But all the men are armed with guns, which they carry day and night.

The grizzly does not usually attack sheep. The California lion, a strong but very cowardly beast, and not a lion at all but a puma, the wild-cat, the fox, and the coyote, are the sheep's enemies.* The last-named is easily poisoned with meat which has strychnine powdered over it. The others are hunted when they become troublesome, and as the lion on the slightest alarm takes to a tree, and will run even from a small dog, it is not accounted a very troublesome beast.

Indians, Spaniards, Chinese, and some Scotchmen, serve as shepherds in California. The last are thought the best; and the Chinese make very faithful shepherds if they are properly and carefully trained. They are apt to herd the sheep too closely together at first, from a nervous fear of losing one out of the band. Dogs I have found but little used on the sheep ranchos I have seen. They are not often thoroughly trained, and where they are neglected become a nuisance.

Of course the shepherds have to be supplied at stated intervals with food. They usually receive a week's rations at once, and cook for themselves. At the Tejon there are two supply stations; and every morning donkeys and mules were sent out with food to some distant shepherds.

---

* A sheep farmer in Santa Barbara County told me that one of his shepherds chased a "lion," in broad daylight, into an oak-tree, but unluckily had left his gun in his house, more than a mile distant. Determined that the beast should not escape, and knowing its cowardice, he took off his shirt, trowsers, and hat, and placed these on sticks around the tree, in sight of the animal. Then, reduced to his shoes, he ran as fast as he could to the house, got his gun, and, on his return, actually found the lion still in the tree, and shot it.

The ration masters count the sheep when they deliver the rations, and thus all the bands are counted once a week, and if any sheep are missing they must be accounted for. The shepherd is allowed to kill a sheep once in so many days, but he must keep the pelt, which is valuable.

Above the ration masters are the mayor-domos. Each of these has charge of a certain number of bands; on a smaller estate there is usually but one mayor-domo. It is his duty to see that the shepherds are competent; that new pasturage is ready when a band has need for it; to see that the corrals are in good order; to provide extra hands at lambing-time; to examine the sheep to keep out scab, which is almost the only disease they are subject to in this State; and to give out the rations for distribution.

On such an estate as the Tejon there is, finally, a general superintendent, and a book-keeper and store-keeper; for here in the wilderness a supply of goods of various kinds must be kept up for the use of the people.

A blacksmith, teamsters, ploughmen, gardeners, and house-servants make up the complement of the Tejon's company. The gardeners and servants are Chinese, as they usually are in this State, and very good men they are—civil, obliging, and competent.

Besides these numbers fed from the home place, there are on this estate about three hundred Indians, who have been allowed to fence in small tracts of land, on which they raise barley and other provisions, and in some cases plant fruit-trees and vines. They form the peasantry of whom I spoke above, and are a happy, tolerably thrifty, and very comfortable people. Their surplus produce is purchased by the superintendent; when their labor is used they are paid, and they all have horses, which pasture on the general fields.

They have learned how to plough, shear sheep, and perform some other useful labor.

Now these Indians came to the Tejon naked except a breech-clout, feeding miserably on grasshoppers, worms, and acorns; ignorant, savage nomads. They were first brought here when a part of this rancho was used by the Government as an Indian reservation. General Beale, the present owner of the Tejon, was then Superintendent of Indian Affairs in this State, and he has seen these people emerge from a condition of absolute barbarism and wretchedness into a degree of comfort and prosperity greater than that enjoyed by the majority of Irish peasants; they have abandoned their nomadic habits, have built neat and comfortable houses, and fenced in ground which they cultivate. Their women dress neatly, and understand how to cook food. The men earn money as sheep-shearers. In some places vineyards and fruit-trees have been brought by them to a bearing condition.

In short, these human beings were savages, and are—well, they are as civilized as a good many who come in emigrant-ships from Europe to New York.

And all this has been accomplished under the eye and by the careful and kindly management of the owner of the Tejon Rancho. It seemed to me a great thing for any man to achieve; and certainly these people were in every way a higher class of beings than the Indians whom I saw on the Tule River Indian Reservation, living at the expense of the Government, idle, gambling, lounging, evil-eyed, and good for nothing.

If the Tule River Reservation were abandoned, the Government would save a handsome sum of money, and the farmers would get a useful laboring force, where now there are three or four hundred idle vagabonds, who, when they do go out to work, as some of them do, still receive rations and clothing from the Government, and consequently use their own earnings for gambling and debauchery.

General Beale's Indians have been raised to a far better condition by his own private efforts than the Reservation Indians have attained after years of expensive support from the Government. They shear all the Tejon sheep, and are thus, of course, of value to the estate; and they are useful in many other ways.

Unluckily their language is Spanish. It seemed to me a pity that when they had to learn a new language English had not been taught them.

The Tehatchapie Pass, by which the Southern Pacific Railroad is to pass from Bakersfield into the Mohave Plain, is part of the Tejon Rancho; and when I came to drive into that great plain, which is just now the home of thousands of antelopes, I saw another fertile region only awaiting the railroad to be "prospected" by settlers.

The Mohave Plains have the name of being uninhabitable; but they furnish abundant pasturage for antelopes and deer, and are thus proved to be fertile. They lack running streams of water; but a German, who is the first settler, has dug a well, and found good water without going far down; and I saw on the plain a fine field of barley almost ready for harvesting, which showed the quality of the soil.

Stretching far into the great uninhabited plain is a singular and picturesque mountain range, called the "Lost Mountains," which relieves the dreariness of a great level, and promises in its cañons springs and streams, and pleasant homes for the future settler, when the railroad opens this great uninhabited tract.

VERNAL FALL, YOSEMITE VALLEY.

CHAPTER XXVI.

A CALIFORNIA CATTLE RANCHO.—A RODEO.—PECULIAR CUSTOMS OF THE
SPANISH CALIFORNIANS.

FROM Anaheim a long but pleasant day's drive brought us, past San Juan
Capistrano—which the readers of Dana's "Two Years Before the Mast"
will remember as the place where he was let down the cliff some hundreds of
feet to knock down a few raw-hides at the risk of his own skin—to the Santa
Margarita Rancho, one of the great cattle ranchos of California, where I had
been promised a *rodeo*.

The business of raising cattle was, as you know, for many long years almost
the only pursuit of Californians. In Dana's time it was the great business of
the province, and, though now a secondary affair, it is still, in some parts of the
State, the calling of a large number of people.

Cattle are not herded as sheep are; they roam at will over large districts,
and those of a dozen or twenty owners feed together on the pastures of all.
Each man marks his own by a peculiar brand, burned into the left hip; and
these marks, or "irons," as they are technically called, are recorded like the ti-
tle-deeds of estates, and it is felony to obliterate a brand.

The following copy of a public handbill will show the Eastern reader both the law and the practice in regard to Rodeos and branding cattle.

NOTICE!

OFFICE OF THE CLERK OF BOARD OF SUPERVISORS,
San Diego County, January 5th, 1872.

NOTICE is hereby given to all whom it may concern, that at a regular meeting of the Hon. Board of Supervisors, in and for the County of San Diego, State of California, on the Fifth day of January, 1871, it was, on motion,

ORDERED, That the following persons be, and the same were, duly appointed

JUDGES OF THE PLAINS,

to hold their office for the term of one year, and until their successors are appointed and qualified, to wit:

For The Coast Range.

Cave J. Couts,   F. P. Forster,   George Selwyn,   Juan Ortego,   James Kerren.

For Temecula Range.

Jose Valencia,   Juan Machado,   Jose A. Estudillo,   Francisco Estudillo.

For Agua Caliente Range.

Charles Ayers,   Joseph Sweikaffer,   J. Wolfskill,   J. Aguilar.

For Southern District.

J. W. Mulkins,   Boon Morris,   Francisco Ames,   William Cant,   R. K. Porter.

For Judges of the Plains at Large.

CHARLES THOMAS,   SYLVESTER MARRON,   JOSE ANTONIO SERRANO.

It was further Ordered, That the three Judges of the Plains at Large appointed as aforesaid meet together at San Louis Rey, in the County of San Diego, on the Second Monday in February, A.D. 1872, or earlier if they deem it necessary to do so, for consultation in all matters appertaining to their duties as Judges of the Plains, and to adopt such rules and regulations as may be authorized by law, governing and controlling their actions during their official term: and a portion of the duties of the said Judges at Large at their meeting as aforesaid shall be, and they are required to appoint the time and places at which all Rodeos for the County of San Diego aforesaid shall be commenced and continued.

And it was further Ordered, That for all services rendered by the Judges of the Plains, they and each of them shall have and receive from the parties required by law to pay the same, FIVE DOLLARS for each day for such services necessarily rendered by said Judges.

By order of the Board of Supervisors.

CHALMERS SCOTT, Clerk.

Sections 5, 6, and 7, of an Act concerning Judges of the Plains and defining their duties, passed April 25th, 1851, and the Amendment thereto:

ART. 2696, SEC. 5. All persons traveling with cattle, sheep, hogs, horses, or mules, shall, in case said animals be not of their own mark and brand, be obliged to procure from the person or persons from whom they obtain such cattle, or from the justice of the peace residing nearest to the farm or place where they obtain the same, a certificate of the number and kind of such cattle, and the mark and brand which distinguished the same; and they shall allow such animals to be subject to the inspection of owners of lands through which they may pass, and upon arriving at any city, town, or village, shall present themselves to a judge of the plains, and state the number and kind of such animals: and it shall be the duty of the judge of the plains to examine the band or drove, and to accompany them out of the precinct of such city, town, or village.

SEC. 6. That if the number and kind of animals do not agree with the report of the owner or person in charge, and with the certificates in his possession, the judge of the plains shall detain the band or drove, and take the owner or person in charge before the nearest magistrate for examination.

ART. 2697, SEC. 7. The judge of the plains shall arrest and take before any magistrate any person who may be accused to him, or whom he has reasonable grounds to suspect of killing, hiding, or otherwise taking away cattle, horses, or other animals belonging to others, and shall execute any warrant delivered to him by any magistrate for larceny or other offense concerning said described property; he shall execute any warrant delivered to him by any justice of the peace, for the purposes herein named, and otherwise shall have and exercise the same powers as any sheriff, constable, or police officer, in the cases provided for by law.

When a horse is sold, it is cross-branded—that is to say, the seller puts his brand also on the shoulder, as a sign that his right is extinguished.   Wherever a man sees an animal with his mark, he has a right to take it.

Every spring, in the cattle country, rodeos are held.   *Rodeo* comes from *rodeár*, the Spanish verb to gather or surround.   A rodeo is, in fact, a collection of cattle or horses, made to enable the different owners to pick out their own, count them, and, if they wish, drive them off to their own pastures.   It is held in the spring, because then the calves still follow the cows, and the great object of the gathering is to brand the calves.

Rodeos are held in the San Joaquin Valley at stated places and preordained times; and one succeeds the other, going from south northward, until at last all the cattle have been seen, and all the calves branded.   In San Diego County, where the Santa Margarita rancho lies, they begin in the same way, far south near the Mexican border, and work northward.

Sometimes 20,000 head of cattle are gathered on a plain, and the work of "parting out," as it is called, and branding, lasts for several days.   A carefully defined set of laws regulates this work, and law officers, called "Judges of the Plains," attend to settle disputes as to ownership, and regulate the procedure. These officers appoint the times and places of rodeos, and attend at each.

In the old times, I have been told, a rodeo was a formal and stately affair. It was held in turns upon the estates of the owners; and each entertained the assembled company.   When I tell you that such a gathering commonly included from twelve to twenty proprietors, each attended by from six to fifteen vacqueros, and with six or eight horses for each person, you will see that there was a little army to keep.

But the old Californians were not only hospitable; they receive visitors with less inconvenience to themselves than any people I have ever known.   I staid this winter for some days, with my wife, at an old Spanish rancho, where the "housekeeping" was so quietly arranged that it seemed as though the house was empty; yet I learned, on inquiring, that from forty to forty-five persons, exclusive of servants, ate in the house every day while we were there.

Partly this is accounted for by the very simple habits of the people.   They eat very moderately, and of few dishes, beef being, of course, the chief article of diet; and they sleep anywhere.   Moreover, they drink only tea or coffee, and very little wine; they are very quiet and decorous in their manners, and they rise early.

In the old times, when the cattle had been gathered, and all was ready, the mayor-domo—an important person on all these estates—came to the proprietor with hat in hand, and formally announced that all was ready.   Then the company, dressed in holiday attire, got to horse and rode out to the plain, and at the word the work began.

Then were seen some really magnificent feats of horsemanship; each vacquero vied with the other in this display; and as the day grew, fresh horses were saddled, and no bull was so wild that he did not find his master.

The state and ceremony have gone out; but the skillful riding still remains, as well as the feats with the lasso, which are really like jugglery or witchcraft. I have a hundred times watched the fling of the riata, and yet have never in a single instance been able to detect the precise moment of the capture. But I am certain that a part of the trick is in the vacquero's intimate knowledge of the animal's motions; for I have seen a riata carelessly thrown down at a bull's heels, and, as the next instant he was fast, he must have stepped into the noose, and he who flung it must have known by experience what would be the animal's next motion.

At the Santa Margarita we attended a rodeo where the horsemen displayed in our honor some of their finest skill; and it was marvelous to see not only the certainty with which the lasso or riata is flung, and the admirable training of the horses, which co-operate with their riders and turn like a flash when a mad bull flies at his pursuer, but the jokes of the field. One of these is to single out a bull or cow, chase it out of the herd, dash after it at full speed, and lean out of the saddle until the rider catches the tail of the flying beast. This he winds quickly about his hand, and at the same time he tucks it under his leg, holding it between the leg and the saddle. At the same instant the horse, feeling the tail on his flank, and perfect in his own part, increases his speed, and both running in nearly parallel lines close together, if the horse's speed is greater than the bull's, the latter is flung heels over head. I saw this practical joke played a dozen times; it is one of the favorite diversions of the rodeo.

The rodeo grounds are usually permanent; and it was to me an odd fact that when the vacqueros went out to gather in the cattle from the hills and valleys for some miles on every side, they had only to begin driving, when all within sight turned at once to the big tree in the centre of the plain, where they were accustomed to be collected.

Half a dozen horsemen sufficed to keep a band of 2500 cattle in a compact mass for many hours. There were nearly a hundred horsemen on the plain; and as the coolest heads rode into the mass of cattle and singled out one by its mark, they turned its head out of the circle, drove it adroitly outside, and there two or three other horsemen stood ready to drive it to the knot to which it belonged, the calf frantically rushing after its mother, who turned again and again to see if it followed. This continued all day long.

The Santa Margarita is an estate of 120,000 acres. It belongs to Don Juan Forster, an Englishman by birth, but a resident of California from his early youth, and married to a sister of Don Pio Pico, the last Spanish governor of California.

At his house more of the old Spanish Californian life remains than at any

other I have visited.   Spanish only is spoken in the family, and the old customs
are kept up, not from any desire to be different from others, but because they
are family habits.   There is something very lovable and pleasant in these
customs.

In the first place the people are kindly and amiable, and though their pursuits might be thought to tend to loud and rough ways, and do so where our
own people manage cattle, here all went on quietly and decorously as though it
was Sunday.   The animals are handled firmly, but with great care and human-
ity.   The work of the house proceeds with absolute noiselessness, and this
though from thirty to fifty persons were fed at the house every day.

Spanish Californian houses, so far as I have seen their interiors, are always
scrupulously clean; and, though their life seems to us strange, and does not
comport with our ideas of comfort, it has the merit of fitting the climate and
the pursuits of the people.

There remains in it, too, something which is too often lacking in our Eastern houses, a degree of trust and confidence and affection between master and
servant, with not the least familiarity, however.   I saw men—Indians—whose
fathers had been in this same service; and of whom the proprietor told me
that he would not hesitate to trust one of them with $50,000 to carry to the
nearest town.   The Spaniards know how to manage the Indians.   Their self-
restraint and courtesy have great effect.   No vacquero addressed the master
without either touching or taking off his hat.   *Padrone* is the master's title.
There was never any excited ordering about, and the work went on apparently
of its own momentum.

In the evening the mayor-domo and the older vacqueros gathered on the
long verandah.   While a lady was singing in the parlor, where the family and
visitors were gathered, I noticed three or four old men—evidently privileged
characters—sitting quietly, listening, on a long bench in the hall.   At meal-
times, if the long dining-table was not full, two or three of these privileged
characters quietly took the vacant places, far down—below the salt—ate and
listened, or answered, if they were addressed.   Meantime another long table
was set, or had been set, under a piazza roof in the quadrangle which every
Californian house incloses, and here others ate.

In the day-time this sheltered quadrangle accommodated three or four Indian women, who sat on the ground and did the family sewing.

People who rise early naturally go to bed betimes, and in the evening after
half a dozen cigaritos had been smoked, the company disappeared, to sleep
soundly somewhere.   As for me, I sat long and questioned Mr. Forster's sons
about the old times.

In the early days, it seems, the missions, which were then rich, made place
and occasion for frequent festivities.   To San Luis Ray, for instance, which
lies near the Santa Margarita, came families from fifty miles around, with their

retainers, for a fiesta. They remained a week or two, and the feast was partly religious, partly secular. The padres, rich in cattle, entertained all who came, and thus the country-side kept up acquaintance.

In those days, said Don Marco Forster, men used to travel from San Diego to Monterey and never spend a cent of money. When night came, you stopped at the nearest house. After supper, you were shown your room. In the morning, a clean shirt was at your bedside; and if you were known to the family, it was customary to place near the bed, on the table, also a sum of money, a hundred or two hundred dollars, from which the visitor, if he needed it, was expected to help himself. Lest my readers might think this incredible, I will add that General Vallejo has fully confirmed to me these and other particulars.

The next day a fresh horse was brought out and the traveler went his way. He usually carried with him a blanket, a hair rope to stake out his horse, and a riata or lasso; and in a bag, tied to his saddle, a small supply of pinola. This is pop-corn, parched, and ground on a stone. It is mixed with water and a little sugar, and a cupful of it makes, as I know by experience, a satisfying luncheon, if you have reason to expect a good dinner later in the day. To the abstemious Spaniard it sufficed, if occasion required, for breakfast, dinner, and supper; and when night came, if no house was near, he staked out his horse, often tying the rope to his own arm, that he might be awakened if the horse was startled by a wild beast; spread upon the ground the huge leather flaps which in those days loosely covered the saddle-tree, rolled himself in his blanket, and lay down to sleep upon the leather.

In San Diego County, I believe, it was a custom in the summer to guard against the approach of rattlesnakes by surrounding this couch with the horse-hair rope which is used to stake out a horse. This, made very ingeniously of the manes and tails of horses, is very rough, the ends of the hairs sticking out all over it, and these, it is said, the snake dislikes, as they probably irritate his skin; and feeling them, he turns aside.

Life on one of the old Spanish ranchos was, I am assured, not so simple as we have been accustomed to think. Various handicrafts had been introduced by the priests; and the Indians, who were the mechanics, were employed not only at the missions but by the more substantial rancheros. A gentleman at Los Angeles described to me the life on one of the great estates in that county "before the Americans came," and I may add that different persons, among them General Vallejo, have confirmed to me every detail.

They milked cows and made cheese; they dressed and tanned sheep and calf skins for clothing; they wove blankets; they made wine; they raised grain enough for their bread, and the Indian women ground this on stones; they preserved the hides of the cattle for the Boston ships; and at the San Fernando Mission, near Los Angeles, I saw the huge stone and cement tanks in which they melted down and kept the tallow, which also was sold to the Boston men.

"In those days," said my friend, "when I went out to see Don Tomas, he received me at the door; he showed me my room; and in a few minutes he came bearing in his own hands a basin of water for my use. But behind him came half a dozen servants, to show me that what he did he did out of respect and welcome to me, and that servants were at hand to do it if he did not choose to trouble himself.

"This old man had sons and daughters, grown and married, living in his house. He always breakfasted alone unless he specially invited his eldest son to eat with him. He arose somewhat later than the family, who had break-fasted before him—the men, I mean; for the women and children ate apart, and had a very merry time over their meals.

"When he had breakfasted, he went out into his corridor or piazza. There stood his sons and his mayor-domo and his vacqueros, hat in hand. Then the horses, which had been saddled since daylight, were brought. The eldest son held his father's stirrup while he mounted; and when he was seated in the saddle, the rest followed.

"Then he gave to each his orders for the day—to Martin the tannery, to Antonio the horses, to Tomas the cheese, or the calves; and when at last all this was received, always in silence, he gave the word, and out into the plain they rode as though shot from a bolt. The old man rode at the head; and as he galloped he called, in that low, soft voice which they almost all have, 'Pedro,' and Pedro drew up alongside: 'I do not want that mañada of horse on the hill yonder.' 'Si, Señor,' says Pedro, and gallops off. 'Antonio, these calves should not be here, they must be nearer the river;' and so on, always in a gallop, see-ing every thing with his practiced eye, and issuing his commands as he rode.

"About four he returned to his dinner, which his sons ate with him. After dinner he sat in his corridor, made and smoked paper cigars, and contemplated himself.

"On Sundays and fast-days," said my friend, "the family rode to church, all on horseback — a graceful cavalcade, for the women rode finely, and the horses, which we Americans ignorantly despise, are yet the best saddle-horses in the world. (In this, by-the-way, every man who has ridden them will agree.)

"Then came the gold discovery, and the Americans, and the sudden and great wealth which spoiled all this simple life. Then they became too proud and too careless to milk, and so now you find no milk on the ranchos. They could buy clothing and all kinds of supplies, and so their useful and ingenious industries perished. They came to the towns dressed in absurd gold and silver lace, and with gold stirrups and gold-mounted saddles, and wasted their money in gambling-houses; and so their business was neglected. Finally they thought it genteel to ride in carriages, and so they gave up the most graceful and healthful exercise which man or woman can have. I still remember my old friend Don Tomas standing here looking with silent disgust at his family climbing into a cumbrous coach, and then turning to me with the words— 'They are young and fool-hardy, and may risk it, but for my part I am determined never to hazard my life in one of those things while I have strength to sit on a horse's back.'"

I do not doubt that it was a happy life they led—these old Californians. But it did not belong to the nineteenth century, and the railroad will, in a year or two, leave no vestige of it this side of the Mexican border.

But one thing I have learned to admire this winter among the old Californians which it is a pity we, their successors, have not copied from them; and that is the moderation of their lives. Their amiable and kindly temper, their abstemiousness, and temperance in eating and drinking, the readiness with which they submit to mere physical inconvenience, their kindness to dependents and servants, the skill with which they know how to manage these, and the politeness and ceremony which they carry into all parts of their lives, seemed to me very admirable indeed.

Going on from the Santa Margarita rancho to San Diego, I came there upon the story of a singular industry. The meat of the abelona shell, which is as much tougher than that of a Long Island quahaug, as that is tougher than an old boot, is a delicacy among the Chinese. I do not know how they cook it— probably it is used to make one of the three thousand five hundred and ninety-two soups from which a red-buttoned mandarin takes his choice when he orders his dinner. The Chinese have discovered that this shell abounds on the coast of the Mexican province of Lower California, and particularly at Ceros Island. Two companies of Chinese have been engaged for several years, in those remote parts, in gathering the abelona meat; they work on shares, having a foreman or chief for each company, who attends to their business affairs. They remain on the island or the main-land, and a little schooner, owned by an old resident of San Diego who is also its master, carries down to these Chinese their supplies of provisions, and brings up the abelona meat in solid bales.

The Chinese cleave the shells from the rocks at low tide, and carry them up to the place where they are prepared. There the meat is cut from the shell and boiled; after boiling, it is salted and dried; and when it is thus cured, it is packed in bales, sent to San Diego, a ten days' voyage, in the little schooner, thence to San Francisco, and from there Chinese merchants ship it to their own country.

The schooner captain, a simple, honest old fellow, told me that he received an eighth of the gross product for carrying to the Chinese their supplies and bringing back their abelona meat; he was bound also to keep them in firewood, and to transport water for them if they chanced to be working where no fresh water was near at hand.   He told me that the Chinese were very honest, dealt with him always fairly, and "knew a heap more than some white folks." He remarked with wonder that they could all read and write.   Will it surprise you if I tell you that most of the food which he carried down for this Chinese colony was imported from China? or that they live, as it seems to me, far better, and at any rate have a more varied bill of fare, than most of the ranch-men of California?

Near San Diego an enterprising person keeps bees on a great scale.   He has this year eight hundred hives; and the profit from these bees is so considerable that he can afford to carry the hives around to different parts of the country, so that the bees may always have an abundant supply of flowers.   I was told that it took him sometimes three weeks to make a move.

While we were in San Diego a party was preparing to go out into the mountains in search of a famous vein of silver, called the "Lost Lead," from the fact that it is known only by a tradition which reports that many years ago one Williams, who had befriended the Indians, was shown by them a deposit of silver of extraordinary richness in the mountains back of San Diego, and allowed to take from it as much as he wanted.   The tradition adds that Williams went home with his silver, and lived in the East in comfort and independence until his death.   *He* would not tell where he got the silver; and several parties have searched through the mountains since, with no success.   They have found indications of silver; but no "Lost Lead."   But when the young men have nothing better to do it seems the more adventurous of them get up a new expedition to look up this rich mine.

It may have been while a solitary adventurer was looking for this "Lost Lead" that he discovered an opal mine, from which he has, for nearly a year, been taking stones, some it is said of fine color and considerable value.   He too has kept his secret—more difficult to keep than the mystery of the "Lost Lead:"   I was told that he had frequently been followed by curious or greedy persons, but so far without success; for he has managed to baffle all watchers; and I could not help wondering whether the pleasure of eluding the trackers and setting at defiance public curiosity was not, perhaps, as pleasing to him as the gains of his discovery.

APPENDIX.

SOUTHERN CALIFORNIA FOR CONSUMPTIVES.

I SUBJOIN here a letter from a friend of my own, a consumptive, who has experienced remarkable relief in Southern California. The writer spent several winters in Southern Europe and one at Aiken, and his letter, as well as the tables of temperature which he has kindly added to it, compare the climates of these regions with that of Southern California. He writes:

"Anaheim, Los Angeles Co., California, July 26, 1872.

"* * *. You speak of the excessive heat. I do wish you and your family were in California; for a more perfect climate I can not imagine.

"You ask me for some account of the climatic differences between some European and American winter resorts, and I send this to you, hoping that others may benefit by the information, as I might have done had I known what I now know; and I again repeat with more confidence than ever, that had I come to California instead of going abroad, to-day I should be a well man.

"Mentone, Nice, and the Rivera generally, are the winter resorts recommended by the faculty; and they are, I believe, the best resorts in Europe; the others being far inferior.

"Meran, in the Tyrol, is too much shut in by mountains. The sun does not shine on the village until after it has been up for an hour, and a mountain to the south-west causes it to set upon the town at three o'clock in the winter. There is also a very cold draught that draws up through the pass.

"Vevey, Clarens, and Montreux, on the shores of Lake Geneva, are great resorts for French, German, English, and American invalids, and many go there because it is cheaper than elsewhere: but the climate only answers for the few. During the four months I was there we had no troublesome winds, but occasionally a *light* breeze.

"I found the climate of Clarens very soothing to the mucous bronchial membranes, but generally invalids did poorly there. It was by no means an unfavorable winter. Some seasons are better and others worse. It is an agreeable and, for those who are not ailing, a healthy place. There are good and comfortable hotels, at prices ranging from forty to sixty dollars per month, according to the accommodations. This account answers for Vevey, Clarens, and Montreux.

"Pau, in the Pyrenees, is much like Montreux in climate; perhaps two or three degrees warmer, and still more sedative than the places I named on Lake Geneva. It is not stimulating as on the Rivera, although more uniform and with less wind, and is very debilitating to many invalids. Some acquaintances of mine, who spent one winter in Mentone and did not like the winds, went to Pau the following winter, but returned to Mentone very much the worse for the experiment.

"The two winters I spent in Mentone, occasionally visiting the other towns on the Mediterranean for a change, led me to be most decidedly in favor of Mentone, as being the most sheltered and the best suited for invalids.

"San Remo I like next. Nice is a tiresome place for the sick, being too full of nonsense and fashion, with terrible winds and dust.   The climate, however, is very stimulating and exciting, and cooler than at San Remo or Mentone.   Oranges and lemons do not flourish there as well as at Mentone and San Remo.

"The first winter I spent in Mentone I did well, and but for the cold winds which blew I should have done very much better, for they gave me very many colds.   I also suffered from the great difference between sunshine and shade.   Even passing into the shade of a house was like going into a cellar, so great was the change.   Many suffered from this cause much more than I did, for experience soon taught me to be extremely careful.

"From carelessness in guarding against cold winds, and the great difference between sunshine and shade, many left Mentone much worse than they would have been had they remained at home. The difference between sunshine and shade was generally thirty-five degrees.   The temperature during the day in the winter season averaged fifty-five degrees, and the difference between wet and dry bulb thermometer five and a half degrees.   Officers in health, and who stood the extreme heat of our Southern States during the rebellion, could not endure the sun in Mentone, but had to do as the rest of us did—use umbrellas.   During the winter my sons, who often went on excursions to the mountains, always noted the direction of the wind, and we found that when we had the wind from a southerly direction it invariably blew on the mountains from the north; thus clearly showing that all the cold winds from the snowy Alps, after striking the ocean a few miles out, are reflected back on Mentone.   The visitors as well as the natives suffer much from pleurisy, owing to these cold reflected winds, together with the great change between sunshine and shade.   I always put on my overcoat when driving through the *old* town, as there was a chilling draught through those narrow shaded streets.   The new town is built on both sides of the old.

" The second winter I spent in Mentone did not agree with me as well as the first, as we had a *great deal* of wet and unpleasant weather.   On one occasion I was confined to the house eight days on account of a storm; and the same winter (1868 and 1869) we had ice in the river at different times, lasting for several days at a time.   The orange and lemon trees were much injured by the severe cold.

" A great objection to going abroad to spend the winter is the danger which the invalid encounters in the transition from land to sea, and vice versa.   My experience among invalids is, that it very frequently results most disastrously, causing the patient to lose all that he had gained during a whole winter's sojourn abroad.   When I went to Europe, and every time I returned, you know how I suffered from that cause; also when crossing the Channel from the Continent to England, as well as when I went south.

" Of all the southern places of resort on the Atlantic side, Aiken and some parts of Florida are admitted to be the best.   Florida has by far too damp a climate; it is not stimulating, but, on the contrary, very enervating.   When I returned from Europe I did not know where to go.   You *then* mentioned Florida; others spoke of Aiken; but my doctor did not like the latter place, telling me that he knew of many who had gone there, and that they did poorly.   He advised me to inquire about Nassau, thinking that might be a good place.   The following spring I met many who had spent the winter in Nassau, and they all told me that they would have been much better in almost any other climate than that, and further said that it was very enervating: and, to their knowledge, no one who passed the winter there did well.

"You know what led me to turn my footsteps this way, and the result you know also.   I shall inclose you an account of my meteorological observations for the winter 1871–1872, and allow me to suggest that you publish them in full, for then an invalid could tell every day that would be fit for him to be out-of-doors.

"Southern California presents a most gloriously invigorating, tonic, and stimulating climate, very much superior to any thing I know of, the air is so pure and so much drier than at Mentone or elsewhere; and although it has those properties, it has a most soothing influence on the mucous membrane, even more so than the climate of Florida, and without the enervating effect of that. It is quite as stimulating as Minnesota, without the intense cold of that climate.

"All the leading physicians of the world agree that a tonic, stimulating, dry climate is the best for the great majority of cases of suffering from pulmonary diseases or from a lowered vitality. The patient needs a climate in which he can spend most of the day out-of-doors. In Mentone, and in the towns on the Rivera, the doctors always advise the patients to be in the house one hour before sundown, the changes are so great; and not to go beyond prescribed limits, because the winds are too cold and the draughts severe. In California I have not been troubled in these respects; nor by the doctors, for I have not had to consult one since I have been in the State. As for going out, I have constantly been out evenings. During the past winter, out of one hundred and fourteen days I spent one hundred and six in the open air. This was in part of November, December, January, and February.

"Italy generally is a poor climate for the invalid, and the ' pure blue Italian skies' are not to be compared to ours; at least, with any thing west of the Mississippi.

"One can come to California and spend the winter as cheaply as in Vevey, Clarens, or Montreux, and these places are the cheapest winter resorts in Europe. For instance, in Santa Barbara or at Horton's in San Diego, one can board by the winter at forty-eight dollars per month.

"I think the tables I send you clearly show that Mentone is by far the best climate in Europe for the invalid, and that California is far superior to Mentone. Such is the fact, and that is what I wish to convey.*   Yours truly,   FRANCIS S. MILES."

---

* The table of temperature for Mentone has not come to my hands as these pages go to press, and the reader must for the present do without it.

TABLES OF TEMPERATURE,

Showing wet and dry bulb thermometer, maximum and minimum for the month, prevalent winds and weather, at Clarens, in Switzerland, Aiken, in South Carolina, and at San Bernardino and Anaheim, California.

CLARENS, SWITZERLAND.

TAKEN AT 9 A.M., 12 M., AND 4 P.M., FOR NO-
VEMBER, 1869.

Average temperature............................... 51°
"   difference of wet and dry bulb...... 4°
     Maximum............................. 60°
     Minimum............................. 39°
Sunshine all day....................... 8 days.
"   and clouds................. 8 "
Cloudy all day...... .... 14 "

     Total.......................... 30 days.
Rain on seven of the above cloudy days.
No strong winds.

DECEMBER, 1869.

Average temperature........................... 42°
"   difference of wet and dry bulb.......$2\frac{1}{10}$°
     Maximum............... .... 50°
     Minimum............. .... 29°
Sunshine all day....................... 6 days.
"   and clouds................. 4 "
Cloudy all day......................... 21 "

     Total.......................... 31 days.
Rain on five of the above cloudy days.
Snow on two "   "   "   "
No strong winds.

JANUARY, 1870.

Average temperature............................. 45°
"   difference of wet and dry bulb...... $3\frac{1}{2}$°
     Maximum............................. 52°
     Minimum............................. 30°
Sunshine all day....................... 10 days.
"   and clouds................. 8 "
Cloudy all day......................... 13 "

     Total.......................... 31 days.
Rain on one of the above cloudy days.
No strong winds.

FEBRUARY, 1870.

Average temperature............................. 41°
"   difference of wet and dry bulb.......$3\frac{1}{11}$°
     Maximum............................. 55°
     Minimum...... .... 32°
Sunshine all day....................... 7 days.
"   and clouds................. 5 "
Cloudy all day......................... 16 "

     Total..........................28 days.
Rain on one of the above cloudy days.
Snow on three "   "   "   "
No strong winds.

AIKEN, SOUTH CAROLINA.

TAKEN AT 9 A.M., 12 M., AND 3½ P.M., FOR DE-
CEMBER, 1870.

Average temperature............................. 45°
"   difference of wet and dry bulb....... 4°
     Maximum............................. 61°
     Minimum............................. 18°
Bright sunshine........................ 15 days.
Sunshine and clouds................. 6 "
Cloudy all day .... 10 "

     Total.......................... 31 days.
Rain on four of the above cloudy days.
Snow on one "   "   "   "
Strong wind, eight days.

JANUARY, 1871.

Average temperature............................. 55°
"   difference of wet and dry bulb....... 6°
     Maximum............................. 69°
     Minimum............. .... 33°
Bright sunshine .... 14 days.
Sunshine and clouds................. 10 "
Cloudy all day .... 7 "

     Total.......................... 31 days.
Rain on three of the above cloudy days.
Strong wind, eight days.

TAKEN AT 9 A.M., 12 M., AND 5 P.M., FOR
FEBRUARY, 1871.

Average temperature........................$57\frac{3}{4}$°
"   difference of wet and dry bulb...... 5°
     Maximum............................. 80°
     Minimum........... .... 38°
Bright sunshine...................... 12 days.
Sunshine and clouds................. 6 "
Cloudy all day......................... 10 "

     Total.......................28 days.
Rain on seven of the above cloudy days.
Strong wind, sixteen days.

MARCH, 1871.

Average temperature............................. 65°
"   difference of wet and dry bulb...... $7\frac{1}{2}$°
     Maximum............................. 85°
     Minimum............. .... 43°
Bright sunshine .... 17 days.
Sunshine and clouds................. 5 "
Cloudy all day......................... 9 "

     Total.......................... 31 days.
Rain on six of the above cloudy days.
Strong wind, ten days.

AT SAN BERNARDINO, CALIFORNIA.

TAKEN 9 A.M., 12 M., AND 5 P.M., NOVEMBER, 1871.

WET BULB.	DRY BULB.	DIFFERENCE.	WIND.	REMARKS.	DATE.
53°	70°	17°	S. Light.	Bright sunshine.	Nov. 8, 1871.
50°	62°	12°	S.E. "	" "	" 9, "
54°	67°	13°	S.E. Very light.	" "	" 10, "
50°	54°	4°	E. " "	{Clouds and rain from 1 P.M. till 8 P.M.	" 11, "
56°	68°	12°	S. Light.	Bright sunshine.	" 12, "
50°	63°	13°	S.W. Light.	" "	" 13, "
52°	64°	12°	S.W. "	" "	" 14, "
50°	64°	14°	S. Very light.	" "	" 15, "
52°	66°	14°	S. " "	" "	" 16, "
50°	67°	11°	W. Light.	" "	" 17, "
50°	64°	14°	W. "	" "	" 18, "
57°	65°	8°	S.W. Very light.	" "	" 19, "
55°	68°	13°	N. Strong.	" "	" 20, "
51°	68°	17°	S. Light.	" "	" 21, "
61°	78°	17°	N.E. Strong.	" "	" 22, "
57°	70°	13°	S. Light.	" "	" 23, "
55°	65°	10°	S. "	" "	" 24, "
56°	60°	4°	S. "	{Sunshine and clouds, and a light shower fifteen minutes, and rain at night.	" 25, "
57°	61°	4°	W. Strong.	Cloudy and rain from 3 P.M.	" 26, "
56°	60°	4°	W. Light.	{Showery until 1 P.M., then sunshine.	" 27, "
50°	56°	6°	W. Very light.	Sunshine and clouds.	" 28, "
50°	56°	6°	N. Light.	" "	" 29, "
46°	59°	13°	N. Strong.	Bright sunshine.	" 30, "

251 = 11°. Difference between wet and dry bulb.
1469 = 64°. Average temperature.
Maximum, 79°; minimum, 45°.

DECEMBER, 1871.

WET BULB.	DRY BULB.	DIFFERENCE.	WIND.	REMARKS.	DATE.
48°	61°	13°	N. Very light.	Bright sunshine.	Dec. 1, 1871.
48°	58°	10°	S. " "	" "	" 2, "
52°	62°	10°	N.E. Very light.	" "	" 3, "
52°	67°	15°	N. " "	" "	" 4, "
55°	71°	16°	N.W. Light.	" "	" 5, "
57°	69°	12°	S.W. Very light.	" "	" 6, "
52°	67°	15°	N.W. Strong.	" "	" 7, "
51°	67°	16°	S. Light.	" "	" 8, "
51°	67°	16°	N.W. Light.	" "	" 9, "
50°	64°	14°	N.W. "	" "	" 10, "
51°	68°	17°	N. Light.	" "	" 11, "
49°	63°	14°	N.E. Very strong.	" "	" 12, "
51°	67°	16°	N.E. Strong.	" "	" 13, "
52°	63°	11°	N.E. Very light.	Sunshine and clouds.	" 14, "
53°	67°	14°	S. Very light.	Bright sunshine.	" 15, "
53°	58°	5°	S. " "	{Sunshine and clouds, and rain at night.	" 16, "
53°	55°	2°	E. Light.	Sunshine and clouds.	" 17, "
55°	65°	10°	S. Very light.	Bright sunshine.	" 18, "
54°	63°	9°	S. " "	" "	" 19, "
55°	66°	11°	S. " "	" "	" 20, "
54°	56°	2°	S. Strong.	Rain all day.	" 21, "
48°	52°	4°	E. Light.	Sunshine and clouds.	" 22, "

DECEMBER, 1871—*continued.*

WET BULB.	DRY BULB.	DIFFER-ENCE.	WIND.	REMARKS.	DATE.
49°	51°	2°	S. Light.	Rain until 3 P.M.	Dec. 23, 1871.
54°	54°	0°	S. Very light.	Rain all day.	" 24, "
55°	58°	3°	S. " "	Sunshine and clouds.	" 25, "
54°	59°	4°	S. " "	" "	" 26, "
52°	56°	4°	S. " "	" "	" 27, "
56°	57°	1°	S. Strong.	Rain until 1 P.M.	" 28, "
55°	57°	2°	S. Very light.	Cloudy all day.	" 29, "
53°	56°	3°	S. " "	Sunshine and clouds.	" 30, "
56°	57°	1°	N.E. Very light.	Rain all day.	" 31, "

272 = 8¼°. Difference between wet and dry bulb.
1899 = 61¼°. Average temperature.
Maximum, 80°, minimum, 43°.

JANUARY, 1872.

WET BULB.	DRY BULB.	DIFFER-ENCE.	WIND.	REMARKS.	DATE.
51°	53°	2°	S. Very light.	Cloudy most of the day.	Jan. 1, 1872.
51°	55°	4°	W. " "	Bright sunshine.	" 2, "
51°	56°	5°	S. " "	Sunshine and clouds.	" 3, "
48°	57°	9°	N. Strong.	Bright sunshine.	" 4, "
49°	56°	7°	N. Light.	" "	" 5, "
52°	59°	7°	N.E. Light.	Sunshine and clouds.	" 6, "
50°	56°	6°	S. Light.	" "	" 7, "
49°	58°	7°	S. "	Cloudy all day.	" 8, "
53°	56°	3°	N. Strong.	Rain all day.	" 9, "
55°	59°	4°	N. Light.	Sunshine and clouds.	" 10, "
53°	60°	7°	N. Strong.	Bright sunshine.	" 11, "
54°	60°	6°	S.W. Light.	" "	" 12, "
53°	61°	8°	S.W. "	" "	" 13, "
58°	65°	7°	S.W. Very light.	" "	" 14, "
58°	65°	7°	S.W. " "	" "	" 15, "
58°	65°	7°	S.W. " "	" "	" 16, "
54°	62°	8°	N. Strong.	" "	" 17, "
56°	63°	7°	N. Light.	" "	" 18, "
51°	60°	9°	N. Very strong.	" "	" 19, "
54°	60°	6°	N. Strong.	" "	" 20, "
52°	61°	9°	S.W. Light.	" "	" 21, "
53°	60°	7°	S.W. "	Cloudy all day.	" 22, "
51°	59°	8°	S.W. "	Sunshine and clouds.	" 23, "
50°	60°	10°	N. Very strong.	" "	" 24, "
49°	59°	10°	N.E. Strong.	Bright sunshine.	" 25, "
44°	53°	9°	S. Light.	" "	" 26, "
47°	55°	8°	S. "	" "	" 27, "
49°	56°	7°	S. "	" "	" 28, "
48°	55°	7°	S. "	" "	" 29, "
49°	56°	7°	S.W. Light.	" "	" 30, "
54°	56°	2°	S. Very light.	Cloudy all day.	" 31, "

210 = 6¾°. Difference between wet and dry bulb.
1798 = 58°. Average temperature.
Maximum, 67°; minimum, 38°.

FEBRUARY, 1872.

WET BULB.	DRY BULB.	DIFFER-ENCE.	WIND.	REMARKS.	DATE.
51°	54°	3°	S. Very light.	Sunshine and clouds.	Feb. 1, 1872.
54°	60°	6°	S. " "	Cloudy all day.	" 2, "
56°	60°	4°	S. " "	Bright sunshine.	" 3, "
44°	57°	3°	S. " "	Sunshine and clouds.	" 4, "
48°	61°	13°	N. Strong.	Bright sunshine.	" 5, "
48°	63°	15°	N.E. Very light.	" "	" 6, "
51°	63°	12°	N. Very light.	" "	" 7, "
53°	64°	11°	W. " "	" "	" 8, "
54°	59°	5°	S.W. Light.	Sunshine and clouds.	" 9, "

FEBRUARY, 1872—*continued.*

WET BULB.	DRY BULB.	DIFFERENCE.	WIND.		REMARKS.		DATE.
55°	64°	9°	S.W.	Very light.	Bright sunshine.		Feb. 10, 1872.
55°	61°	6°	S.W.	Light.	" "		" 11, "
54°	61°	7°	S.W.	"	" "		" 12, "
53°	66°	13°	N.E.	"	" "		" 13, "
55°	67°	12°	S.W.	"	" "		" 14, "
55°	67°	12°	S.W.	Very light.	" "		" 15, "
57°	68°	11°	S.W.	Light.	" "		" 16, "
60°	72°	12°	S.W.	Very light.	" "		" 17, "
61°	74°	13°	S.W.	Light.	" "		" 18, "
55°	67°	12°	N.	Strong.	" "		" 19, "
56°	74°	18°	N.W.	Light.	" "		" 20, "
56°	69°	13°	S.W.	"	" "		" 21, "
51°	53°	2°	S.	"	Rain till 12 M., then sunshine and clouds.		" 22, "
53°	60°	7°	S.W.	"	Bright sunshine.		" 23, "
48°	51°	3°	S.W.	Strong.	Rain most of the day.		" 24, "
48°	53°	5°	S.W.	Light.	Sunshine and clouds.		" 25, "
50°	56°	6°	S.W.	"	Bright sunshine.		" 26, "
51°	58°	7°	S.W.	"	Sunshine and clouds.		" 27, "
46°	52°	6°	S.W.	"	" "		" 28, "
48°	59°	11°	N.	Strong.	Bright sunshine.		" 29, "

257 = 8¾°. Difference between wet and dry bulb.
1793 = 62°. Average temperature.
Maximum, 81°; minimum, 47°.

MARCH, 1872.

WET BULB.	DRY BULB.	DIFFERENCE.	WIND.		REMARKS.		DATE.
54°	64°	10°	W.	Light.	Bright sunshine.		March 1, 1872.
55°	67°	12°	W.	Very light.	" "		" 2, "
59°	71°	12°	E.	" "	" "		" 3, "
61°	71°	10°	W.	" "	" "		" 4, "
55°	59°	4°	W.	Light.	Sunshine and clouds.		" 5, "
51°	56°	5°	S.W.	"	Bright sunshine.		" 6, "
56°	63°	7°	W.	"	" "		" 7, "
53°	62°	9°	W.	Strong.	" "		" 8, "
54°	60°	6°	W.	"	" "		" 9, "
61°	70°	9°	S.	Light.	" "		" 10, "
59°	68°	9°	S.W.	Very light.	" "		" 11, "
52°	60°	8°	S.W.	Light.	" "		" 12, "
52°	62°	10°	N.	"	" "		" 13, "
55°	62°	7°	S.	"	" "		" 14, "
64°	69°	5°	S.W.	"	" "		" 15, "
52°	59°	7°	S.W.	"	" "		" 16, "
52°	64°	12°	W.	Very light.	" "		" 17, "
63°	70°	7°	S.	Light.	" "		" 18, "
55°	61°	6°	S.	"	" "		" 19, "
54°	62°	8°	W.	Very light.	" "		" 20, "
56°	63°	7°	S.W.	Light.	" "		" 21, "
57°	62°	5°	S.E.	Strong.	" "		" 22, "
56°	63°	7°	S.W.	"	Sunshine and clouds.		" 23, "
55°	63°	8°	S.	Light.	Bright sunshine.		" 24, "
57°	64°	7°	N.W.	Strong.	" "		" 25, "
58°	66°	8°	W.	Light.	" "		" 26, "
60°	68°	8°	W.	"	" "		" 27, "
55°	62°	7°	W.	"	" "		" 28, "
56°	62°	6°	S.W.	Very light.	" "		" 29, "
57°	65°	8°	S.W.	Light.	" "		" 30, "
57°	67°	10°	W.	Strong.	" "		" 31, "

244 = 7¾°. Difference between wet and dry bulb.
1985 = 64°. Average temperature.
Maximum, 80°; minimum, 51°.

The days marked sunshine and clouds were invariably clear and fine, but with a few fleecy clouds in the sky. On the days marked bright sunshine there was not a cloud to be seen. The wind that is marked "very light" was just enough to tell the direction from which it blew. The strong winds blew hard, but not so strong as those we call strong in the East. The average temperature is higher than in Mentone, and the air drier, as you will perceive.

ANAHEIM, CALIFORNIA.

TAKEN AT 8 A.M., 12 M., AND 6½ P.M., JULY, 1872.

WET BULB.	DRY BULB.	DIFFER-ENCE.	WIND.		REMARKS.		DATE.
63°	70°	7°	S.W.	Light.	Bright sunshine.		July 1, 1872.
63°	70°	7°	"	"	"	"	" 2, "
64°	70°	6°	"	"	"	"	" 3, "
65°	71°	6°	"	"	"	"	" 4, "
63°	69°	6°	"	"	"	"	" 5, "
62°	68°	6°	"	"	"	"	" 6, "
65°	71°	6°	"	"	"	"	" 7, "
65°	72°	7°	"	"	"	"	" 8, "
62°	68°	6°	"	"	"	"	" 9, "
66°	69°	3°	N.W.	Very light.	{ Cloudy all day, and rained from 1 A.M. till 12 M. }		" 10, "
66°	72°	6°	S.W.	Light.	Bright sunshine.		" 11, "
67°	72°	6°	"	"	"	"	" 12, "
67°	74°	7°	"	"	"	"	" 13, "
66°	72°	6°	"	"	"	"	" 14, "
65°	72°	7°	"	"	"	"	" 15, "
66°	72°	6°	"	"	"	"	" 16, "
67°	74°	7°	N.W.	Light.	"	"	" 17, "
67°	74°	7°	S.W.	Light.	"	"	" 18, "
66°	72°	6°	"	"	"	"	" 19, "
65°	72°	7°	"	"	"	"	" 20, "
65°	72°	7°	"	"	"	"	" 21, "
67°	75°	8°	"	"	"	"	" 22, "
67°	74°	7°	"	"	"	"	" 23, "
66°	75°	9°	"	"	"	"	" 24, "
66°	75°	9°	"	"	"	"	" 25, "
67°	76°	9°	"	"	"	"	" 26, "
67°	77°	10°	"	"	"	"	" 27, "
66°	77°	11°	"	"	"	"	" 28, "
66°	74°	8°	"	"	"	"	" 29, "
68°	77°	9°	"	"	"	"	" 30, "
68°	78°	10°	"	"	"	"	" 31, "

222 = 7⅛°. Difference between wet and dry bulb.
2255 = 72¾°. Average temperature.
Maximum, 83°; minimum, 66°.

At Anaheim, in July, sometimes early in the morning it is cloudy, but the clouds soon disappear after sunrise.

SANTA BARBARA.

I take the following table of mean temperature for the year from the *Santa Barbara Press*.

MONTHLY MEAN, 1870-1.

April, average of the 3 daily observations	60.62°	Oct., average of the 3 daily observations 65.96°
May, " " " "	62.35°	Nov., " " " " 61.22°
June, " " " "	65.14°	Dec., " " " " 52.12°
July, " " " "	71.49°	Jan., " " " " 54.51°
Aug., " " " "	72.12°	Feb., " " " " 53.35°
Sept., " " " "	68.08°	March, " " " " 58.42°

Average temperature for the year............................ 60.20°

COLDEST DAY.	WARMEST DAY.
April 12th, 60°.	April 16th, 74°.
May 15th, 66°.	May 23d, 77°.
June 1st, 69°.	June 3d, 80°.
July 26th, 76°.	July 11th, 84°.
August 11th, 77°.	August 8th, 86°.
September 23d, 66°.	September 27th, 90°.
October 23d, 60°.	October 20th, 92°.
November 7th, 64°.	November 20th, 87°.
December 15th, 52°.	December 28th, 71°.
January 11th, 56°.	January 3d, 76°.
February 22d, 42°.	February 28th, 71°.
March 13th, 56°.	March 27th, 83°.

Coldest day in the year, February 22d, 42°.
Warmest day in the year, October 20th, 92°.
Variation, 50°.

LATEST IMPROVEMENTS IN THE YOSEMITE ROUTE.

As this book is going through the press, a well-informed friend writes me from San Francisco:

"The prospects are good for a new wagon-road into the Yosemite Valley, to be completed in time for next season's travel, whereby the tourist will avoid all horseback travel. This new wagon-road is laid out from Clarke's, and will be a continuation of the new stage-road of this year. Travelers into the Yosemite will then reach Merced by rail at sundown, remain all night at the new hotel there, set out in comfortable coaches the next morning, and reach the hotel in the Valley the evening of the same day, through all the way on wheels, and without change of stages. The day's drive will be about eighty miles from Merced, by way of Mariposa, White's, Clarke's, and Inspiration Point, into the Valley.

"For the pleasure of those who prefer horseback, the saddle-trail between Clarke's and the Yosemite, by way of Glacier Point, will also be kept open."

THE END.

Another Bestselling Book from Ten Speed Press!

RUNNING THE ROOKERIES—GATHERING MURRE EGGS.

NORTHERN CALIFORNIA, OREGON, AND THE SANDWICH ISLANDS

Charles Nordhoff

Nordhoff continues his travel guide for tourists and adventurers of another era with this volume which includes details of agriculture and the wine industry in California, logging in Oregon, a side trip to the Washington Territory, and a glimpse of the colorful people of the Hawaiian Islands. Centennial Edition, first printed in 1874.

256 pages, 6 x 9 inches   ISBN 0-89815-419-7   Paper, $7.95

VALUABLE AND INTERESTING

WORKS OF TRAVEL

PUBLISHED BY

HARPER & BROTHERS, NEW YORK.

☞ HARPER & BROTHERS *will send either of the following works by mail, postage prepaid, to any part of the United States, on receipt of the price.*

NORDHOFF'S CALIFORNIA. California: for Health, Pleasure, and Residence. A Book for Travellers and Settlers. By CHARLES NORDHOFF, Author of "Cape Cod and all Along Shore," &c. With Illustrations. 8vo, Paper, $2 00; Cloth, $2 50.

PRIME'S TRAVELS. Around the World. By EDWARD D. G. PRIME, D.D. With numerous Illustrations. Crown 8vo, Cloth, $3 00.

PALMER'S DESERT OF THE EXODUS. Journeys on Foot in the Wilderness of the Forty Years' Wanderings; undertaken in connection with the Ordnance Survey of Sinai and the Palestine Exploration Fund. By E. H. PALMER, M.A., Lord Almoner's Professor of Arabic, and Fellow of St. John's College, Cambridge. With Maps and numerous Illustrations from Photographs and Drawings taken on the spot by the Sinai Survey Expedition and C. F. Tyrwhitt Drake. Crown 8vo, Cloth, $3 00.

HAZEN'S SCHOOL AND ARMY IN GERMANY AND FRANCE. The School and the Army in Germany and France, with a Diary of Siege Life at Versailles. By Brevet Major-General W. B. HAZEN, U.S.A., Colonel Sixth Infantry. 12mo, Cloth, $2 50.

THIRTY YEARS IN THE HAREM; or, The Autobiography of Melek-Hanum, Wife of H. H. Kibrizli-Mehemet-Pasha. 12mo, Cloth, $1 50.

ANDERSSON'S OKAVANGO RIVER. The Okavango River: a Narrative of Travel, Exploration, and Adventure. By CHARLES JOHN ANDERSSON. With Steel Portrait of the Author, numerous Woodcuts, and a Map showing the Regions explored by Andersson, Cumming, Livingstone, and Du Chaillu. 8vo, Cloth, $3 25.

ANDERSSON'S LAKE NGAMI. Lake Ngami; or, Explorations and Discoveries during Four Years' Wanderings in the Wilds of Southwestern Africa. By CHARLES JOHN ANDERSSON. With numerous Illustrations, representing Sporting Adventures, Subjects of Natural History, Devices for Destroying Wild Animals, &c. 12mo, Cloth, $1 75.

ATKINSON'S AMOOR REGIONS. Travels in the Regions of the Upper and Lower Amoor, and the Russian Acquisitions on the Confines of India and China. With Adventures among the Mountain Kirghis, and the Manjours, Manyargs, Toungous, Touzempts, Goldi, and Gelyaks, the Hunting and Pastoral Tribes. By THOMAS WITLAM ATKINSON, F.G.S., F.R.G.S. With a Map and numerous Illustrations. 8vo, Cloth, $3 50.

ATKINSON'S SIBERIA. Oriental and Western Siberia: a Narrative of Seven Years' Explorations and Adventures in Siberia, Mongolia, the Kirghis Steppes, Chinese Tartary, and Part of Central Asia. By THOMAS WITLAM ATKINSON. With a Map and numerous Illustrations. 8vo, Cloth, $3 50.

ADVENTURES OF A YOUNG NATURALIST. By LUCIEN BIART. Edited and Adapted by PARKER GILLMORE. With 117 Illustrations. 12mo, Cloth, $1 75.

ALCOCK'S JAPAN. The Capital of the Tycoon: a Narrative of a Three Years' Residence in Japan. By Sir RUTHERFORD ALCOCK, K.C.B., Her Majesty's Envoy Extraordinary and Minister Plenipotentiary in Japan. With Maps and Engravings. 2 vols., 12mo, Cloth, $3 50.

BAIRD'S MODERN GREECE. Modern Greece: a Narrative of a Residence and Travels in that Country. With Observations on its Antiquities, Literature, Language, Politics, and Religion. By HENRY M. BAIRD, M.A. Numerous Illustrations. 12mo, Cloth, $1 50.

BARTH'S NORTH AND CENTRAL AFRICA. Travels and Discoveries in North and Central Africa. Being a Journal of an Expedition undertaken under the Auspices of H. B. M.'s Government, in the Years 1849–1855. By HENRY BARTH, Ph.D., D.C.L. Illustrated. 3 vols., 8vo, Cloth, $12 00.

BALDWIN'S AFRICAN HUNTING. African Hunting, from Natal to the Zambesi, including Lake Ngami, the Kalahari Desert, &c., from 1852 to 1860. By WILLIAM CHARLES BALDWIN, Esq., F. R. G. S. With Map, Fifty Illustrations by Wolf and Zwecker, and a Portrait. 12mo, Cloth, $1 50.

BURTON'S LAKE REGIONS OF CENTRAL AFRICA. The Lake Regions of Central Africa. A Picture of Exploration. By RICHARD F. BURTON, Captain H. M.'s Indian Army, Fellow and Gold Medalist of the Royal Geographical Society. With Maps and Engravings on Wood. 8vo, Cloth, $3 50.

BURTON'S CITY OF THE SAINTS. The City of the Saints; and Across the Rocky Mountains to California. By Captain RICHARD F. BURTON, Fellow and Gold Medalist of the Royal Geographical Societies of France and England, H. M.'s Consul in West Africa. With Maps and numerous Illustrations. 8vo, Cloth, $3 50.

BELLOWS'S TRAVELS. The Old World in its New Face: Impressions of Europe in 1867, 1868. By HENRY W. BELLOWS. 2 vols., 12mo, Cloth, $3 50.

BROWNE'S APACHE COUNTRY. Adventures in the Apache Country: a Tour through Arizona and Sonora, with Notes on the Silver Regions of Nevada. By J. Ross Browne. Illustrations. 12mo, Cloth, $2 00.

BROWNE'S AMERICAN FAMILY IN GERMANY. An American Family in Germany. By J. Ross Browne. Illustrations. 12mo, Cloth, $2 00.

BROWNE'S CRUSOE'S ISLAND, CALIFORNIA, &c. Crusoe's Island: a Ramble in the Footsteps of Alexander Selkirk. With Sketches of Adventure in California and Washoe. By J. Ross Browne. With Illustrations. 12mo, Cloth, $1 75.

BROWNE'S LAND OF THOR. The Land of Thor. By J. Ross Browne. Illustrations. 12mo, Cloth, $2 00.

BROWNE'S YUSEF. A Crusade in the East. A Narrative of Personal Adventures and Travels on the Shores of the Mediterranean, in Asia Minor, Palestine, and Syria. By J. Ross Browne. Illustrations. 12mo, Cloth, $1 75.

BUFFUM'S SIGHTS AND SENSATIONS. Sights and Sensations in France, Germany, and Switzerland; or, Experiences of an American Journalist in Europe. By Edward Gould Buffum, Author of "Six Months in the Gold Mines," &c. 12mo, Cloth, $1 50.

BAKER'S CAST UP BY THE SEA. Cast up by the Sea; or, The Adventures of Ned Grey. By Sir Samuel W. Baker, M.A., F.R.G.S., Author of the "Albert N'Yanza Great Basin of the Nile," "The Nile Tributaries of Abyssinia," &c. With Ten Illustrations by Huard. 12mo, Cloth, 75 cents.

THE MUTINEERS OF THE BOUNTY. Some Account of the Mutineers of the Bounty and their Descendants in Pitcairn and Norfolk Islands. By Lady Belcher. Illustrated. 12mo, Cloth, $1 50.

REINDEER, DOGS, AND SNOW-SHOES. A Journal of Siberian Travel and Explorations made in the Years 1865-'67. By Richard J. Bush, late of the Russo-American Telegraph Expedition. Illustrated. Crown 8vo, Cloth, $3 00.

CURTIS'S HOWADJI IN SYRIA. The Howadji in Syria. By George William Curtis. 12mo, Cloth, $1 50.

CURTIS'S NILE NOTES. The Nile Notes of a Howadji. By George William Curtis. 12mo, Cloth, $1 50.

CUMMING'S HUNTER'S LIFE IN AFRICA. Five Years of a Hunter's Life in the far Interior of South Africa. With Notices of the Native Tribes, and Anecdotes of the Chase of the Lion, Elephant, Hippopotamus, Giraffe, Rhinoceros, &c. Illustrations. By R. Gordon Cumming. 2 vols., 12mo, Cloth, $3 00.

DURBIN'S OBSERVATIONS IN EUROPE. Principally in France and Great Britain. By Rev. J. P. Durbin, D.D. Illustrations. 2 vols., 12mo, Cloth, $3 00.

DURBIN'S OBSERVATIONS IN THE EAST. Chiefly in Egypt, Palestine, Syria, and Asia Minor. By Rev. J. P. Durbin, D.D. 2 vols., 12mo, Cloth, $3 00.

DARWIN'S VOYAGE OF A NATURALIST. Journal of Researches into the Natural History and Geology of the Countries visited during the Voyage of H. M. S. *Beagle* round the World, under the Command of Captain Fitzroy, R. N. By Charles Darwin, M.A., F.R.S. 2 vols., 12mo, Cloth, $2 00.

DAVIS'S CARTHAGE. Carthage and her Remains: being an Account of the Excavations and Researches on the Site of the Phœnician Metropolis in Africa and other Adjacent Places. Conducted under the Auspices of Her Majesty's Government. By Dr. N. Davis, F.R.G.S. Profusely Illustrated with Maps, Woodcuts, Chromo-Lithographs, &c. 8vo, Cloth, $4 00.

DILKE'S GREATER BRITAIN. Greater Britain: a Record of Travel in English-speaking Countries during 1866 and 1867. By Charles Wentworth Dilke. With Maps and Illustrations. 12mo, Cloth, $1 00.

DOOLITTLE'S CHINA. Social Life of the Chinese: with some Account of their Religious, Governmental, Educational, and Business Customs and Opinions. With special but not exclusive Reference to Fuhchau. By Rev. Justus Doolittle, Fourteen Years Member of the Fuhchau Mission of the American Board. Illustrated with more than 150 characteristic Engravings on Wood. 2 vols., 12mo, Cloth, $5 00.

DIXON'S FREE RUSSIA. Free Russia. By W. Hepworth Dixon, Author of "Her Majesty's Tower," &c. With Two Illustrations. Crown 8vo, Cloth, $2 00.

DU CHAILLU'S AFRICA. Explorations and Adventures in Equatorial Africa; with Accounts of the Manners and Customs of the People, and of the Chase of the Gorilla, the Crocodile, Leopard, Elephant, Hippopotamus, and other Animals. By Paul B. Du Chaillu, Corresponding Member of the American Ethnological Society, of the Geographical and Statistical Society of New York, and of the Boston Society of Natural History. With numerous Illustrations. 8vo, Cloth, $5 00.

DU CHAILLU'S ASHANGO LAND. A Journey to Ashango Land, and Further Penetration into Equatorial Africa. By Paul B. Du Chaillu. New Edition. Handsomely Illustrated. 8vo, Cloth, $5 00.

EWBANK'S BRAZIL. Life in Brazil; or, A Journal of a Visit to the Land of the Cocoa and the Palm. With an Appendix, containing Illustrations of Ancient and South American Arts, in recently discovered Implements and Products of Domestic Industry, and Works in Stone, Pottery, Gold, Silver, Bronze, &c. By Thomas Ewbank. With over 100 Illustrations. 8vo, Cloth, $3 00.

ELLIS'S MADAGASCAR. Three Visits to Madagascar, during the Years 1853, 1854, 1856. Including a Journey to the Capital, with Notices of the Natural History of the Country, and of the Present Civilization of the People. By the Rev. William Ellis, F.H.S. Illustrated by a Map and Woodcuts from Photographs, &c. 8vo, Cloth, $3 50.

GERSTAECKER'S TRAVELS ROUND THE WORLD. Narrative of a Journey round the World. Comprising a Winter Passage across the Andes to Chili; with a Visit to the Gold Regions of California and Australia, the South Sea Islands, Java, &c. By F. Gerstaecker. 12mo, Cloth, $1 50.

GIRONIERE'S PHILIPPINE ISLANDS. Twenty Years in the Philippines. By Paul de la Gironiere. Revised and Extended by the Author expressly for this Translation. Illustrations. 12mo, Cloth, $1 50.

HALL'S ARCTIC RESEARCHES. Arctic Researches and Life among the Esquimaux: being the Narrative of an Expedition in Search of Sir John Franklin, in the Years 1860, 1861, and 1862. By Charles Francis Hall. With Maps and 100 Illustrations. 8vo, Cloth, Beveled, $5 00.

HERODOTUS, LIFE AND TRAVELS OF. The Life and Travels of Herodotus in the Fifth Century before Christ: an Imaginary Biography founded on Fact, illustrative of the History, Manners, Religion, Literature, Arts, and Social Condition of the Greeks, Egyptians, Persians, Babylonians, Hebrews, Scythians, and other Ancient Nations, in the Days of Pericles and Nehemiah. By J. TALBOYS WHEELER, F.R.G.S. Map. 2 vols., 12mo, Cloth, $3 50.

HOLTON'S NEW GRANADA. Twenty Months in the Andes. By I. F. HOLTON. Illustrations and Maps. 8vo, Cloth, $3 00.

HUC'S TRAVELS THROUGH THE CHINESE EMPIRE. A Journey through the Chinese Empire. By M. HUC. With a Map. 2 vols., 12mo, Cloth, $3 00.

KINGSLEY'S WEST INDIES. At Last: A Christmas in the West Indies. By CHARLES KINGSLEY, Author of "Alton Locke," "Yeast," &c., &c. Illustrated. 12mo, Cloth, $1 50.

LAMONT'S SEASONS WITH THE SEA - HORSES. Seasons with the Sea-Horses; or, Sporting Adventures in the Northern Seas. By JAMES LAMONT, Esq., F.G.S. With Map and Illustrations. 8vo, Cloth, $3 00.

LIVINGSTONE'S SOUTH AFRICA. Missionary Travels and Researches in South Africa; including a Sketch of Sixteen Years' Residence in the Interior of Africa, and a Journey from the Cape of Good Hope to Loando on the West Coast; thence across the Continent, down the River Zambesi, to the Eastern Ocean. By DAVID LIVINGSTONE, LL.D., D.C.L. With Portrait, Maps by Arrowsmith, and numerous Illustrations. 8vo, Cloth, $4 50.

LIVINGSTONE'S EXPEDITION TO THE ZAMBESI. Narrative of an Expedition to the Zambesi and its Tributaries; and of the Discovery of the Lakes Shirwa and Nyassa. 1858–1864. By DAVID and CHARLES LIVINGSTONE. With Map and Illustrations. 8vo, Cloth, $5 00.

LAYARD'S NINEVEH. A Popular Account of the Discoveries at Nineveh. By AUSTEN HENRY LAYARD. Abridged by him from his larger Work. With numerous Wood Engravings. 12mo, Cloth, $1 75.

LAYARD'S FRESH DISCOVERIES AT NINEVEH. Fresh Discoveries at Nineveh and Babylon; with Travels in Armenia, Kurdistan, and the Desert. Being the Result of a Second Expedition undertaken for the Trustees of the British Museum. By AUSTEN HENRY LAYARD, M.P. With all the Maps and Engravings in the English Edition. 8vo, Cloth, $4 00.

MARCY'S ARMY LIFE ON THE BORDER. Thirty Years of Army Life on the Border. Comprising Descriptions of the Indian Nomads of the Plains; Explorations of New Territory; a Trip across the Rocky Mountains in the Winter; Descriptions of the Habits of Different Animals found in the West, and the Methods of Hunting them; with Incidents in the Lives of different Frontier Men, &c., &c. By Brevet Brig.-General R. B. MARCY, U. S. A. 8vo, Cloth, Beveled Edges, $3 00.

MOWRY'S ARIZONA AND SONORA. Arizona and Sonora. The Geography, History, and Resources of the Silver Region of North America. By SYLVESTER MOWRY, of Arizona, Graduate of the U. S. Military Academy at West Point, late Lieutenant Third Artillery, U. S. A., Corresponding Member of the American Institute, late U. S. Boundary Commissioner, &c., &c. 12mo, Cloth, $1 50.

MACGREGOR'S ROB ROY ON THE JORDAN. The Rob Roy on the Jordan, Nile, Red Sea, and Gennesareth, &c. A Canoe Cruise in Palestine and Egypt, and the Waters of Damascus. By J. MACGREGOR, M.A. With Maps and Illustrations. Crown 8vo, Cloth, $2 50.

NEVIUS'S CHINA. China and the Chinese: a General Description of the Country and its Inhabitants; its Civilization and Form of Government; its Religious and Social Institutions; its Intercourse with other Nations; and its Present Condition and Prospects. By the Rev. JOHN L. NEVIUS, Ten Years a Missionary in China. With a Map and Illustrations. 12mo, Cloth, $1 75.

NEWMAN'S FROM DAN TO BEERSHEBA. From Dan to Beersheba; or, the Land of Promise as it now appears. Including a Description of the Boundaries, Topography, Agriculture, Antiquities, Cities, and Present Inhabitants of that Wonderful Land. With Illustrations of the Remarkable Accuracy of the Sacred Writers in their Allusions to their Native Country. By Rev. J. P. NEWMAN, D.D. Maps and Engravings. 12mo, Cloth, $1 75.

OLIN'S (DR.) TRAVELS. Travels in Egypt, Arabia Petræa, and the Holy Land. Engravings. 2 vols., 8vo, Cloth, $3 00.

OLIPHANT'S CHINA AND JAPAN. Narrative of the Earl of Elgin's Mission to China and Japan, in the Years 1857, '58, '59. By LAURENCE OLIPHANT, Private Secretary to Lord Elgin. Illustrations. 8vo, Cloth, $3 50.

ORTON'S ANDES AND THE AMAZON. The Andes and the Amazon; or, Across the Continent of South America. By JAMES ORTON, M.A., Professor of Natural History in Vassar College, Poughkeepsie, N. Y., and Corresponding Member of the Academy of Natural Sciences, Philadelphia. With a New Map of Equatorial America and numerous Illustrations. Crown 8vo, Cloth, $2 00.

PAGE'S LA PLATA. La Plata, the Argentine Confederation, and Paraguay. Being a Narrative of the Exploration of the Tributaries of the River La Plata and Adjacent Countries during the Years 1853, '54, '55, and '56, under the Orders of the United States Government. New Edition, containing Farther Explorations in La Plata during 1859 and 1860. By THOMAS J. PAGE, U. S. N., Commander of the Expeditions. With Map and numerous Engravings. 8vo, Cloth, $5 00.

PFEIFFER'S SECOND JOURNEY. A Lady's Second Journey round the World: from London to the Cape of Good Hope, Borneo, Java, Sumatra, Celebes, Ceram, the Moluccas, &c., California, Panama, Peru, Ecuador, and the United States. By IDA PFEIFFER. 12mo, Cloth, $1 50.

PFEIFFER'S LAST TRAVELS AND AUTOBIOGRAPHY. The Last Travels of Ida Pfeiffer: inclusive of a Visit to Madagascar. With an Autobiographical Memoir of the Author. Translated by H. W. DULCKEN. Steel Portrait. 12mo, Cloth, $1 50.

PRIME'S (S. I.) TRAVELS IN EUROPE AND THE EAST. Travels in Europe and the East. A Year in England, Scotland, Ireland, Wales, France, Belgium, Holland, Germany, Austria, Italy, Greece, Turkey, Syria, Palestine, and Egypt. By Rev. SAMUEL IRENÆUS PRIME, D.D. Engravings. 2 vols., large 12mo, Cloth, $3 00.

PRIME'S (W. C.) BOAT-LIFE IN EGYPT. Boat-Life in Egypt and Nubia. By WILLIAM C. PRIME. Illustrations. 12mo, Cloth, $2 00.

PRIME'S (W. C.) TENT-LIFE IN THE HOLY LAND. Tent-Life in the Holy Land. By WILLIAM C. PRIME. Illustrations. 12mo, Cloth, $2 00.

READE'S SAVAGE AFRICA. Western Africa: being the Narrative of a Tour in Equatorial, Southwestern, and Northwestern Africa; with Notes on the Habits of the Gorilla; on the Existence of Unicorns and Tailed Men; on the Slave Trade; on the Origin, Character, and Capabilities of the Negro, and on the Future Civilization of Western Africa. By W. WINWOOD READE, Fellow of the Geographical and Anthropological Society of London, and Corresponding Member of the Geographical Society of Paris. With Illustrations and a Map. 8vo, Cloth, $4 00.

SMITH'S ARAUCANIANS. The Araucanians; or, Notes of a Tour among the Indian Tribes of Southern Chili. By EDMUND REUEL SMITH, of the U. S. N. Astronomical Expedition in Chili. 12mo, Cloth, $1 50.

SQUIER'S CENTRAL AMERICA. The States of Central America: their Geography, Topography, Climate, Population, Resources, Productions, Commerce, Political Organization, Aborigines, &c., &c. Comprising Chapters on Honduras, San Salvador, Nicaragua, Costa Rica, Guatemala, Belize, the Bay Islands, the Mosquito Shore, and the Honduras Inter-Oceanic Railway. By E. G. SQUIER, formerly Chargé d'Affairs of the United States to the Republics of Central America. With numerous Original Maps and Illustrations. 8vo, Cloth, $4 00.

SQUIER'S NICARAGUA. Nicaragua: its People, Scenery, Monuments, Resources, Condition, and Proposed Canal. With One Hundred Maps and Illustrations. By E. G. SQUIER. 8vo, Cloth, $4 00.

SQUIER'S WAIKNA. Waikna; or, Adventures on the Mosquito Shore. By E. G. SQUIER. With a Map and upward of Sixty Illustrations. 12mo, Cloth, $1 50.

SPEKE'S AFRICA. Journal of the Discovery of the Source of the Nile. By Captain JOHN HANNING SPEKE, Captain H. M.'s Indian Army, Fellow and Gold Medalist of the Royal Geographical Society, Hon. Corresponding Member and Gold Medalist of the French Geographical Society, &c. With Maps and Portraits and numerous Illustrations, chiefly from Drawings by Captain Grant. 8vo, Cloth, $4 00.

STEPHENS'S TRAVELS IN CENTRAL AMERICA. Travels in Central America, Chiapas, and Yucatan. By J. L. STEPHENS. With a Map and 88 Engravings. 2 vols., 8vo, Cloth, $6 00.

STEPHENS'S TRAVELS IN YUCATAN. Incidents of Travel in Yucatan. By J. L. STEPHENS. 120 Engravings, from Drawings by F. Catherwood. 2 vols., 8vo, Cloth, $6 00.

STEPHENS'S TRAVELS IN EGYPT. Travels in Egypt, Arabia Petræa, and the Holy Land. By J. L. STEPHENS. Engravings. 2 vols., 12mo, Cloth, $3 00.

STEPHENS'S TRAVELS IN GREECE. Travels in Greece, Turkey, Russia, and Poland. By J. L. STEPHENS. 2 vols., 12mo, Cloth, $3 00.

THOMSON'S LAND AND BOOK. The Land and the Book; or, Biblical Illustrations drawn from the Manners and Customs, the Scenes and the Scenery of the Holy Land. By W. M. THOMSON, D.D., Twenty-five Years a Missionary of the A.B.C.F.M. in Syria and Palestine. With Two elaborate Maps of Palestine, an accurate Plan of Jerusalem, and *Several Hundred Engravings*, representing the Scenery, Topography, and Productions of the Holy Land, and the Costumes, Manners, and Habits of the People. Two large 12mo Volumes, Cloth, $5 00.

VÁMBÉRY'S CENTRAL ASIA. Travels in Central Asia: being the Account of a Journey from Teheran across the Turkoman Desert, on the Eastern Shore of the Caspian, to Khiva, Bokhara, and Samarcand, performed in the Year 1863. By ARMINIUS VÁMBÉRY, Member of the Hungarian Academy of Pesth, by whom he was sent on this Scientific Mission. With Map and Woodcuts. 8vo, Cloth, $4 50.

VIRGINIA ILLUSTRATED: containing a Visit to the Virginian Canaan, and the Adventures of Porte Crayon and his Cousins. Illustrated from Drawings by PORTE CRAYON. 8vo, Cloth, $3 50.

WALLACE'S MALAY ARCHIPELAGO. The Malay Archipelago: the Land of the Orang-Utan and the Bird of Paradise. A Narrative of Travel, 1854-'62. With Studies of Man and Nature. By ALFRED RUSSEL WALLACE. With Maps and numerous Illustrations. Crown 8vo, Cloth, $3 50.

WELLS'S EXPLORATIONS IN HONDURAS. Explorations and Adventures in Honduras; comprising Sketches of Travel in the Gold Regions of Olancho, and a Review of the History and General Resources of Central America. By WILLIAM V. WELLS. With Original Maps and numerous Illustrations. 8vo, Cloth, $3 50.

WHYMPER'S ALASKA. Travel and Adventure in the Territory of Alaska, formerly Russian America —now ceded to the United States—and in various other Parts of the North Pacific. By FREDERICK WHYMPER. With Map and Illustrations. Crown 8vo, Cloth, $2 50.

WILKINSON'S ANCIENT EGYPTIANS. A Popular Account of the Ancient Egyptians. Revised and abridged from his larger Work. By Sir J. GARDNER WILKINSON, D.C.L., F.R.S., &c. Illustrated with 500 Woodcuts. 2 vols., 12mo, Cloth, $3 50.

☞ *For a full list of Harper & Brothers' Publications, see* HARPER'S CATALOGUE, *which comprises a large proportion of the most esteemed works in the English language, being particularly extensive in the departments of Travel, History, Biography, Juvenile and Religious Literature. This Catalogue will be sent by mail on receipt of Six Cents; or will be given, free, on personal application to the Publishers.*